Love (Try) Angle

Manali Desai

Ukiyoto Publishing

All global publishing rights are held by

Ukiyoto Publishing

Published in 2021

Content Copyright © **Manali Desai**

ISBN 9789354901201

www.ukiyoto.com

Dedication

To my 'funny' husband,
I hope this book proves (once and for all) who is funnier.
P.S: You'll have to read the book for that.

Acknowledgements

Hello there. I hope you don't start by reading this page before you read the full book. If so, please read it and come back here. If you're already done reading it, yay! Congratulations to both of us, because you've just finished reading my debut novel.

Ever since my first book came out, the one question asked by every person (irrespective of whether they read my books or not) was, *"When are you writing a novel?"*

It would be an awkward question to answer because of two reasons:

a.   I didn't have a worthy enough story idea.
b.   I lacked the courage, patience, and confidence to engage in long-form creative writing.

But every time I was hit by this question, I would kick my brains to hit me with an inspiring and worthy enough story idea to write my debut novel.

After many ideas were discarded (read 'not-worked-upon') I thought to myself, "Okay, Manali. You're funny. So why not a humorous book?". That's when I knew it had to be a romcom.

Reading romance books, has, and continues to be a guilty pleasure. So, I thought why not combine my 'fun' element into a romance story that will resonate with most millennial readers. And here is the result in your hands.

Ayesha, Viren and Abhi represent so much more than just their physical appearances and their intellect. Their story is of growth, maturity, passion, and ambition. I'm sure you found yourself or someone you know within the pages of this book.

Although I'm the creator of the trio's world, the end result would not have been possible without a few people.

First off has to be 'the love of my life' (eye rolls cue), Manan Desai, who endured my erratic moods and constant absenteeism. Having a spouse who chooses to write on weekends and Valentine's Day is surely not a cakewalk. I would throw a tantrum if the tables were turned. Well, he did that too. But it was in vain. Because, obviously, using my tricks on me doesn't work. So, here's me saying, you got a keeper Mr. Husband. But I got lucky too. Thanks a lot, the yin to my yang.

One can only improve in their work if they receive honest feedback on it. For that, I have the constant critiquing of Upasana Arora to be grateful for. If you've enjoyed reading this book, it's more because of her than me. Trust me when I say, the story might have turned out completely drab if not for her comments like "This needs to improve", "Please remove this scene" or "We need more specifics here" and many such valuable inputs.

Then there was my most faithful fan, Kinnari Desai. She was kind enough to read my first draft and be the editor as well as proofreader. Thanks to her keen eye, a lot of typos and grammatical errors were (thankfully) done with. Thank you for always being my number one fan and motivator. But a ton of gratitude for reading my book without bias and telling me exactly where it needed improvement.

There's also of course my family, especially my parents and my in-laws. I'm not an easy person to be and deal with on a daily basis. I wonder many times how you all tolerate me. So, thanks for being by my side and helping me see through this book in your own way.

Then there are friends, which include quite a few people. So, without getting into specific names (mostly because I don't want to piss someone off in case, I forget to name them), here's a thank you to everyone who knows me personally.

For the others who know me (or knew me once-upon-a-time) and wonder why I don't call, or drop a message saying 'Hi', here's a disclaimer: I'm not great at keeping in touch. But if you've read my work sometime, someplace, and it brought a smile to your smile, that's me saying 'hi'. Also, thanks for your support. I can promise to call or text, but we both know that's not going to happen. So, let's call it a truce? Oh, and yeah, do keep reading my books and all my social media content. It doesn't help pay the bills much, but it helps me stay motivated to continue writing. I promise to forgive you for not wishing me on my birthday or forgetting to send me gifts.

Lastly, it's YOU. If this is the first book of mine you're reading, I admire your courage in picking up a book penned by someone you've never read before. So, thank you.

But if you're someone who has read all my books (or more than one book), here's a virtual Hi5 from me. It's because of souls like you that I gathered up the courage and motivation to work on this book. Thanks for sticking by. I promise to keep providing more books, each one better than the previous. So, stay with me on this journey.

That's all folks (for now at least)

Keep reading.

Love & Luck Always,

Manali M. Desai

(A Rustic Mind)

Epigraph

"Learning from your mistakes and getting inspired from other's success is the way to growth."

\- Ayesha Banerjee
(Who is basically a fictional character so it's my quote)

Praise For *Love (Try) Angle*

CONTENTS

2014

Prologue

"Not wanting a girl child is as stupid as getting into a journey without knowing your destination."

-Ayesha Banerjee

"Our next participant is Ayesha Banerjee. An all-rounder in all senses, Ayesha's recent achievement has been winning the State Level Debate Championship for the second year in a row. Let's welcome her on stage for her poetry recital."

A scrawny, dusky girl, with pigtails, walked on to a roaring applause onstage. She had an air of confidence about her that would shame people double her age.

"Good evening, dear friends, parents, esteemed judges and respected principal and teachers."

She smiled and continued, "I haven't given any title to the poem that I am going to recite today. The simple reason being that I believe it is not my right to name something which belongs to all."

She paused a bit to look at the audience before starting her recital. Every person seated in the auditorium felt like she was looking directly at them. Such was her presence, that it made everyone feel involved and had them on the edge of their seats. They hung on to her next words with undivided attention.

"I hear voices, happy voices and rejoicing all around,

As the news of my soon arrival starts doing the rounds.

Though I'm just beginning to take form,

By happiness and blessings, I'm already being swamped.

Everyone takes such good care of my mother and me,

We're always surrounded by love, good food and all-around glee.

Mom and dad talk about me all the time,

With kicks I sometimes respond to put in my chime.

My mother's tummy begins to swell,

As I slowly grow within her protective shell.

They do not yet know if I'm a girl or a boy,

I hope this, in no way, affects their happiness and joy.

In a few days I become too big for the womb,

I want to get out as for breathing and moving I need more room.

That's when my mother begins to scream in pain,

Because all I wanted was to come out of this reign.

Soon the agony ended for her and me,

And for the first time my parents I could see.

Mother looks tired but happy as she holds me in her arms,

Father stays distant and unaffected by my presence and charms.

In just a few hours I encounter all human emotions and behaviour,

My mother's yelling, screaming, pleading, and crying, failed to be my saviour.

I was snatched and taken away by my own father,

Who threw me into a dump without any bother?

Oh! Mother, the foul smell is suffocating me,

And there is only darkness around as far as I can see.

But it is the ants and insects tearing into my skin that hurt more,

As slowly the numbness engulfs me, and I see your happy face as I enter another door."

As she ended the poem, there was a 10 second pin-drop silence. This was followed by an applause so loud that anyone passing from outside the auditorium would have thought there was an explosion inside.

Most of the audience was standing as they clapped hard, and some were even wiping away their tears slyly before anyone could notice. But

Ayesha's eyes didn't miss these things. It was this that made her love being on the stage, performing and making people hear her stories.

The event ended with Ayesha bagging the first prize. As she was given the trophy, the Principal of the school could only say, "Ayesha Banerjee is someone the school will always be proud of, because we expect nothing but greatness from her in the coming years."

Ayesha bowed in respect and collected the trophy. She smiled and wondered what the future held for her and what kind of greatness she was meant for.

A New Beginning

"Silence is a privilege when your mind is in chaos".

-Viren Joshi

"And just how do you justify charging so outrageously for such a short distance?"

"Sir, that's not for me to decide. The meter shows the reading, and you need to pay the amount that it reads. Also, it seems you are new to the city. So let me tell you that the rates are different after midnight."

Viren was shaken out of his reverie by the loud, arguing voices drifting in through the open window of his bedroom. He was irritated to be disturbed at an hour he considered holy. Holy because it was past midnight already. But mostly because it literally was the only time, he could concentrate on his studies without the unholy sounds of the city he called home.

Mumbai can't be the city it is without its sounds though.

Shh. We'll argue about that later.

He moved out of his chair to look out the window and understand the unholiness properly. Viren took in the scene in front of building number 2 of Sunrise Housing Society. He saw a middle-aged man and woman alongside a young girl. They seemed to be standing with their luggage, waging a war with one of the 'always in a mood to argue' taxi men of Mumbai.

The taxi driver looked irritated and kept gesturing towards the meter of his taxi. Clearly unconvinced, the middle-aged man was visibly shaking with anger.

Viren thought things were about to get ugly. Just then, the girl, who had so far been standing behind and observing, came forward. Viren could make out her confident posture even from such a distance. Her hair was tied up in a bun and the shorts she was wearing did complete justice to her long, shapely legs.

Creep!

Well, I can't see her face and her legs are exposed. What am I to do?

If you say so.

A baggy t-shirt and a pair of sneakers completed her casual look. Viren couldn't help but admire her boldness at wearing such an outfit while travelling in a compartment probably full of leering men in an Indian railways train. It was obvious they had travelled by train. Even someone visiting Mumbai for the first time wouldn't call the distance between the airport in Andheri to the Sunrise Housing Society in Matunga, "a short distance", as proclaimed by the annoyed passenger.

The girl gently held the middle-aged man's elbow and had a whispered conversation with him. At this point Viren had gauged that she was the daughter and the other two of the trio, probably, her parents.

The middle-aged man grunted loudly and handed over the taxi fare without any word after this little scene.

As the taxi moved out and the trio slowly made their way towards the entry of building number 2, Viren wondered what the girl had said. But he remembered he had bigger problems. So, he shrugged and got back to his study table. He was soon deep in concentration, digging into his UPSC[1] guide. It was much later when he stretched out of his chair and prepared to go to sleep that he realized they now had new neighbours. He chuckled about how migrants were always getting into arguments with the auto and taxi drivers of the city.

"Just a forgettable unholy incident".

But those legs.

Goodnight creep.

---

[1] The Union Public Service Commission (ISO: Saṅgh Lōk Sēvā Āyōg), commonly abbreviated as UPSC, is India's premier central recruiting agency. It is responsible for appointments to and examinations for All India services and group A & group B of Central services.

He went to sleep peacefully soon. He obviously didn't have an inkling that his life was about to encounter many such unholy incidents in the coming days.

Slow And Furious

"Being a Mumbaikar[2] comes with the price of having to explain to an outsider why you prefer to travel by public transport even when you have a car."

- Abhi Agarwal

"Oh goddamit! Will you just move please? I can't go ahead because you are in the way."

These outsiders. Why do they keep blocking our way?

Abhi was already in a bad mood. He had been reluctantly sent by his parents to drop off their guests at VT station. [3]

Let's be clear. It was not parents. Just one parent. Singular!

"But it makes more sense to go by the local train. What is the need to drop them off by car? I'll ensure that they are properly seated before I leave."

"No Abhi, you will do no such thing. Can you imagine how disrespectful and discomforting it will be for the Mehtas to travel in the local train? Take my car if you have to, but you will drop them off in the proper and respectful manner."

Sigh! It's so much easier to convince strangers than your own family.

Especially your father.

He knew that tone of his father. There was no room for further discussion. Hence, a disgruntled Abhi had driven through the narrow lanes and jammed streets to the VT station. He had dropped the

---

[2] a native or inhabitant of the city of Mumbai

[3] Chhatrapati Shivaji Terminus (CST), formerly known as Victoria Terminus (VT), is a UNESCO World Heritage Site and a historic railway station located in the heart of Mumbai.

Mehtas near the station entry. They were waiting for him to join them as Abhi looked for a spot to park the car.

He had found a perfect one but was unable to reach it. Two women, who seemed to have just gotten out of the station, were standing at the same spot for the last two minutes. They were oblivious of blocking his way to drive further. Even after honking a couple of times, they hadn't moved, which had led to his outburst.

"Excuse me? Can you please speak politely? I'm sorry we have been blocking your way. But we have just entered here and are confused about what to do next. Is this how the residents of this city treat their people?'

Abhi looked at the speaker and was left speechless for a minute. Her piercing brown eyes felt like they were passing a judgement on everything. Yes, they seemed to be scanning him whole, right from his car to his open necked shirt that exposed a bit of his chest.

Is she making you uncomfortable?

Huh! Not at all and who is she anyway?

He mumbled, "I'm sorry. I just need to park my car before that space is occupied". He noticed her flared-up pointed nose. He heard a small grunt as she moved aside grabbing the elbow of the woman with her.

She mumbled, "Please go ahead". Then she did a dramatic flip of her hand to point towards the vacant spot.

Well well, she's a fiery one.

Abhi mumbled another 'sorry' as he drove ahead and parked the car. He couldn't help checking out the speaker's long legs in the rear-view mirror.

Sexy, right?

Well, what I'm supposed to do when she's wearing shorts!

He observed the women getting into a taxi along with a middle-aged man. He sighed thinking about the growing incoming crowd into the city and got out.

Abhi and the Mehtas slowly made their way towards the platform where their train was already stationed. He helped them locate their compartment and seats. Once inside, Abhi stowed their luggage below the seats and sat down for a while to ensure all was okay.

"Thank you, Abhi. It's alright if you want to leave now. I understand it might take you a while to reach back home because of the traffic", said Mrs. Mehta kindly.

"No, aunty. In fact, it will be a little better while going back. Because it's the opposite route. So, I'm not worried about the traffic now. I'll get some refreshments for you", saying so he stepped out of the compartment. He bought two bottles of water, a packet of chips and biscuits, and three cups of tea. Barring one teacup, everything else was passed on to the Mehtas.

He gave them company as he stood on the platform. He leaned his arm on the window outside their seats while savoring his tea.

"Here, have some snacks with it dear," Mr. Mehta offered.

"No uncle, just this tea is what I need. I avoid junk food and such beverages too. But driving in Mumbai can be tiring. This tea is my antidote for that. I always joke that the reason Mumbai is called the city of dreams and the city that never sleeps is because the people spend so much time outside their homes. They're stuck in traffic and travelling most of the day. Hence, there's no time for the city and its people to sleep anyway."

Mrs. Mehta chuckled and said, "You are such a funny boy. We are sorry for the inconvenience, but your father just wouldn't listen."

"No worries, aunty. He is a tough man to convince once he has made up his mind. When it comes to hospitality, he is very particular."

Soon the horn signalling the train's departure blared. He bid the Mehtas farewell and a safe journey. Whistling lightly, he made his way back to the spot where he had parked his car.

As he drove back home, he recalled the flared-up nose of the girl he had earlier run into. It brought a smile to his face. There was something incredibly attractive about the girl's anger.

She looked even sexier with that rage.

Though he hated admitting it, he had been more at fault than she was. Not to mention, a little impolite too. He sighed and thought "Let

bygones be bygones" and turned on the music. The lyrics of *Maahi Ve*
[4]immediately filled his heart with peace. He soon forgot all about that
flared-up nose.

Little did he know of how much entertainment that specific facial
expression was going to lend him in the coming days.

---

[4] A Hindi song from the movie *Kaante*

A Musical Meeting

"Music can make any task easier, less tedious, and take the boredom out of the mundane"

- Ayesha Banerjee

"Maut se darr nahi lagta mujhko, sirfff tumse judaai ka darrr haiiiiiiiii…"

Ayesha crooned at the top of her voice as she swayed around the room. She had her earphones plugged in. Hence had zero idea that she was at that moment being watched infuriatingly by her parents.

It took a tap on the shoulder by her mother to bring Ayesha back to the real world. She was annoyed at being brought out of her trance. It was helping her get through the enormous task of unpacking her clothes and books.

You have just too many books.

Duh, what helps you top the class and win those debates?

"Oh, hello. Sorry I didn't see you there. Err, when did you both return?"

"About a minute ago, and we have some company too. Apparently, your singing can be heard till two floors down and it is causing this young gentleman a disturbance in his studies."

At this, Ayesha followed her mother's pointed finger to notice a bespectacled guy standing at the door of their house. He was wearing a simple grey t-shirt and beige cargo capri shorts. Even a cursory glance at his messed up wavy hair was enough to tell that he must be having a hard time taming that mane.

She sheepishly pulled out her earphones and mumbled, "Sorry, I can get carried away with music sometimes."

As their eyes met, his mocking expression was unmissable. His twinkling eyes felt like they were judging her choice in music.

Probably your shabby clothes too.

He is for sure, checking you out babe.

"It's alright, umm, maybe just listen and not sing next time? I'm sure Neha Kakkar[5] would appreciate that too. Since she's a musical maestro, the rest of us can never come close to her singing level."

Oh! the nerve.

She forced a smile as she said, "Of course. I assume you need to catch up on your studies. See you around."

Saying so, she shut the door in his face before he could humiliate her further.

Huh! Just what does Mr. My-Choice-In-Music-Is-Better-Than-Yours think of himself?

What a snob to presume she was listening to the Neha Kakkar version of Maahi Ve!

She was brought out of her fuming trail of thoughts when her father mumbled, "Be polite to the neighbours, Ayesha. We're new here and don't want to start off on the wrong foot before we've even settled down."

Ayesha nodded and hugged her father. She mumbled a sorry again. He was one person whom she never deliberately annoyed.

I aspire to be like him one day.

"Okay, let that be. Tell me, what did you guys bring?"

"We bought some basic things from the nearby store. Oh, and you are going to love this! The society has a nice park of its own. It's tiny though. But there are quite a few parks in the neighbourhood itself. We can pick and choose any for our morning walks."

---

[5] An Indian singer

"Perfect, I was wondering about that too. So that's sorted now. Did you get a notepad for me? I'm still having a hard time recalling how I forgot mine in the train."

"Yes. We bought two just in case you lose or forget one somewhere again, like before."

Ayesha hugged her mother as she rolled her eyes and said, "Here's your Crackle too. God knows when you'll get rid of your chocolate obsession."

Ayesha grabbed it right away, ducked into the chocolate and continued, "But how did you guys run into him?", she said pointing towards the door. Despite her annoyance she couldn't help being curious about him.

"His name is Viren and he seems like a nice fellow. He stays on the 3rd floor with his parents and sister. Bless his kind heart. He offered to help with the groceries and anything else we might need while settling in."

Ayesha gritted her teeth. She was still not over the cheekiness of Mr. Viren with his hi-fi musical taste. But she muttered an "Okay" with a straight face to show her assent.

"We met him in the elevator. The usual initial introductions followed. During that chat he also told us about the loud singing. It led him to come up and request the perpetrator to keep their voice down. It was when we came home that we realized it was your singing that had been disturbing him."

Ayesha blushed and felt bad. She nodded embarrassingly and gave an apologetic look.

Her parents then began to take out the other groceries and got busy arranging them around. Ayesha too resumed her unpacking and plugged her earphones back in. She couldn't help rolling her eyes as she controlled her urge to sing out loud again.

I can enjoy the music in my mind too.

It's not the same though.

Sushh you!

Call Me Maybe?

"Chivalry is often confused with flirting."

-Viren Joshi

It felt like the perfect beginning to a long day of studies again. The sun had just started to spread its light. Viren felt good as he stretched his arms and legs before his morning jog.

Another day drowned in books awaits.

Only a few more months now.

He soon began his first round and noticed the new girl with her father Mr. Banerjee.

So, they have found their way to the popular Kings Circle Garden.

He wasn't surprised. It was literally an oasis right in the middle of Mumbai's concrete jungle. And a marvel for anyone new to the city.

As he drew close to the duo, Viren couldn't help but chuckle as he recalled their brief encounter yesterday.

She's cute.

You mean sexy cute?

"Way to make a good first impression, Mr. Joshi", he mumbled to himself. As he jogged past them, he smiled and waved to Mr. Banerjee while trying to ignore her annoyed expression.

But he was a man in his early 20s. Mostly spending his days locked up in a room and with almost zilch socializing. Not to mention the only women he got to see lately were his mother and his younger sister. So, could he be really blamed for noticing her shapely legs and her long wavy hair as he continued to jog?

What's with this girl and shorts?

A little uneasily, he observed that he wasn't the only one enticed by her. Most men his age and even some younger and older ones were hardly hiding their leering expressions as they checked out Ms. Banerjee.

She was wearing a pink sleeveless tank top. It hugged her chest as sweat beads trickled down her neck and made her dusky skin glisten. She walked briskly with those damn earphones plugged in. This only helped add to her overall mysterious aura. Not to mention, it made everyone in the park either gawk at her or envy her at that moment. She had an almost hourglass shaped figure, so why wouldn't people admire it?

As Viren was close to passing by them again, he noticed that her shoelaces had come off. She, of course, was oblivious to it. Although the thought of her tripping over made him chuckle, he did the right thing.

"Hey, your shoelaces are undone", he said tapping her shoulder. As he overtook them he couldn't help adding, "I'm sure Ms.Kakkar will appreciate catching a breath too while you tie them."

The grunt that followed could be heard even with his back turned to them. The smirk stayed on his face as he slowly sat down on a vacant bench. He wanted to relax for a while before making his way back home.

After a few minutes, he noticed that she was walking back alone towards their society. So, he quickly jumped up not wanting to miss another opportunity to pull her leg.

Surely, you mean figuratively, right?

He quickly caught up with her.

"Hi there, I believe a round of introductions is long due now. I'm Viren Joshi, who is probably making it difficult for you to follow the 'Love thy neighbour' rule."

An eye-roll and then, "I'm Ayesha Banerjee. You can stop acting all chivalrous now. It can impress people like my father and those of that generation. But I know it's just a façade to flirt."

Ouch!

"My my, aren't we being all judgemental? Okay, Ms. Banerjee. I'll try not to be polite and helpful. I mean if that's what makes you uncomfortable."

Her voice rose a notch as she turned her face towards him. Viren couldn't help noticing how her nose flared up.

She's cute when she's angry.

Sexy is more appropriate.

Focus, she is saying something.

"Who are you to talk about being judgemental when you presumed Neha Kakkar to be on my playlist and have not left even one opportunity to pass a snide comment about it? Before you go all Chandler Bing on me again, let me clarify that I wasn't listening to her version of *Maahi Ve*. And I certainly wasn't listening to any of her songs during my morning walk today."

"Gosh! Are you feeling better now? That was quite a monologue. Okay, so I'm sorry about those comments. It was wrong of me to be prejudiced about you. My opinion was based on an entire generation of teenagers who swear by Neha Kakkar being the only good singer. Can we start afresh now?"

The nose is still flared-up.

But she seems calmer.

"I guess so. Also, I'm 18 and almost out of my teens now. So, I don't belong to the generation you're referring to."

She held her hand out as a peace offering. A tiny smile played around her thin lips as she looked at him piercingly. As he shook his hand with hers, he couldn't help but notice how hers felt so soft and tiny in his.

She was still smiling as their brief handshake ended. He couldn't help smiling back too.

"Noted your age, mademoiselle. Since we're neighbours and even friends now, would it be too soon to exchange numbers? My phone is anyway non-existent for me these days, so I assure you, no 'Will you be my frannd?' messages and friend requests from 'Angel Priya' from me."

She chuckled at that. The ringing sound of her laugh made his heart beat a little faster. They had reached their society by now. He pressed the elevator button once they were inside building number two. They stood facing each other while waiting. The ghost of her chuckle still lingered around those tiny lips. It was the first time he noticed her dimple, albeit just a small one.

It only appears when she smiles wide.

Ah! Time to put those unfunny jokes to use.

They're funny alright!

"Sure, you can have my number. Here", she punched her number into the phone he extended towards her. As their hands brushed, she quickly diverted the topic and asked, "So, what's keeping you so busy anyway? Weren't you disturbed in your studies by my singing? What an unusual hour to study."

"All hours are unusual in this city to study. Anyway, I'm preparing for the UPSC. So, even 24 hours seem less. But I'm getting by so far."

"That's great! Hey, my father can help you. He knows many people in the civil services."

The elevator dinged and announced its arrival. Ayesha seemed uncomfortable, and added, "I'll just check on my father and return home with him or my mother will bombard me with questions I'll not have any answers to."

It was hard not to notice her reluctance in being alone with him. He shrugged and said, "Sure, I have your number now anyway. So, I'll call you maybe?"

There's an unfunny joke again.

She smiled and nodded. Viren got into the elevator hoping that she understood his lame referential joke. The smile didn't leave his face till he showered and had breakfast. He prepared himself to join his only friends these days; the UPSC course books.

Before drowning into them though, he sent a text saying, 'Hi, try to keep the music down today ☐ "

"I'll try. But you've to promise to make up for my boredom."

Stop blushing like a teenager and get back to your books.

That blush was soon going to be a regular feature on his face though.

April 2016

Jai Shree Ram

"Belief in religion is preferencing, belief in spirituality and a higher force is pragmatizing."

- Ayesha Banerjee

The chants of 'Jai Shree Ram' were getting louder by the minute. As were the sounds of the bells tolling in the temple[6]. The clapping of hands by the huge crowd assembled there, intensified too.

Ayesha was consumed by it all. Though there was noise around, it gave her mind some much-required peace. It was her first Ram Navami [7]in Mumbai, where it felt mellowed in comparison to the northern states where she had spent her childhood. She wasn't naïve enough to fall for religious fanaticism. But she did believe there was a higher force than mortals, beyond humans and animals. Hence, she preferred being called spiritual rather than religious.

As the Aarti[8] reached its crescendo, a calmness washed over Ayesha. She spotted Viren in the crowd and passed him a smile. Dressed in a light orange cotton kurta[9], he surely looked better than what she had seen of him so far.

His eyebrows rose in a manner of asking her 'Are you checking me out?' So, she quickly averted her eyes towards the idol in the front. She could feel his eyes on her and felt a blush creeping up her cheeks.

---

[6] a building where people pray to a god or gods

[7] Rama Navami is a spring Hindu festival that celebrates the birthday of the Hindu God Lord Rama. The festival celebrates the descent of Vishnu as shri Rama avatar, through his birth to King Dasharatha and Queen Kausalya in Ayodhya

[8] A Hindu ceremony in which lights with wicks soaked in ghee are lit and offered up to one or more deities.

[9] a long, loose shirt worn by men and women in south Asia

"So, I see you took my recommendation and decided to come." Viren said as he walked up to her after the Aarti ended.

"Yes, thank you for the suggestion. I was feeling very nostalgic about missing the grand celebrations up north. It's huge out there. One year we went to Ayodhya[10]. It was so captivating that as a child I remember feeling like I had walked into a fairyland."

"I'm not much of a religious person. But that sounds like a grand experience. This is the most popular Lord Rama [11]temple around here and I thought it would serve your purpose."

"Yes, it did."

They slowly made their way towards the gate of the temple together. Ayesha was acutely aware of the quickly dissipating initial animosity and discomfort between them. Suddenly, Viren turned around. Somebody had tapped him on the shoulder and was offering the prasad[12]. Ayesha held out her hand too. While putting the laddu in her mouth she saw the offeror's face.

Where have I seen this guy before?

He smiled and said, "We met at VT station the other day. Sorry about that again."

Oh! It's that Mr.Rude.

"Hi. Never mind. It's all in the past now."

"That's great. Anyway, I'm Abhi Agarwal and abhi (now) I must finish this work. But nice seeing you again. Bye."

She couldn't help smiling at the lame joke as she said, "Okay, bye. And I'm Ayesha by the way."

He waved and walked away continuing with his sweet's distribution. The lemon-coloured kurta he wore, complimented his fair complexion

---

[10] An ancient town in North India, in Uttar Pradesh State. As the birthplace of Rama, it is sacred to Hindus.

[11] A deity or deified hero of later Hinduism worshipped as an avatar of Vishnu

[12] A devotional offering made to a god, typically consisting of food that is later shared among devotees.

very much. He had added a dupatta[13] to it too. This further completed his traditional look. Ayesha couldn't help noticing how the girls seemed to engage him in chit chat before he could move on to the next person for offering the prasad.

Viren made a coughing sound, making her realize he was still there.

"Shall we go on or would you like to stay behind? I mean if you would like to talk to the gentleman until he is done with his current task at hand. Seems like there will be a queue for it though."

The sarcasm didn't go unnoticed by Ayesha. But she ignored it and said "No, let's go. I wanted to try out Mumbai's popular Vada Pav[14]. Is there a good place around here?"

"Wrong question. You're in the mecca[15] of Vada Pavs. Of course, there is a good place at every corner here. The important question is, which one is worth trying? You're in luck because you have me, your unofficial and unpaid guide to the many secrets of Mumbai."

"Are you always such a snob or is it my presence which brings out this charming side of yours?"

"I'm going to take that as a compliment and continue with my city guide. Follow me mademoiselle to the best of Vada Pav this side of town has to offer. You don't mind walking a bit, do you? If not, we can take the famous kaali peeli."[16]

"How far is this place?"

"Roughly around 10-15 minutes walking distance from here."

"I'm not even wearing the right footwear for that. Let's take a taxi please."

---

[13] A dupatta is a scarf worn by people in India

[14] Vada pav, alternatively spelt wada pao, is a vegetarian fast food dish native to the state of Maharashtra. The dish consists of a deep-fried potato dumpling placed inside a bread bun (*pav*) sliced almost in half through the middle.

[15] a place that many people wish to visit because of a particular interest

[16] a kaali peeli is a black and yellow taxi that runs on the streets of Mumbai

"Your wish is my command milady." Saying so he put his hand out. As if he had conjured something right out of a magical wand, a black and yellow taxi appeared within seconds.

He opened the door and indicated for her to go in first. The chivalry wasn't lost on her. Soon they were moving across the city at a pace that would shame a snail.

"Is it always this bad, the traffic?"

"Yes, it's worse during the morning and evenings. But don't worry, we'll reach our destination in 10 minutes even with all this traffic."

He suddenly brushed aside a hair strand from her face. It was threatening to invade her eyes soon. The unexpected touch sent shivers down her spine, and she froze for a second.

Where did that come from, girl?

She quickly hid her flustered face under the pretence of getting her hair in place.

"Umm.. So, tell me, why UPSC? Is it the lure of money or doing good for the society that beckons you?"

"Neither actually. I see it more as a challenge currently. I've worked in the corporate world for a bit to know that I'm not cut out for that. So, it was either a government job or doing something of my own. I wasn't sure what I could do on my own, hence UPSC beckoned."

That's an interesting motivation.

She was genuinely intrigued by his persona and simply nodded.

"Oh, we're here."

She made to get the money out of her wallet, but he was already getting out. The taxi drove away immediately once she was out and before she could offer to pay.

When did he pay him?

She shrugged and turned around. A huge board read 'Kirti College Vada Pav Center".

"Welcome to one of the best Vada Pav joints in the city, madame."

She asked him to take care of the order as she felt completely lost in the crowd. This was further propelled by the menu which offered a variety of Vada Pavs.

"Good call. I think you should start just with the basic Vada Pav. Try the other items as and when you can."

He went up to the counter and she got a chance to sneak a look at him again. Viren was not someone you might call 'handsome' but there was this charm about him she couldn't quite resist. While making small talk with the person seated at the counter, he smiled and ran his hand through his curly hair. Suddenly she felt the urge to do the same and wondered what it would be like to run her hands through his mane.

What is going on? Get a grip girl!

She reprimanded herself but couldn't stop the warmth spreading over her body as he made his way back to her. He was smiling as he carried two plates of Vada Pav. The twinkling eyes and his childish eagerness would make someone think he had just bought her tickets to Disneyland.

They ate in silence as she savoured her first bite of the dish.

"This is delicious. Having spent most of my life in North India, I have grown to enjoy spicy food. So, this is kind of perfect. At least my taste buds will be happy here. The rest of me is still adjusting."

Once over her foodgasm, she realized that Viren had been looking at her with a most peculiar expression.

He quickly looked away and suggested they should return soon. It was hard for her to not notice the change in his body language as they took another taxi and made their way back.

Why is he acting so cold suddenly?

"Where exactly have you moved from? You only mentioned North India, but which city?", he asked, breaking the awkward silence.

"We have moved here from Chandigarh. That's where we were for the past 7 years. Before that we were in Agra for 7 years. And before that in Kolkata. I was born in Kolkata, and we moved to Agra when I was 4. So, I have been here and there since I was a child, which explains my fused-up cuisine preferences."

Viren smiled and nodded absentmindedly.

Why isn't he talking?

"What about you? Were you born and brought up in Mumbai?"

"Yes. I'm the living embodiment of the working middle class of Aamchi Mumbai.[17]"

The drive back didn't take long and was mostly spent in some more small talk about family and past lives.

On reaching, he hopped out of the taxi and bade her a quick goodbye. He disappeared into the society and building before she could say anything.

She paid the taxi driver and walked into the building, wondering about how strange the boys in this city were. There was Abhi Agarwal, who had seemed so rude in that first encounter but was so gracious today. Then there was Viren, who oscillated between being friendly and weird.

"Oh well, at least I got my Ram Navami nostalgia satisfied."

"Jai Shree Ram", she chanted as she entered her house.

Right away, she got busy narrating the events of the whole evening to her parents. As she chatted away about the beautiful temple décor and her Vada Pav expedition, the boys were forgotten, at least for the time being.

---

[17] It means Our Mumbai. "Aamchi Mumbai" is the loving phrase used by Maharashtrians in general, and Mumbaikars in particular, to refer to their beloved city, the economic capital of the country, Mumbai.

Temple Run

"You either do or you don't, there's no in between when it comes to faith."

- Abhi Agarwal

The lyrics of "Waah Waah Ramji, jodi kya banaayi" [18]hit Abhi's ears as he entered his house.

What is this?

"Really mom? Do we literally have to play each song with 'Ram' in it?" He asked in a mildly irritated tone.

"It was you who put on the playlist. I'm too preoccupied with the preparations to bother changing the song."

Abhi sighed and turned off the music completely.

How am I supposed to know what kind of songs come out by using the filter 'Ram'?

Anyway, it was better to work in silence for a while than barking at each other from one end of the house to the other.

The Agarwals lived in a luxurious 3 BHK apartment in Pashmina Serene. That in itself spoke volumes about their strong financial standing. Add the location factor to it and eyebrows were raised right away. Abhi had yet to meet someone who didn't go "Dude, you're rich" when he told them he lived in the posh area of Hindu Colony in Dadar.

Radha Agarwal was a staunch believer of Lord Rama. Abhi often joked that if she weren't tied down with responsibilities of being a wife and a mother, she would have been a frontline crusader of the 'Mandir Yahi Banega' [19]movement.

---

[18] A Hindi song from the Bollywood movie *Hum Aapke Hain Kaun*

[19] A slogan to build "Ram Mandir" in Ayodhya as a place of birth of Lord Ram. Mandir: Temple

It was the most coveted day of the year in the Agarwal household, the *Ram Navami* festival. So, everyone was on high alert. Nobody dared cross the *home minister* on this day. It was a good thing Mr. Agarwal was a believer himself, or Abhi worried there would have been literal fireworks in the house. Not that there weren't already.

He sometimes amused himself by thinking of the questions his parents must have asked each other in their arranged marriage meeting.

"Hello, I'm Radha. Is there a Lord Rama temple in your locality?"

"There isn't, but I'll build one soon enough. Jai Shree Ram. Oh! and my name is Shyam."

"Did you buy the sweets and flowers as instructed? Last time you got boondi ladoos [20]instead of besan ladoos. [21]That just wasn't right. It's not Sai Jayanti. [22]It's Ram Navami." Shyam Agarwal's gruff voice brought Abhi back to the present.

"Yes, and don't worry so much. I even checked the décor while coming back. The temple looks just like you had visualized. In fact, even better than that, I feel."

"I sure hope it does. I haven't spent half my life toiling around it to be disappointed by the outcome. The least we can do is ensure it looks good on such an auspicious day. If we are all ready, I think we should start making our way to the temple."

Both the Agarwal brothers, Abhi and Varun, helped their mother, Radha, in carrying the necessary items required for the big Aarti. All the four Agarwals settled down in the car after two rounds of ensuring that everything was taken. It was a rare occasion when Abhi agreed with the rest of the family that taking the car would be more convenient. What with all the things they needed to carry and not to mention their heavy Indian traditional attires. Yes, walking to their destination, though less than a kilometre away, would be a fool's errand in such a scenario. Of course, Varun was driving so that was another

---

[20] Boondi laddu or bundiar laddu is made from bengal gram flour based boondi

[21] Besan laddu is a popular Indian sweet dish made of besan (chickpea flour or gram flour), sugar, and ghee

[22] Birthday of Shirdi Sai baba in India

factor in Abhi's peaceful consent. Being the younger sibling came with many such perks and Abhi never shied away from those.

The drive from Pashmina Serene to today's destination, the Lord Rama temple in Wadala, was hardly a five-minute affair.

"Abhi and Radha, you carry the lighter items. Varun and I will park the car and get the heavier items."

Shyam Agarwal instructed once they reached the temple. The mother-son duo did as they were told. The Lord Rama temple looked resplendent with a combination of fairy lights and earthen lamps lighting the exterior as well as interior.

There was a huge rangoli [23]at the entrance depicting the holy trio of Lord Ram, his wife Sita and his younger brother, Laxman. There were earthen lamps placed around its border. Flowers were dispersed in a random yet symmetrical manner in between the rangoli design. A few mosaic glasses were placed here and there too. The lights reflecting from the earthen diyas [24]created beautiful shadows over the floor and ceiling. There were other smaller rangolis across the perimeter of the temple adorned in a similar manner. These represented various scenes from the epic Ramayana. [25]Annam Vilakku lamps [26]were placed in between each rangoli, lending the exterior an overall alluring aura.

All the visitors, including Abhi and Mrs. Agarwal, were spellbound. It was easy to see why people weren't heading straight inside.

---

[23] Rangoli is an art form, originating in the Indian subcontinent, in which patterns are created on the floor or the ground using

[24] A diya, diyo, deya, divaa, deepa, deepam, or deepak is an oil lamp usually made from clay, with a cotton wick dipped in ghee or vegetable oils. Diyas are native to the Indian subcontinent often used in Hindu, Sikh, Jain and Zoroastrian religious festivals such as Diwali or the Kushti ceremony.

[25] Rāmāyana is one of the two major Sanskrit epics of ancient India and an important text of Hinduism, the other being the Mahābhārata. The epic, traditionally ascribed to the Maharishi Valmiki, narrates the life of Rama, a legendary prince of Ayodhya city in the kingdom of Kosala

[26] The Nachiarkoil lamp, also called Annam lamp or Nachiarkoil Kuthuvilakku, is an ornamental brass lamp made of series of diyas, a handicraft product which is exclusively made by Pather (Kammalar) community in Nachiyar Koil town in Tamil Nadu, India.

"I told you it looks better than we anticipated."

"Yes, it does. Come on, now. Let's not forget our main task."

They hurried inside and headed straight towards the attending priest. All the items they were carrying were handed over to him and his handful disciples.

"It looks marvellous, Trivedi ji. You have outdone yourself." Said Mr. Agarwal as Varun and he joined them soon.

"You are too kind, Shyam ji. But it was yours and Radha ji's vision. And of course, a team effort by the florists and the womenfolk of our families, including Radha ji herself."

The head priest Mr. Trivedi had been the caretaker of this temple for the past twenty years. Since its inception, to be precise.

"Come, please take the lord's blessing before we begin the final preparations."

All four of them went into the inner sanctum and bowed in reverence. Abhi didn't always agree with his parent's religious beliefs and inclinations, but he wasn't an atheist either. This temple was probably one of the few inheritance endowments he and his brother would be blessed with. After all, their father was the founder and chief financer. The thought wasn't entirely a pleasant one for Abhi, but he shrugged it off. After all, that was a probable scenario way into the future. So why worry about it from now on?

As the time for the Aarti drew closer, the preparation began in full fervour. A gold-plated thali[27] and a brass diya [28]were handed over to Mr and Mrs. Agarwal respectively. Today was one of those few occasions during the year when the Agarwal couple did the Aarti.

---

[27] Thali (meaning "plate") or Bhojanam (meaning "full meal") is a round platter used to serve food in South Asia and Southeast Asia. Thali is also used to refer to an Indian-style meal made up of a selection of various dishes which are served on a platter.

[28] Diya is an oil lamp with a cotton wick dipped in ghee or vegetable oils. Brass is a hard yellow metal that is a mixture of two other metals (copper and zinc).

A conch[29] was blown by one of the junior priests indicating the commencement of the Aarti. Abhi was handed over a hand bell and he saw Varun holding a pair of cymbals. As the singing began, Abhi got lost in the all-consuming uplifting aura. He rang the bell in his hand with as much fervour as his spiritual heart could invoke.

He looked around as the Aarti was reaching its crescendo. He had never seen the temple so crowded. The management had literally outshone their own last year's footfall. His eyes suddenly caught a movement in the crowd, and he soon spotted the source. She was smiling at someone, but he identified her right away. It was Ms. Sexy Legs from the day he had gone to drop the Mehtas.

She was wearing a peach-colored sleeveless kurta. She had paired this up with a white dupatta that was adorned with mirror work. The reflection from the mirror work was what had caught his eye. Her dangling earrings shone off the light from the many diyas that illuminated the temple. She was constantly head bobbing to the tune of the Aarti, which made the earrings and her dupatta even more prominent. Though he couldn't hear it in the crowd, Abhi was sure the many bangles[30] on her wrists created a tune of their own as she clapped away fervently. With all the adornments, and her dimpled smile over her peaceful face, it was hard for anyone in the crowd not to notice her. At that moment though, she was looking at a guy wearing an orange-colored kurta. A pang of jealousy rose within him.

Who is he?

Why does it matter to you though?

Abhi's mother coughed as the Aarti was ending. It was a clear call to get his attention back to where it mattered. She handed him and Varun two plates of the ladoos he had bought earlier.

"Go start distributing the prasad before all the people leave."

Abhi headed straight towards Ms. Sexy Legs. His earlier jealousy was shooting high as he noticed her talking to the same orange kurta guy.

---

[29] The shell of a sea creature. In India certain kind of conches are played by blowing into them on auspicious occasions

[30] a circular metal band that is worn around the arm or wrist for decoration

He offered the prasad to the guy first. His aim was to get her attention to himself.

It worked. He saw a flicker of recognition in her eyes.

He smiled and said, "We met at VT station the other day. Sorry about that again."

"Hi. Never mind. It's all in the past now."

She looked even more appealing from so close by. The peach kurta suited her dusky skin.

She looks hot even in Indian attire. Rather, hotter!

Perfect package, huh?

He wanted to talk some more but remembered his mother's instructions. Varun seemed to be doing a better job and he didn't want to hear the usual "Learn from him" again.

"That's great. Anyway, I'm Abhi and abhi (now) I must finish this work. But nice seeing you again. Bye."

She smiled. He couldn't believe his lame joke worked!

 "Okay, bye. And I'm Ayesha by the way."

He noticed her dimple as she continued to smile. Then he waved to her and walked away reluctantly before getting consumed by her charms.

Let's focus on this task.

But you might never see her again!

As he continued his sweet's distribution, he hoped she would wait awhile. The task was getting on his nerves because the aunties and some of the teenagers seemed to deliberately engage him in chit chat. He didn't want to seem impolite either, so relented.

He went from one to the next person as quickly as he could. As he approached the last few visitors, he noticed that she was leaving with orange kurta.

"Ah! Let it be. If you love someone, let them go, blah blah..."

He laughed at his own joke and turned towards the remaining visitors. Most of the crowd had dispersed. Those who remained were just friends and acquaintances of the Agarwals. His parents were talking to the priests, probably congratulating them on the success of the event. His mother walked towards him with a few of her female friends and their daughters.

He knew what was coming and dreaded it.

"Hello Abhi beta[31], how are you?", asked Mrs. Kulkarni. Without waiting for his response, she went on, "Did you hear the good news? Gayatri is soon starting out at your college."

Abhi smiled politely and said hello to both the mother and the daughter. He sometimes wondered how Sharad, his closest friend, was an offspring of this nosy woman. But he was used to her eccentricities by now. He and Sharad were classmates at Mithibai College[32], so he already knew Gayatri cursorily.

"Congratulations. Though I must warn you that it's not as fancy as it is made out to be. Also, no concessions for you on the ragging front."

Gayatri merely nodded and smiled. She quickly excused herself and walked out citing 'my friends are waiting for me' as a reason.

She's pretty as well.

But you obviously like Ms. Sexy Legs.

Abhi observed her walking away. He could not help drawing a comparison between the two young women he had met today. The alluring Ms. Ayesha and this demure Ms. Gayatri.

"Women and their mysterious ways", he mumbled to himself and prepared to leave with his parents soon. He couldn't stand Mrs. Kulkarni anyway. Surely not without Gayatri as a shield.

---

[31] A person's son

[32] Mithibai College of Arts, Chauhan Institute of Science & Amruthben Jivanlal College of Commerce and Economics is a college affiliated to the University of Mumbai

May 2016

Have A Good Day

"Finding your footing in a new place means getting a chance to explore new sides of your own personality."

- Ayesha Banerjee

"Hey, I wish I could join. But it's just not possible. It'll take away 2-3 hours from my study time. Sorry."

You're on your own girl.

Ayesha read Viren's text and groaned. She dreaded the prospect of going by herself to her new college. She had mostly had either of her parents accompany her when it came to form filling and fee submissions. And school was a different ball game. Even with the change in schools a couple of times over the years, Ayesha had managed to get things done. If her parents were sometimes unavailable, things didn't seem that intimidating because she had figured out her way around.

She was completely new to the college scene and the city was still unknown for her. Her parents were busy with their jobs. Plus, they wanted her to be an "adult" and learn to do such things on her own now. Self-confidence was one of the virtues Ayesha prided herself in, but this time she was a bit nervous.

As a last resort she had messaged Viren and asked him if he could accompany her. She expected him to deny it but tried her luck anyway. Her phone beeped again.

"I didn't know Ms. Ayesha could get nervous too. Where is your confidence? We've been through the route and it's just a form submission. You'll be fine, don't worry. Good luck and have a good day. Let's meet in the evening if possible."

He's such a kind soul.

Or is he flirting?

Such a pessimist you are.

She smiled and left the house, a little less nervous now.

It's not going to be so difficult. Come on girl.

Yeah, anyway Mr. Chivalrous has explained the route so well.

They had been running into each other quite frequently during their respective morning walks. She had asked him about the route a few days back.

"Mithibai is just a 15-minute walk from the Vile Parle station. You can take the slow local from Matunga. One important thing by the way. If you are planning not to walk, you will have to catch a rickshaw. [33]There are very few taxis running in that part of the city. The rickshaws aren't allowed beyond Bandra. That's why you see so many taxis here."

"Okay. I'll keep that in mind. But tell me, how far is Matunga station from here and how do I get there?"

"Umm.. it's actually not very far. Would you like me to show you the way? We can go today evening."

She had obviously agreed. Reaching Matunga station had taken around 15 minutes, but she didn't mind walking. Viren constantly kept her engaged, explaining to her the route and how to remember it.

"So, this is the King's Circle Garden which you already are well-versed with now."

"Yes, I am still enchanted by it every time. The location is what amazes me. Bam in the middle of a crossroads, below a bridge. There's such an urban hustle outside, with the vehicles and so many shops on both sides of the street. But once you're inside the park, it feels you're cut off from it all, despite being just a few steps away."

Why is he looking at me like that?

"Did you know it is one of the very few such parks in the world? Also, Matunga is popular for many such parks and gardens. The lane you see

---

[33] A small light vehicle with two wheels used in some Asian countries to carry people over short distances. The rickshaw is pulled by a person walking or riding a bicycle

there has 5 gardens in close vicinity to each other, on the same street. Hence the street is called 5 Gardens. Then there's the walkway below the flyover too. It is very aesthetically done. You can come there too for your morning walk. Or you could go to any of the five gardens in that lane."

Ayesha listened in fascination and looked at the places he was pointing out. She was glad her family had landed in such a great locality.

Also, glad to have got Viren right?

Of course, duh.

"So, you cross this circle, which is the King's Circle Garden and go walk straight for about fifteen minutes. Ask anyone if you are confused. And here you are."

Ayesha saw the board that read 'Matunga'. There was a constant flow of people going in and coming out of the station.

"This is quite close by."

"I told you. So, that's the ticket window. I suggest for tomorrow you just buy a return ticket which will allow you to travel from here till Vile Parle and back home. Later you'll probably be getting a concession for your daily travel pass. Most colleges provide that."

Ayesha nodded as he continued, "So, when you buy the ticket tomorrow, ask the attendant to help you out with the next train going to Borivali. He will mostly direct you to platform number 1. But let's not take a chance. When you are on the right platform, ask anyone where the ladies' compartment will be. That way you don't need to worry about creepy uncles and dudes on your first day of travel. I'm confident that you'll figure out your way once you get familiar with the city and this route. Also, since tomorrow you aren't time bound, I suggest you travel after 11 am so that there's less crowd. Even on your daily commute after tomorrow, I don't think you will face the problem of crowds. Because you are traveling in the opposite direction and most of the crowd will get down at Bandra. The tricky part for you might be boarding the train. You might also find the train a little more crowded when you return. Here too boarding and alighting will be challenging."

This is so overwhelming.

Viren probably gauged her nervousness, so he smiled encouragingly and went on, "It's not as difficult as it sounds, trust me. Might I also suggest that you download the M-Indicator app right away. It's your answer to every mode of travel in Mumbai."

Ayesha nodded. She was still apprehensive about all of this, but Viren made it seem simple.

He's so caring and considerate.

Sometimes he can look good too.

What has that got to do here?

While returning, Viren had insisted they try out something at the popular Koolar & Co. It was located right opposite Kings Circle.

They ordered Irani Brun Butter Cucumber and Masala Omelette as per Viren's recommendation. Ayesha was regaled with tales of how the café was considered iconic.

"You must have seen it in many movies, most recently it appeared in *The Lunchbox and Singham Returns.*"

There was a different spring in his step and a twinkle in his eyes the whole evening. As he had gone on to talk about the neighbourhood and then the eatery, Ayesha saw a side of him which was quite a delightful revelation for her.

He's so easy to be with.

Another food adventure passed pleasantly before they made their way back and retired to their respective homes.

They had bonded well in the little time they had spent together during the last few weeks. She was glad to have found someone who could be her local guide. Sometimes her heart fluttered when he smiled or when their hands touched accidentally. But other than that, he was just a great companion to be with.

Viren's instructions played in her mind once she reached the railway station. She was excited and nervous at the same time. This whole experience of being on her own and finding her way around, was a heady feeling.

She did exactly as Viren had told her the other day. She bought a return ticket and asked about where to board the next Borivali train from. As predicted by Viren she was told to go to platform number one. The people were kind enough to guide her to the right platform and then direct her towards the ladies' compartment.

It's not that difficult. I can surely do this every day.

You go girl.

Her optimism faded as she realized that a huge crowd had slowly gathered around her to board the train along with her. Once the train came in, there was frantic movement among the people waiting to board. Her nervousness increased as she looked at the people literally hanging on to the edge of the compartment doors. Once the train started to slow down, people began to jump off it even before the train halted.

What is the rush?

Ayesha soon got pushed as more people hopped off. Surprisingly, the people who had been waiting, cleared away slightly and waited patiently for those who were getting off, to get done. Once they had all alighted, only then the waiting ones started boarding, but then too all at once. She too rushed forward and with a little pushing and shoving, got in just in time. The compartment was sparsely filled, and most of the people seemed to be gathered near the two doors itself. Ayesha pushed her way through the crowd to get further in. It dawned on her that they were probably waiting to get down at one of the next stations. Once comfortably inside the compartment and away from the assembled crowd near the doors, she settled herself at a vacant window seat. The train halted for a while, and the compartment got almost empty. Ayesha remembered Viren's words, *"you are traveling in the opposite direction and most of the crowd will get down at Bandra."*

She smiled at that. Viren had prepared her quite well. Apart from the slight hitch while boarding the train, (which too Viren had warned her about), things were going pretty okay till now. The gentle blowing of the wind coupled with her favorite companion, music, made the remainder of the journey quite pleasant for Ayesha.

Once she got off at Vile Parle, she was confident about finding her way around. Of course, technology was at her aid too. So, she sought help from Google maps and reached her soon-to-be college in 15 minutes. She didn't mind walking today, but she would probably have to take a rickshaw if she were running late or something.

Once there, she took in the college building from outside. As she read the words "Mithibai College", she felt her heartbeats getting louder. This was it, her first step towards her future. All her hard work in securing good grades and never missing out on any co-curricular activities, had been to reach here. She had wanted to get into St. Xavier's but sadly they didn't offer BA Hons. Political Science course. Hence, she chose this. Why do a simple BA when she was sure about her majors?

"Hey, you lost or something?"

She turned to the voice and saw a girl staring at her intently, but kindly. The speaker was about an inch shorter than Ayesha. She was wearing a blue sleeveless V-neck kurti, paired with black jeans. She even had light makeup on and the many bangles on her hand jingled in a melody of their own as she unbuckled her hair.

Ayesha suddenly felt underdressed in her plain black t-shirt and blue jeans.

"Oh, no. I'm at the right place. But yes, I'm definitely lost about what to do next. Can you tell me where I can submit my admission form?"

"Of course. Which course? I'm here to submit my form as well. Come, let's do it together. My brother is already a student here, and he's waiting inside for me."

"Thank you so much. I'm Ayesha and I'm joining the B.A. Hons Political Science course. What about you?"

"What a coincidence. We're going to be batchmates then. I'm Gayatri. Oh! There is my brother." Gayatri pointed a little further and the duo made their way towards two boys. They had apparently been waiting for them. She recognized Abhi Agarwal right away.

Is he stalking me?

Probably. It's weird that you keep running into each other like this.

"Hello, Ayesha. Are you stalking me or what?"

"You wish! But how come you are here?"

"I'm a student here, mademoiselle. This is Sharad by the way, and the young lady with you is his sister."

She waved and said hello to Sharad. She could see the resemblance between him and Gayatri. Both had the same button shaped nose, deep-set black eyes, and a fair complexion. Sharad's was albeit a shade darker than hers. The only difference was in their heights; Sharad's 5.11 towered well over Gayatri's 5.4.

The four of them made their way towards what seemed like a never-ending queue.

"You girls wait here. We'll get this done in just a few minutes. Ayesha, you have all your necessary documents, right?"

"Yes, I believe so."

Both the boys confidently walked to the front of the line. Ayesha was impressed and worried at the same time.

"Don't worry. They've good camaraderie with most of the admin and management. They'll work their charm and get the task done without having to wait in the queue."

Ayesha simply nodded at this bit of information relented by Gayatri. She couldn't help but notice how chic Mr. Abhi looked. He was wearing a white t-shirt over which he had put on a black shirt that was left open. The sleeves of the shirt were rolled up to his elbows and one could not, not admire the well-toned muscles hiding beneath. He had paired this with a pair of black chinos and light brown loafers. His perfectly-in-place wavy hair was slightly disarrayed because of the crowd. *Sexy* was the word that came to Ayesha's mind as he made his way back towards them. She noticed many of the girls in the crowd either waving to him or giggling as they passed by him.

Jealous, are we?

Uh oh! He looks annoyed.

"Did you not get your Migration Certificate and the application for Provisional Eligibility Certificate?"

"Huh? Why?"

"Uff, you outsiders. Why do you people not research properly before going in all blind? You will require a migration certificate from Mumbai University to complete your admission formalities. Did you not have the common sense to read all the conditions before barging in here?"

His voice had risen by ten decibels at least. Ayesha noticed that everyone had stopped talking or moving. It felt like the entire hallway was holding its breath.

"I did my research. It was nowhere specified that I would need to submit the migration certificate along with the admission form. I have already arranged for the certificate and have clearly made a note in the form that I will submit it on the first day of college. But since you precious Mumbaikars seem hell bent on making an outsider feel unwelcome, I will come and submit it later, along with the damn migration certificate. And, the application for a Provisional Eligibility Certificate too."

She snatched the form from him and turned away before the tears threatened to make an entry. She was so blinded with rage and embarrassment that she didn't bother to respond to Gayatri's pleas to come back. She ran out as fast as she could. She wanted to put as much distance as possible between herself and that snob!

Her initial judgement about him had been right. He was a privileged, arrogant typical *bade baap ki bigdi aulaad.* [34]

What does he think of himself? Just because he is rich and looks good, he can get away with being rude every time?

But….

The tears fell in earnest as she made her way back home, dejected and demoralized to the core. Not only was she angry at him, but she was also disappointed in herself.

Who does he think he is talking to like that!

She was Ayesha Banerjee, school topper and someone who never took crap from the likes of him. She was determined to either ignore Mr.

---

[34] Aimless kids with too much money to spend from their filthy rich parents' bank accounts.

Agarwal or show him just who she was, or rather *who he was* by putting him in his place.

The same journey that had excited her an hour back felt like a burden as she contemplated her days ahead in the course. Pursuing Political Science from one of the best colleges in the city had been keeping her optimistic about leaving behind her friends. She was looking forward to meeting new people and making new friends. But it felt the most hostile of welcomes now.

If today was anything to go by, she didn't know how long it would be before she started to regret coming to this city. Because she was already dreading the move.

The only tiny ray of hope in her life currently was Viren. A little smile broke through her tears as she remembered their plans of meeting up in the evening.

See, the welcome to the city is not as hostile.

But.. What about college?

Let's worry about that later.

Everything's Gonna Be A-Okay

"When you are looking forward to something, the time seems to just drag on."

- Viren Joshi

"Hey, are we meeting?"

His heart fluttered as he read the text.

What is this girl doing to me?

He felt like a stupid teenager trying hard to woo the girl he had a crush on.

Nonetheless, he replied, "Yes, see you at the gate in half an hour."

He took extra care dressing-up today. Obviously, the clothes he was currently wearing wouldn't do. A drab grey t-shirt and boxer shorts would hardly impress any girl.

He quickly changed into something more presentable and washed his face. He was whistling and combing his hair when he heard his mother from behind.

"Are you going somewhere?"

He should have expected such behaviour wouldn't go unnoticed.

Sadhna Joshi stood with hands on her waist, amused by this sudden change in her son's evening routine. As far as she could recall, he hadn't stepped out at this hour since the past six months.

"Yes, I'm meeting Ayesha. Remember the Banerjees I told you about?"

"Oh yes, Ayesha is their daughter, right? And she was the one you helped with the station route too, correct?"

"Yes"

"So, what are you helping her with today?"

The sarcasm was blatantly ignored.

"Nothing, I thought I'll just take a small break."

"It's good to see you stepping out of the house more often. Frankly, it's a bit of a relief to see you haven't lost your ability to socialize. 22 and already acting like an uncle. Huh!"

Viren laughed and replied, "Let's not get carried away, mom. Our definitions of "socializing" are poles apart. Gossiping with the women of Sunrise for two hours under the pretext of evening walks, is not socializing."

"It's more of a social service actually. We share our woes and help each other with suggestions. Not much unlike how you're helping the young lady."

He had no comeback for such a ridiculous justification. He loved his mother to bits but was not blind to her idiosyncrasies. She was a schoolteacher and took care of the household with meticulous precision. None of the Joshis could ever match her level of perfection. When it came to mundane things though, she had her own eccentric ways. Neither Viren nor his sister Nalini were such oddballs, and he was glad for it.

"I hear she's quite the all-rounder. She has won many creative writing and poetry debate competitions in school. Her mother told Mrs. Sinha all about it. She has just cleared her HSC[35] with 94% and is joining Mithibai soon."

That was news to Viren. The bit about her being a star student. But then he wasn't surprised.

Well, that explains her fiery attitude and confidence.

Viren simply nodded and deliberately kept his face void of any expression lest his mother start another round of aunty type jokes. So, he bid her a goodbye and made his way towards the door. Just before stepping out, he asked, "Anyway, do you want me to pick something up while coming home?"

---

[35] The Higher Secondary Certificate (HSC/INTERMEDIATE) is a public examination in Bangladesh, India, Nepal and Pakistan. HSC is equivalent to GCE A Level in England and 3rd and 4th year of high Schools in the United States

"Whatever you're 'helping' the young lady with. Because I'm sure you're taking her to some food joint. Oh, and get three of whatever it is. Nalini should be back by then and your father will be home too."

Nodding his head, Viren walked out whistling.

Look at you all cheery about meeting her.

I'm just happy to be stepping out.

Okay, you can tell yourself that lie.

Ayesha was already waiting at the gate. One glance at her was enough to get his heart racing.

Shut it! You're not in college anymore.

She was wearing a beige-coloured dress with multi-coloured floral patterns. The dress ended just above her knees, exposing her smooth long legs. Her hair looked different today. It was left loose from behind. She had put on a bow headband to probably keep it from flying all around in the windy weather.

We're going retro today it seems.

She certainly carries it off well.

Ayesha smiled and waved at him. It was clear that something was troubling her. The smile didn't quite reach her eyes and her wave was very unenthusiastic.

Uh-oh. Is she upset about me not joining her in the morning?

Viren hoped not. This outing itself was cutting thin into his study schedule. So, he didn't know how to defend the absenteeism if it came up. He decided to lighten up the mood.

"Why do you look like you've just seen a ghost? I must warn you that there are some ghost stories about our society…."

Without any preamble, she rushed forward. Quickly bridging the few steps between them, she engulfed him in a hug. The suddenness of it sent him a few steps behind. He could not react for a second or two but was soon embracing her in return.

She smells like a garden.

Her dewy fragrance consumed his head and body completely. It was a completely hedonic feeling for him. Involuntarily his hands found their way to her open hair. Her hands were teasing the back of his neck too, giving him goosebumps right from head to toe. He could feel her trembling and started to move his hands up and down her back to pacify her. She moved away a bit without leaving her hold on him and looked up into his face.

Oh my God! Why is she crying?

Viren's heart was gutted at the thought of what must have broken her heart. Without bothering about the consequences, he leaned down and kissed her on the forehead. The physical proximity to her body and the touch of his lips to her skin, set his mind ablaze. His breaths became deep and shallow. It took all his self-control to not kiss the rest of her face. But he did cup it up in both his hands and stroked her cheeks gently to make her understand that he felt her pain.

This made her hug him tighter. She leaned her head on his chest and Viren heard her sigh. He continued to cuddle and caress her back to calm her down. Slowly her breathing became normal, and thankfully, as did his.

Whoa! And you think there's nothing between you two huh?

Can you disappear for a bit?

As if brought back to the reality of the present at the same time, they broke apart.

"Sorry about that. I've had a rough day. Can we go somewhere where we can just sit and talk? But I'm hungry too. So first, let's eat something."

She avoided eye contact. Her nervousness was obvious in the rapid way she talked. She quickly wiped away the tears from her flushed cheeks. Then began fidgeting with her hair, trying to get them in place as she waited for him to respond. It was a little amusing for him.

She's so cute when she acts all sorted.

Trying hard not to laugh he said, "Yes, sure. Have you had a dabeli[36] before? Let's try that today. There's a roadside stall nearby that is extremely popular."

"Yes, I have had it once before and loved it. Let's go then."

They made their way out of the society and towards Matunga Dabeli. Viren noticed that Ayesha was walking further than usual from him. It was obvious to him that she was trying to keep a physical gap between them.

The popular roadside food stall wasn't far. They reached there in an uncomfortable silence within just a few minutes.

"The stall has been around for many years and people from various parts of the city come to devour this street delicacy. You know, it is my backup plan to open a franchise of this somewhere in South Bombay."

Viren joked, trying to dissipate the sudden awkwardness between them.

She merely smiled.

Your jokes are really bad dude.

But she smiled and you better stay shut.

Dejected, Viren went ahead and placed an order. He glanced at her while waiting for the order. She still looked anxious. Wondering what was bothering her, he carried back two plates. He offered her one plate, wishing that food would do the magic he couldn't.

One bite into it and her face broke into a smile.

Phew!

Well, she clearly likes the food more than you.

Umm.. so?

---

[36] Dabeli, kutchi dabeli or double roti is a popular snack food of India, originating in the Kutch or Kachchh region of Gujarat. It is a sweet snack made by mixing boiled potatoes with a special dabeli masala, putting the mixture in a ladi pav (burger bun), and serving it with chutneys made from tamarind, date, garlic, red chilies and other ingredients

He heaved a sigh of relief and said, "Clearly this guy knows how to woo girls. I need to take lessons from him." Viren said, pointing towards the man busy handing out dabelis to the huge crowd around him.

Ayesha laughed and punched him playfully on the shoulder. The touch gave him goosebumps again. But he shook himself out of it and dug into his own dabeli.

"Would you like another one? I'm getting three of them packed for my family. Would you like to take it for your parents as well?"

Ayesha looked at him in a peculiar way, "Yes, please. Not for me I mean. Please get two of them packed for my parents."

Her voice sounded almost like a squeak. It made his heart melt.

Is she still sad?

Yes, mostly because of your stupid jokes.

Oh, go away.

He got back with two bags and handed one to Ayesha. There was no need to decide on what to do next. Viren knew where they both wanted to go. They made their way in silence to their now common favourite spot, the King's Circle Garden.

Ayesha had probably not seen it during the evening yet. She looked at the yellow lights lit around the periphery of the garden in awe. Viren pointed to a bench below a tree, and they made themselves comfortable.

"I'm so glad I have you to find my way around this city. I wish all Mumbaikars were like you. Welcoming and kind."

Aww, she likes you.

She is miserable. Can you give it a rest?

Viren didn't respond. He knew she needed to vent out whatever had upset her. He moved his hand towards her palm which lay on the bench. His intention was only to console her, but she quickly moved it away.

Well, bad luck buddy.

I'm fine, really.

Okay. Good for you.

"I had the most unwelcoming experience at the college today. You remember that guy Abhi Agarwal we met at the temple on Ram Navami? He's a senior in the same college."

Viren nodded and listened to her narration without interruption. He knew what being a good listener came with. He "hmmed" at the right places to let her know he was on her side. He noticed that flared-up nose. She was even more beautiful when vulnerable like this. Viren controlled his urge to pat her back or console her physically. He didn't want to bring her any more discomfort for the day.

This Abhi Agarwal is a conceited pig.

Who talks to someone new in the city like this?

It had clearly been a harrowing experience for Ayesha, and it angered him. He wanted to punch that idiot in the face for his insolence.

"So, that's that. The migration certificate is here now. I have also written an application for the Provisional Eligibility Certificate. I'll go back tomorrow, and I hope I don't see that moron again."

"I hope so too. Are you feeling better now though?"

She nodded and smiled nervously.

"Oh c'mon. You can kick his ass once college starts. From what I hear, you're quite a debater. "

"Thank you. I feel better now." The smile was much wider now.

Well done, buddy.

"That will be 1000 Rs. plus, taxes. I charge by the hour for my counselling."

The laughter that rang out from her mouth warmed his heart. He was finding it hard to see this dejected side of her. The confidence she emanated was one of the things he found highly attractive about her.

Are you sure it's just that?

No.. it's….

Bringing himself out of his reverie, he said, "We should be heading back. It's not that we're getting late. But the dabelis won't be as delectable when they're cold. Your parents won't enjoy it. My family has had it umpteen times, so it doesn't matter."

There was that peculiar look again.

What's up with her today?

She stood up and pulled him up too, to indicate her assent. As their hands touched again, a shadow crossed her eyes. She looked directly into his eyes and before he could understand anything, gave him a peck on the right cheek.

Oh my!

Congratulations, mate.

He was sure he turned red. He hoped she couldn't hear his heartbeats which were threatening to burst out of his body.

She brushed her hand on his cheek and said, "Thank you for everything and for today, especially."

Just as abruptly, she removed her hand from his and started walking out. He followed, still reeling from the titillation that her lips had sent over his entire being.

La la la la la la….

Let's head back home and to the books. You better shut up now.

My Dream Is To Fly

"Without ambition there's no purpose to life."

- Ayesha Banerjee

"This isn't ragging, come on, don't look so glum! We would rather call it an 'ice breaking session'.", Sharad was addressing the huge crowd gathered in one of the halls at Mithibai college.

Sharad, Abhi and a few other seniors were up on a makeshift stage. It was the first day of college for the new students.

Ayesha and Gayatri were standing next to each other. It wasn't just students of their department. The various course students had all been asked to assemble there before commencing their classes.

"So, it's quite simple. As your seniors, we want you all to feel welcome to this college. All we want is for you to introduce yourself to us and everyone here. The catch is that it must be something that describes you in the best possible manner."

At this point, Abhi took the mic from Sharad and continued.

"See, we don't want an essay about your name, your achievements, how well you did in your school and blah blah. It's boring stuff. Put that on your CV rather than telling us here about how great you are."

He sounds so arrogant.

But he's still hot.

Some girls chuckled at that. Ayesha simply nodded, that too while looking at Sharad. She, however, did notice that Mr. Agarwal was *dressed for the occasion* as always. He was wearing a casual black blazer over an aqua-blue round neck t-shirt, with black denims. A pair of white sneakers completed his semi-formal look. A few weeks back, this might have impressed Ayesha, but today she knew it was all just a façade hiding the arrogance inside.

She couldn't help but notice that Mr. Rich and snooty, Abhi Agarwal, was looking at her with a sly smile on his face.

It's as if he knows you checked him out.

Snob.

He went on, "This is a reputed college so we're aware that all of you scored over 80% in your HSC boards. We don't care about that. You've made the cut to be among the best. What we are looking for are people who can maintain the prestige of the institute and hopefully take it a notch higher. So, be as creative as possible."

He had the audience captured. They all seemed eager to impress. Some of the girls were already giggling, poking each other, and discussing what they would be doing.

I see he's got a fan club among the freshers already too.

Are you jealous babe?

"So good luck, or shall I say may the odds be in your favour", he winked and pulled out a chit from a bowl placed on the stage.

"Ayesha Banerjee"

Uh-oh. What are the chances?

Being the first one made her feel like a guinea pig. Gayatri held her hand and pressed it as a way of reassurance that she had her back. Nervous and hesitant, yet confident in her stride, Ayesha made her way to the stage.

As she moved closer, she noticed how Abhi seemed ready to make her feel embarrassed. Now, Ayesha felt anything but nervous. She felt as if this was the perfect opportunity to let everyone, including Mr. Agarwal know that she had arrived.

That's right. You show him girl!

Getting to be on stage after so many months was exhilarating. Performing for a live audience always made her feel alive. And she was glad her name got picked first, even though out of sheer coincidence.

A mocking smile was already playing around Abhi's lips as he handed the mic to her.

"I won't be needing that. Thanks."

With raised eyebrows he asked, "Will it be a dance performance then? We're all eager to see your moves, Ms Banerjee."

Cheapo.

On any other day and occasion, the mocking comment would have annoyed and maybe even demotivated Ayesha. But this was her time to shine. The self-confidence that had gone astray since she moved to Mumbai, was bubbling to burst forth now.

She straightened her back and answered haughtily, "No, may I please have the tune of heartbeats in the background? I'd prefer the one from Kal Ho Naa Ho[37]."

Abhi nodded slightly. The sly smile was still pasted on his face.

The heartbeats reverberated through the hall as Ayesha faced the crowd. She felt her own heartbeats rise, but with excitement and exhilaration. Sweeping her eyes through the audience, she began

"You look at me and see a girl,

Someone who you probably think is 'pretty'.

Some of you might even label me 'average looking'.

A few of you also see me as an 'outsider'.

Because I don't belong to your beloved city.

You have heard my name already,

Is that what my identity is?

A name on paper and what I look like to you?

Or someone who can be known by their geographics?

That's what I am here to change,

I want to go beyond your definitions of me.

I am here to change perceptions,

I am here to prove my worth,

---

[37] A Bollywood movie

I aim to learn and grow,

I aim to change lives as I go.

My dream is to fly,

My dream is to achieve all that I aim for.

But also remind you every day,

My dreams are my goals.

Watch me as I chase and accomplish them, and be envious,

Or hold my hand and let's together be marvellous!

There was an awkward silence for a few seconds. Then Gayatri began clapping. The rest of the crowd joined in, but Gayatri's claps remained the loudest.

"Well, that was quite an introduction. And highly creative too I must say."

It was Sharad who had taken over the mic again. Ayesha felt a little let down by the lackadaisical applause. She bowed down in acknowledgment, nonetheless.

Have I lost my charm?

Maybe.

But that was one of my best ones.

Ayesha noticed that Abhi looked ashen. His face had gone pale and there was a slight embarrassing look about him.

Is he feeling bad about calling you an outsider?

I hope so.

"Now, before you go. Why don't you pick a chit so we can call on our next performer?"

"Gayatri Kulkarni.", she read out from the chit and quickly made her way down. She felt Abhi's piercing eyes following her. So, the further she kept herself from him, the better she would feel. The whole thing felt planned to her now.

Did he deliberately read out my name first?

Is he making it a point to humiliate me every time?

You're overthinking this. Relax.

Ayesha passed Gayatri on her way down. She gave her a thumbs up to wish her luck. Gayatri too smiled encouragingly and gave a thumbs up to show that she liked her performance.

"Since you have your classes to attend to as well, we are time-bound. So, once Gayatri is done, she will be picking up another chit from the bowl in the same manner. We'll see how many performances we can do for an hour."

It was Abhi back on the mic now. He was smiling in the most charming manner.

Why does he look so pleased suddenly?

Whatever. Let's focus on Gayatri's performance.

Passing on the mic to Gayatri, Abhi said "Good luck, Gayu."

Gayu?

The endeared shorter version of Gayatri's name didn't go unnoticed by Ayesha. A little pang of jealousy rose within her, but she quickly brushed it off. As she looked around, she was not surprised to notice many girls looking enviously at Gayatri already.

Hmm. Interesting.

Gayatri whispered something in Sharad's ear and in a few seconds, Beyonce's voice reverberated through the halls.

She began her graceful, yet saucy movements to the tune and lyrics of *Diva*[38]. Ayesha was spellbound.

Oh my. This girl can dance!

A lot of the boys in the audience were looking at Gayatri with their mouths agape. Mr. High on his Horse, Abhi, looked most impressed. Ayesha couldn't really blame them. The way Gayatri moved to Beyonce's lyrics, made Ayesha feel like the song was created just for this dance by Gayatri. At one point, she did the moonwalk combined with the floss and a twist, which made Ayesha go "Wooo" and quite

---

[38] A song by Beyonce

loudly so. She was glad she wasn't the only one who did that though. Gayatri had impressed most of the crowd with that move.

Abhi stepped forward as the song ended and clapped the loudest. The crowd went crazy with its acknowledgment too. Ayesha was sure the thunderous applause could be heard on the street outside as well.

"That was stupendous. Well done, Gayu. I'm tempted to be your dance partner at a duet performance, if you can allow me the pleasure."

Wait, what? Is he flirting with her?

You are so jealous girl. Just admit it.

Gayatri blushed and nodded shyly. This was followed by a lot of envious looks, this time from the boys and girls alike.

"Your message was loud, clear and I must add very graceful and enticing too. Please choose the next performer. I am sure, whoever it will be is going to curse their luck to be the successor to such a mind-blowing performance. And I'm already feeling bad for your predecessor who you have completely outshined."

What the hell? I don't need your sympathy.

But you clearly want his admiration.

She felt her cheeks reddening as he looked at her. This was so embarrassing.

Gayatri read out the next name "Abhishek Saxena".

"Finally, a guy to defend our honour. I must say, the girls in this batch are killing it. I can only hope the boys do well too. But I'm also kind of nervous for them already."

Gayatri was beaming. Ayesha could only manage a weak smile when Gayatri joined her. As the rest of the performances continued, Ayesha was only half aware. All she wanted now was to get away from the ridiculing expression and piercing grey eyes of Mr. Abhi Agarwal.

He's looking at you.

I don't want him to.

What do you want him to do then?

She was glad they were not in the same class or even the same batch. That way she wouldn't have to endure him every day at least.

Sharad soon announced, "Okay, that's enough show off from you all today. Now it's time to get to your classes or the professors will catch us. As your seniors, we'll only blame you. You don't want that now, do you?"

Ayesha had never felt more relieved as the crowd chuckled and dispersed slowly. She walked out with Gayatri. Together they made their way towards their first lecture of the day.

"Hey, Gayu. Why don't you go on? I'll make sure your friend gets to sit next to you even if she gets a bit late."

It was Abhi, who had apparently run towards them. Ayesha was dreading this already. She didn't need favours from Mr. Sorry-I-Acted-Like-A-Jerk.

"Let's talk after the lectures please. I don't want to make a bad impression as an 'outsider'."

He winced at that. But Ayesha didn't care anymore. She put her hand through Gayatri's and dragged her towards the classroom. Gayatri's, "Give him a chance to explain, at least" fell on deaf ears.

All Ayesha wanted now was to focus on her own lines, My *Dream is to fly*. The only way to do that currently was by being a good student. Something she wanted to continue excelling in.

Good girl.

You stay out of this.

Party All Night

"With great power comes great responsibility, but also the chance to meet new people and grow your network."

\-   Abhi Agarwal

"Hey, Gayu. How's college treating you so far?"

Abhi and Sharad were in the college canteen when they noticed the girls and walked up to them.

"Hey, hi Abhi. It's going quite well. I loved Citizens and Constitutions the most so far. But Ayesha was all ears during Making of the Constitution. Or maybe I should say 'all eyes'."

Ayesha punched her playfully, but the blush on her face was unmissable.

So, she has a crush on the scrawny Mr. Das?

A pang of jealousy shot through Abhi.

What does she see in that boring professor?

"You do know he is dating Ms. Pillai, right?"

"It hardly matters to me. I only like the subject; hence I like him. He teaches well. That's all. Anyway, we have to rush to our next lecture."

"Don't get so lost in daydreaming about Mr. Das that you forget about your nightly adventure of the freshers party tonight."

Ayesha scrunched up her face and gave an almost imperceptible nod. Gayatri had the good sense to pull Ayesha up and make a quick exit before things got ugly. Ayesha passed on a pleasant smile to Sharad as both she and Gayatri waved goodbye. Abhi couldn't help noticing that she deliberately looked anywhere but at him. She had been doing that every time they crossed each other's paths. Either she turned or changed her route or looked the opposite side without making eye contact.

What the hell is her problem?

He continued staring at her retreating figure. She was wearing a grey-coloured layered skirt which ended a little above her knees. She had paired it with a dark blue polka dot blouse. If one wasn't drawn to her exposed legs right away, the sequin ballerinas ensured it. She had worn a pearl anklet on her right foot, which further drew attention to her shapely legs. Abhi couldn't help but notice her arched back as she marched confidently ahead. In just a few days, she had found her footing as an 'outsider'.

Are we still hung up on that?

Well, she started it.

Actually, you did.

The boys who passed by, hardly concealed their desire or admiration for the two girls as they made their way to class. Gayatri waved at a few of them. Ms. Banerjee however, seemed unfazed.

He admired her growth. It felt like just yesterday that she had run out of the college corridor with tears in her eyes. The word had already spread around that she was a fiery one. In fact, she and Gayatri had been nicknamed the 'sinful sisters' by a few of the seniors.

It's an obvious derogatory reference to their looks.

Does that bother you though?

The professors were noticing her too. He knew it because the class representatives had to be elected soon. He was coordinating with the teaching staff to help shortlist the best candidates. Surprisingly, Ayesha's name had been suggested by more than one professor.

"In case you are done with your bird watching, can we focus on the task at hand?"

Sharad hit Abhi on the back of his head with a book. He smiled sheepishly and took a seat at the now empty table. The dewy fragrance left behind by Ms. Banerjee still lingered. It made him suddenly want to embrace her and lose himself in the intoxication of her aroma.

Get a grip boy.

"Okay, so we have it all under control. I spoke to the manager, and he said the venue will be ready in a few hours. So, let's head home and meet there sometime before the freshers start coming in."

Sharad nodded and replied, "You go on. I think I'll wait for Gayu. It's her last lecture for the day."

Abhi couldn't help feeling a little jealous of Sharad. After all, he was obviously getting to see more of Ms. Sexy Legs because of Gayatri. Also, Sharad was not at the receiving end of *Miss Ice Princess*, unlike him.

He walked out of the canteen and whistled his way out of the college. The thought of the evening ahead cheered him. Overseeing events like these and getting to engage with new people always gave him a heady feeling.

Not to mention, the curiosity of seeing what Ms. Banerjee would don at the party.

Well, yeah, a little bit.

An unbidden image of her sexy legs conjured up in his mind, leaving him a little titillated.

Heck!

She was affecting his thoughts way too much than he liked to admit.

On reaching home, Abhi dozed off with the hopes of making things right with Ayesha tonight. It felt that just in a few minutes he was shaken awake by his mother.

"Your phone has been buzzing constantly."

He groaned but got up and about in a matter of seconds. Radha Agarwal was surprised at his proactive behaviour. She looked on amusingly as her son took his own sweet time to finalize an outfit. It was obvious that he was taking extra care to look good today. Multiple shirts, t-shirts, jackets, blazers, and shoes were tried on before he was satisfied with what he saw in the mirror. His aim was to *dress to impress* for tonight.

"You look great. Now move on."

He hugged his mom affectionately, "You say that for anything that I wear."

"Have the bowl of sprouts before leaving. It's kept on the dining table."

He mumbled a "Thank you" while quickly gorging on the healthy yet delectable sprouts.

"See you soon." He said walking out enthusiastically into the glorious sunset.

My Regular Place aka MRP Bistro was just a five-minute walk for Abhi from the Hindu Colony. Mr. Sawant, the manager, was there, overseeing the last bits of the décor. They had cleared away the tables from the centre to make space for dancing. Dim yet sparkling lights gleamed on the floor from the ceiling. A disco ball hung from the ceiling was adding its own shimmering effects.

There were a handful of tables on each side of the dance floor. Tealight candles had been placed inside aesthetic metal and acrylic holders on all the tables. The lights and shadows thrown off by these candles added a charm of their own to the overall aura. There was a small podium at the end of the floor where all the musical equipment had been set up. A DJ was already playing some light music.

"This looks great Mr.Sawant. Thank you so much for doing everything at such short notice."

"It is our pleasure, Abhi. Are we expecting everyone to arrive now?"

"Not yet. Just a few others from the organizing committee."

"Oh, great. Because we haven't put up the plaque outside yet. You wanted a banner behind the DJ as well, right?"

"Yes. I'll take care of that. You please ensure that the rest is in place."

Abhi was putting up the banner when he heard from behind.

"Do you need a hand with that?"

Sharad had arrived just in time. He looked suave in a grey waistcoat and white shirt. The sleeves of the shirt were rolled up till just below his elbows. He was wearing ankle length trousers and loafers. Abhi raised his eyebrows admirably. If truth be told, he had never seen Sharad look so presentable before.

"Someone's dressed for the occasion. Yes, please finish this off. I'll take the other one outside."

Gayatri walked in as Abhi made his way outside with the plaque. She looked stunning in a netted teal green dress. The contrasting, red-coloured pumps made her appear much taller than her actual height. She was wearing a red belt over the dress and a long neckpiece with red and green beads hung around her shapely neck, reaching to her navel. The colours brought out her fair complexion quite well. Abhi was sure a few hearts were going to be stolen tonight. That's if they weren't already robbed.

"You look amazing, Gayu. Make yourself comfortable. I'll join you in a bit once I am done putting this outside."

"You look quite dashing too, but your snooty self probably knows that already."

She winked and made her way towards one of the tables. Abhi chuckled and walked out. He was checking the placement of the plaque and its visibility when an unpleasant sight caught his eye.

Ayesha was hugging someone while she laughed playfully. She then pulled the guy's cheek and said, "Thanks. I'll see you in a couple of hours. Bye."

Abhi realized it was the same bespectacled guy she had been staring at during the Ram Navami Aarti. Pangs of jealousy overtook his entire being as he narrowed his eyes annoyingly.

Maybe it's her boyfriend.

Thanks for your help!

The thought brought a painful and uncomfortable feeling up his heart.

The guy squeezed Ayesha's hand as she walked away from him and stepped forward. Both Ayesha and the guy noticed Abhi at the same time. Ayesha merely ignored him and walked inside right away. The flared-up nose didn't miss Abhi's eyes though. The guy stared at him coldly in a challenging manner for a few seconds, then shrugged and walked off.

Abhi felt dejected suddenly. Nonetheless, he walked back inside, determined to forget the whole episode. He made his way towards Sharad and the girls while humming "party all night[39]" and whistling to himself.

Sure, Ms. Banerjee looked ravishing in her pink sleeveless short dress. But he swore not to let himself get distracted by it.

---

[39] A Hindi song from the Bollywood movie *Boss*

Do You Wanna Partner?

"Regrets have the power to either make you weaker or stronger. The choice is yours."

- Ayesha Banerjee

"This should be fun. I'm really excited."

Gayatri tugged at Ayesha's arms and dragged her to the front. Abhi was announcing the plans for the evening that the seniors had made. It was a combination of some light-hearted games and dancing. Even Ayesha felt a little better.

The thought of attending this party had been making her skittish since the past few days. As the day came closer, her anxiety had only increased. What if a repeat of the first day happened again? The thought of another public embarrassment terrified her. Yes, she had been doing well in the lectures and was already building up a reputation as an ideal student. It was outside the class that she became unsure of herself. The two previous encounters which involved the presence of Mr. Snooty had left their marks on her. She knew it would be hard to ignore him at the party. Especially when he was one of the organizers. She had been close to giving it a miss completely. But Viren had intervened.

"Take it from someone who has experienced college life. You do not want to miss such events. They're always enjoyable. You'll be making a lifetime of precious memories. Not to mention they're a great platform to make friends and grow your network."

Ayesha hadn't been convinced. So, he had gone on and on about it every time they met.

"Come on. How can you let one person's presence dictate your life decisions? I'll come to drop you off and pick you up. That's a huge sacrifice by the way. The prelims are only a few weeks away now. I need to give in more hours of study than usual."

In the end, she had relented just to end the emotional blackmailing. He had of course followed through on his promise too. Though the venue was close by, Viren had insisted they take a taxi. Ayesha had noticed him giving her a head-to-toe scan before declaring that decision. Anyways, she was glad for his company as they made their way to the party venue. Mostly because his constant chatter and lame jokes had helped calm her nerves a bit.

She was almost excited for it as they had got down and she hugged him as a way of gratitude. He obviously had to make a departing joke in his signature style.

"Jaa Ayesha jaa, jee le aaj ki raat."[40]

She had chuckled and pulled his cheek playfully.

"Thanks. I'll see you in a couple of hours. Bye."

The physical discomfort between them was slowly but surely dissipating. Especially after her breakdown on that godawful day. A warmth spread through her body as he gave her hand a final reassuring squeeze. She was ready to face the music, quite literally.

But expect Mr. Conceited to ruin it right away!

What was he doing at the gate anyway?

She did not like the way his grey eyes stared at her accusingly. She had an uneasy feeling in the pit of her stomach ever since then. Ayesha refused to admit that the source of it was Mr. Snob.

Oh, but it is darling.

Whatever.

"Are you ready to *party all night?*"

She focused on the now, albeit half-heartedly. Abhi was shouting into the mic as the crowd cheered a unanimous yes. He noticed the two of

---

[40] Go and enjoy the time of your life tonight. Inspired from an iconic dialogue 'Jaa Simran Jaa, Jee Le Apni Zindagi' from a popular Bollywood movie *Dilwale Dulhaniya Le Jaayenge* where this dialogue is said by the female protagonist's father to encourage her to chase a life of her dreams.

them coming forward and smiled flirtatiously at Gayatri. The uneasiness in Ayesha's stomach went a notch higher.

"We have an evening of dancing, games and food planned for you all. Now, those who do not wish to partake in the games can dance away, and those who wish to do neither, can just enjoy the food. But be prepared for the onslaught of leg-pulling for the rest of the course."

A few people chuckled, again, mostly girls. Ayesha groaned inwardly. Unlike on most other days, she had first noticed Sharad today. This might be because she hadn't really looked at Mr. Chic yet. But she couldn't deny the fact that Sharad looked extremely dapper in the grey waistcoat and white shirt.

Now, as Abhi had all eyes, including hers, on him, she was forced to note his appearance. Today, he was dressed in a crimson shirt and white pants that exposed a bit of his ankles. He had removed the grey jacket paired with it and was carrying it draped over his left arm. The shirt, as always, was rolled up till his elbows. The muscles on his arms and his biceps were more prominent than usual. Probably because he was wearing a slim fit shirt. The top few buttons were undone, exposing his chiselled chest. He was wearing a black wristwatch with a huge dial on one wrist. A thin grey leather bracelet with an om charm decked the other wrist. On his feet were a pair of grey loafers with red and grey ankle socks, completing his impeccable party look.

Ayesha couldn't help admiring his well-toned physique despite her irritation.

And as always, he looks gorgeous.

Can we focus on just having fun tonight?

"To ensure that everybody who wants to dance gets to dance, we have added a twist to the game we're going to play first."

The crowd was hanging on to his words with bated breath. Even Ayesha was feeling giddy by now.

"I'm going to pick up five chits each from the two bowls here. One has boys' names and the other has girls' names. Whoever's names I read out will take their seats on the tables on the two sides, one boy opposite one girl. That way each table will have one couple. Understood so far?"

An excited yes was roared out by the crowd as he went on, "Great. On each table we have placed two boxes with chits containing questions. Each boy and girl will pick 5 of these questions, so in total 10 questions per couple. You need to write your answer to each question on the back of that chit. But here's the catch. You won't be answering for yourself. You need to guess your partner's answer to that question. So, for example, if the chit says, 'Favourite colour' you need to jot down your guess about what your partner's favourite colour might be."

Gayatri was beside herself with excitement. But she asked sceptically, "What if am I paired with Sharad though? That won't be any fun and we would know the answers too."

"Smart question, Gayu. In that case I pick up another chit and pair you with someone one else, hopefully me." He winked at that and Gayatri scoffed.

Why don't you two just get a room!

Really, you care that much, huh?

"If both of you guess more than 3 answers correctly individually, the dance floor is all yours for 2 minutes. Meaning you get to do a duet dance performance. The game is called *Do you wanna partner*[41]. So, are you ready to find your partner?"

Everyone shouted out a loud 'woohoo' to indicate their assent.

Sharad read out ten names one after another. The girls and boys took their seats as their names were announced. Abhi's wish came true as he was paired with Gayatri.

There goes your wish.

No way was that my wish.

Oh, don't lie.

They walked over to one of the tables excitedly with hands looped through their elbows. Ayesha felt a tinge of jealousy but ignored them. She was more eager to know who her partner would be. She beamed

---

[41] A Hindi song from the Bollywood movie *Partner*

when Sharad read out his own name after hers. He looked up and smiled mischievously at her.

Before he walked over to her though, he announced, "Okay, the rest of you have the dance floor to yourself till then. Don't worry, you'll all be getting a chance to play. In case you're already hungry or don't want to dance, help yourself to the food. Two tables have been left out on that side. So, you can use those to sit and eat. Or you can sit and chit chat and play your own set of ice breaking games. Let the fun begin."

Ayesha looped her arm through Sharad's as he guided her to the one last empty table.

"I hope you are ready to dance off. I want to beat those two arrogant asses who probably think they're the best dancers of the college."

She laughed and said, "Let's first win the game."

She noticed Abhi looking at them with raised eyebrows as they passed their table.

Is that jealousy I see?

Who cares?

Sharad pulled out the chair for her before taking his seat.

How chivalrous! How can two best friends be so different from each other?

She wondered not for the first time about the opposing personalities of Sharad and Abhi. Where Sharad was the most kind and gentle guy in the seniors' batch, Abhi seemed to be the most unapproachable and conceited of the lot.

"Shall we begin then?"

"Yes, please."

Ayesha quickly picked out 5 questions and began writing down her answers. She was on her third question when there was movement behind them which made her turn around.

Abhi and Gayatri were making their way to the dance floor. Abhi walked over to the DJ and whispered something.

Probably the song they will be dancing to.

Before he walked back towards Gayatri, he picked up the mic and said, "We declare ourselves the first winners and performers. Try beating our 9 on 10, you all. Also, the challenge is now on for the best performance too!"

Arrogance thy name is Abhi.

So, is jealous thy name?

Gayatri was already standing in a pirouette position. Ayesha was filled with dread and admiration at the same time. As the beats of *Bang Bang* [42]began playing, Abhi waltzed over towards Gayatri.

Whoa. He can dance too.

The chemistry between them was unmissable. His lifts and her twirls set the stage on fire. Never once did they lose eye contact with each other as they held onto each other's arms and waists while moving around the floor. As the song was reaching its climax, Abhi lifted Gayatri with both hands over his head and held her from the waist. She continued waving her arms and legs like a bird as he held her in the air. The move needed trust and comfort which was obvious as they gazed at each other endearingly and almost provocatively. The envying looks from the onlookers were unmissable. Ayesha felt herself going red in the cheeks too. Abhi brought Gayatri back down with a graceful twist of his arms. They held each other by the waist as the song ended and they bowed down to the audience.

That was a steamy performance.

The steam could be coming from your heart too.

There was tumultuous applause but also resentful looks. After all, they made a gorgeous pair, and a lot of hearts must have been broken at that moment. Ayesha felt herself clapping non-enthusiastically too.

Poor baby, are you still denying you're jealous?

Sharad scoffed and mumbled, "Bloody show-offs" as they sat down again. He didn't seem much affected though.

Gayatri and Abhi had disappeared into the crowd that had assembled back on the floor. Ayesha concentrated on the game again. She was

---

[42] A Hindi song from the Bollywood movie *Bang Bang*

determined to burn out the image of Abhi and Gayatri's close dancing, from her mind.

Why is it affecting you so much, girl?

Because you wish it was you instead of Gayatri duh.

"Okay, I'm done", Sharad declared after a few minutes, bringing Ayesha out of her gloomy mood.

"I am done too. Shall we do this then?"

Ayesha smiled and mentally chided herself to enjoy the game.

That's right girl.

It turned out to be quite enjoyable as Sharad joked around his answers. He had mostly guessed them right. But it was his mocking disbelief on the wrong guesses that made Ayesha laugh hysterically.

"What? C'mon! All girls' have DDLJ[43] or Titanic as their favourite movies. What species are you to like Rang De Basanti[44]?"

Ayesha laughed away as she either nodded or shook her head to his answers.

She had guessed 4 answers correctly and Sharad 3, bringing their total score to 7.

"So, do we get to dance?"

"Hell, yeah we do! I'm the organizer and I say we win! Now off we go."

Ayesha laughed as Sharad pulled her up and almost dragged her towards the dance floor.

He leaned in towards her ear and said, "What say we show those bozos their position by choosing an even more stimulating song?"

Ayesha noticed Mr. Snob staring at them with a grim expression.

Yeah, we won too you snob. Now see as we burn the dance floor.

---

[43] A popular Bollywood movie titled ***Dilwale Dulhaniya Le Jaayenge*** often abbreviated to DDLJ

[44] A Bollywood movie

Good girl.

Sharad's suggestion had ignited a fire within her too. This was propelled further as an image of a sullen Abhi came to her mind. Ayesha suddenly grabbed Sharad's elbow tightly and whispered her thoughts animatedly into his ear. All the while, she could feel the cold grey piercing eyes of Abhi glowering at her.

"That's brilliant, Ayesha. I'll get the ball rolling."

Sharad winked at her as he walked towards the DJ to explain what was to be done. Ayesha felt herself flushing with exhilaration. She had goosebumps all over as she moved to the center of the dance floor. A few cushions were laid out as props and Ayesha took her position as she sat on them. She had her back to the audience, with her right hand held upright above her head. Her palm was spread out in the formation of a swan. As the beats of their chosen song reverberated through the restaurant, Ayesha swayed her body in the manner of flowing water. There were already sounds of woot and whistles from the audience, but Ayesha stayed focused.

You've got this girl.

Soon she felt Sharad's hands run over her back and pull her up. They swayed, twisted, twirled, and enticed each other to the lyrics of *Ang Laga de.* [45] The whistling from the audience became loudest when Sharad lifted Ayesha and she embraced him with her legs around his waist. She took her time landing her feet on the floor again as she moved her hands over Sharad's chest and arched her back gracefully to the song's beats. As the climax of the song neared, Sharad lifted her up again and then bent down to land her gracefully, with a split on the floor.

They didn't stop looking into each other's eyes till the song ended. What followed was an applause unlike Ayesha had heard before. Not at least after coming to Mumbai. There was some catcalling and whistling too. Ayesha felt herself going red in the face.

That must be the boldest dance performance you have ever done, girl.

---

[45] A Hindi song from the Bollywood movie Ram-Leela

She still couldn't fathom what had come over her.

How did you muster up the courage to do it and pull it off so well?

A certain set of piercing eyes might be the answer.

Sharad hugged her then and they bowed in acknowledgement to the applause. She excused herself and made her way towards the food section to have some water. Her throat was dry, probably out of the exhilaration.

Or maybe out of nervousness that came from a piercing stare?

"That was quite a performance I must say."

When and how did he follow her?

Ayesha almost choked as she turned around. The water she was drinking got caught in her throat and she began to cough uncontrollably. Her eyes teared up soon. Abhi had come up behind her so unexpectedly that she panicked. He rushed forward and rubbed his hand on her back to help control the coughing. It didn't stop even then.

Omg. I'm dying.

At least you'll die in his arms.

He grabbed her hand and made her sit on a nearby chair while continuing to pat and rub her pack. There were worry lines on his forehead and his eyes were most anxious. Ayesha was able to calm down after a few seconds as the coughing settled. She didn't realize that she had been holding on to Abhi's palm all this while. She let go of it, suddenly feeling very awkward and conscious.

Oh why? We were finally making progress, girl.

'Are you okay?'

She nodded embarrassingly.

Why do I always make a fool of myself around him?

Do I need to answer that?

"Hey, there you are, Ms. Seductress. Are you trying to steal my brother, you vamp?"

Gayatri barged in looking angry. She stood with her hands on her waist and stared coldly at Ayesha.

Uh oh! This wasn't expected.

Ayesha felt flustered and tried to think of a justification. Suddenly, Gayatri just shrugged and pulled Ayesha into a warm embrace. For the next few seconds, Ayesha couldn't stop laughing over the scene Gayatri had tried to create.

"Right. Like I would dare to do that with his sister watching us like a hawk." Ayesha said while punching Gayatri on the shoulder playfully.

She then turned towards Abhi. Before she could acknowledge his question or thank him, Gayatri dragged her back to the dance floor. Almost everyone was there now. A few people were sitting at the tables, munching on the food or just chit chatting.

Clearly Gayatri was in no mood to either sit or eat. So, Ayesha decided to join in the dancing too. Sharad danced his way towards them and twirled Ayesha before turning to Gayatri and doing the same. The duo then began a dance routine of their own.

"May I have the pleasure to dance with you too?"

Abhi's voice breathed down Ayesha's back.

What's with him creeping up on me like this?

She was glad there was no water this time or her coughing fit would have made an appearance again.

But then he would have been so considerate again.

He's surprisingly kind, isn't he?

His voice had made the hair on her neck and back stand. A titillating sensation rose in her stomach as she turned around. But she didn't realize how close he had been standing so she bumped into him.

Oh God. I'm going to slip and fall flat on the floor.

Her hand went up defensively while trying to maintain balance and landed on his exposed chest. She heard a gasp escape his mouth. His hands went around her waist to keep her from falling. Their eyes met at that moment and impulsively, her other hand reached out to his left cheek. Another gasp escaped his mouth as their heads drew closer without their eye contact breaking. Desire was writ large across his face and in eyes as he came closer, and his hands became tighter around her.

Her hand too was moving in a circular movement on his exposed chest. Her other hand had slowly moved from his cheek to his hair. A giddiness and tingling sensation spread over her body. She felt herself trembling as her heart beats became faster and louder. She had no control over her movements as she slowly began to lose herself in his spicy fragrance.

'Ahem'

Sharad coughed uncomfortably from behind them.

What was I about to do?

Just wanted you wanted. Trust Sharad to ruin the perfect moment and opportunity.

Shut up.

The moment ended abruptly, bringing them back to reality. Ayesha quickly straightened up and broke eye contact with Abhi.

"Sorry, I was just wondering if you would like to join us? Gayatri and I are heading towards the food counter."

Ayesha was still reeling over what had just transpired. She couldn't even gather the courage to look up and answer Sharad.

But she heard Abhi say, "No, you guys go on. We'll join you in a while."

Ayesha felt so uncomfortable that she continued to look down.

Abhi placed both his hands on her shoulders and turned her towards him. When she still refused to look up, he put his hand on her chin and gently pulled up her face. Even that little physical touch sent shivers down Ayesha's body. There was an apologetic look in his piercing grey eyes.

"I am sorry. Please don't be embarrassed. I don't know what came over me."

Ayesha could feel tears pricking her eyes. But she nodded to tell him that it was okay. He pulled her into a bear hug then. A few tears rolled down Ayesha's cheeks. He continued to embrace her as he placed his face on her head. His hands were gently patting and moving over her back to soothe her.

He's so dreamy when he's being nice for a change.

But you found him dreamy even when he was not nice to you.

It helped calm her down. Slowly he began to sway to the beats of the music. She felt herself moving along with him too.

"Do you want to go have some food now?"

She nodded without saying anything. He looked down at her. His eyes were so kind and unlike what she had seen so far. He held her face in his palms and wiped away the tears from her cheeks gently with his thumbs. Before she could comprehend anything, he planted a kiss on her forehead and slowly let go of his hold on her.

Ayesha felt herself blushing. She had a tingling sensation on her face where he had touched and kissed her.

He held out his hand and she readily took it as they made their way towards the food counter. The touch made her feel giddy again, but she jerked herself to focus on the present.

Tonight's gonna be a good night. [46]

Yeah yeah. Gloat away.

---

[46] A song by *Black Eyed Peas*

The Way You Look Tonight

"They talk about growing up, but nobody really prepares you for the responsibilities."

-Viren Joshi

"Ready or not, here I come."

Viren hit the send button on the text and waited with bated breath. An image of Ayesha's smiling face as she read his message, conjured up in his mind. It sent a strange satisfaction and warmth over his body.

"Off to be the knight in shining armour again?"

The sarcasm in his mother, Sadhna Joshi's voice didn't miss his ears.

"Firstly, she's no damsel in distress. And secondly, mommy dearest, how are you home at this hour?"

"I can also compromise one day of my evening walk for my son. We're all about helping each other lately, aren't we?"

Viren was slowly understanding where his own dry sense of humour came from. What he couldn't understand was why his mother was behaving like Karan Johar lately. Every time he had walked out of the house in the past few weeks, she was sure to ask or comment about Ayesha. Sometimes she would also break into random Bollywood songs.

What was worse was that she had even got his sister, Nalini into the mix. Dinners were becoming increasingly about putting him on the spot. The mother-daughter duo would sing love songs in chorus and discuss what they would be wearing at his wedding. Such extras!

The teasing had begun from that day he had bought dabelis for them.

"The dabelis are cold which means the weather outside was definitely hot, isn't it Nalini?"

They had then broken into peals of laughter, giggling away at their own joke. It was obvious Nalini had been told about his meeting with Ayesha. They had probably also made a plan of action on how to pull his legs. Viren had ignored them and walked away at that time. But this had become a routine from the next day.

Viren was glad Nalini wasn't around today at least. He could handle one drama queen at a time. Together, they were insufferable.

As he checked himself in the mirror and made to walk out of the house, the usual scene followed. His mother broke into *Sajna hai mujhe sajna ke liye[47]*. Viren scowled at her and exited without commenting. He knew the best way to cope with it was to ignore their behaviour completely.

Viren couldn't believe how Ayesha had fit herself so easily into his routine though. They saw each other and made small talk during the morning walks every day. But this was restricted as Ayesha would be with her father. Not that Mr. Banerjee had any issues about it, but it would be rude to expect Ayesha to walk with him and leave her father alone. On most days though, after the walk, Mr. Banerjee would stay behind to sit and chat with his newfound friends. So, Ayesha and Viren would walk back alone together. The five-minute distance was mostly spent in catching up on her college life and his study progress. But sometimes they also talked about their past lives and future plans.

It was clear to Viren that Abhi was making life on campus difficult for Ayesha. But he was glad to learn that she was enjoying the course and the lectures. She was a quick learner and a fiery one. It seemed she had adjusted to the daily commute well too. Not once had she complained about the crowd on the stations and in the trains, which meant she had adjusted to it already. Viren was kind of proud of her for settling into the Mumbai lifestyle so well. But he was also annoyed by how much she was letting this Abhi guy affect her. What an arrogant prick! It had been a task convincing her to attend the party tonight. But he was glad she'd finally agreed to go. The girl needed to enjoy her youth. And also, of course, get to experience the Mumbai nightlife. He was looking forward to the day when he would be able to do it with her.

---

[47] A Hindi song from the Bollywood movie *Saudagar*

Viren saw Ayesha waiting for him as he reached down. Looking at her made him forget his trail of thoughts.

Like it always does, dude.

His heart fluttered as he took in her appearance.

Maybe there is some smoke to the fire being lit by your mother and sister?

Either way, he couldn't stop admiring how she looked today. A short, pink sleeveless dress hugged her hourglass figure. His eyebrows shot up as he noticed the length of the dress. Sure, she looked ravishing. But Viren suddenly felt jealous of the boys who would be partying with her tonight. The maroon-coloured lipstick and the maroon plus black mascara added to her overall *sexy* look. Her eyes looked even more enticing than usual because of the eye makeup. She had worn black stilettos, making her almost the same height as him today. He gave her a head-to-toe scan again and decided upon what he had already thought would be a wise choice. As he neared her, he declared it to her as well.

"Hi, there. Let's take a taxi? I am sure you wouldn't like to walk either."

Ayesha nodded and they soon got into a taxi. She was fidgety and kept putting her hair behind her ears. Sensing her anxiety, he kept his barrage of jokes on, to try and improve her mood. It probably worked because as soon as they got down, he noticed her smiling in an excited manner.

She hugged him gratefully. The physical contact made the hair on his back stand on edge. To hide his discomfort, he cracked another joke. But this only made her chuckle and pull his cheek playfully. That was an unexpected reaction! He felt a pleasing tickling sensation where her fingers had touched his skin.

How can I let her go now?

It took all his strength to give her hand a reassuring squeeze and see her walk away.

Just when she turned to go, he noticed the prick staring at them coldly.

Way to ruin a moment you ass!

Viren noticed Ayesha's hurried steps and flared-up nose as she walked in straight without looking at him.

Viren had half a mind to confront the guy about his behaviour around Ayesha. But thought, "Well, let's not spoil their evening" and shrugged as he turned and made his way back.

His mind and body were highly unsettled even after reaching home. He just could not give his 100% concentration to the books today. It annoyed him to no end. Even dinner was a quiet affair. His parents and sister had probably figured out his pensive mood and thought of letting him be. He was glad about that. A round of teasing would have only escalated his angst.

He hoped the unease would settle after dinner. But it was in vain. He tried his best to focus on the paper set he had been trying to crack. But his thoughts kept wandering towards what would be happening at the party.

Is she enjoying herself?

Yes, but you are only bothered because you aren't with her.

Would the boys be leering at her?

Obviously, they were.

Is she going to dance with the boys?

Duh! Of course. But you are worried about only one boy in particular.

He let out a loud 'arghh' in frustration. Finally, he just shut the book, laid out on the bed, and forced himself to sleep. That seemed to be the only way to put a stop to the unsettling thoughts.

It didn't help much either though. Because he dreamt that Ayesha was dancing with the arrogant ass. He could hear the lyrics of *The way you look tonight* [48] playing softly in the background. When the song ended, Viren walked up to her and asked if she could be his partner for the next song. But she shook her head and continued dancing with the prick. Surprisingly, the same song started playing again as he gazed at them mutely, feeling distraught.

---

[48] A song by Frank Sinatra

He woke up in a fit of frustration. The only thing that cheered him was that it was time to go pick up Ayesha. The thought of spending time with her again, all alone, improved his mood immensely.

Nalini and his mother raised their eyebrows questioningly as he walked out from his room whistling to himself. He could hear them singing *pyaara bhaiya mera dulha raja banke aa gaya* [49] as he shut the door.

He chuckled. Somehow even the idiosyncrasies of Nalini and his mother helped elevate his excitement. He walked to the venue continuing to whistle and reached there in just under ten minutes.

A lot of crowd was gathered at the gate. Most of them were waving goodbyes and dispersing. He couldn't locate Ayesha though.

Where is she?

His anxiety increased when she hadn't come out even after ten minutes.

Is she okay?

He decided to walk in and check. What he saw next shattered him completely, His enthusiasm about spending time with Ayesha ebbed away. Abhi was carrying her in his arms. He seemed to be headed towards one of the tables. Overcome by worry and jealousy, Viren rushed to see what was happening.

Ayesha noticed him and he saw that her face was flushed.

What is going on here?

She looked slightly embarrassed as well, as if he had caught her doing something bad. An uncomfortable feeling rose within him as he came near her. He noticed that Abhi was still holding her hand. His other hand was caressing her back. It made Viren want to push him away from Ayesha. He controlled his anger though. Ayesha spoke sheepishly as Viren came and stood amidst some 4-5 people gathered around the table.

"Hi. Sorry about being late. Did you have to wait long?"

---

[49] A Hindi song from the Bollywood movie *Kya Kehna*

"Leave that. What's wrong with you? Did you hurt yourself or something?"

He reached out for her other hand and started rubbing it gently.

"I slipped. I think I have twisted my right ankle. But otherwise, it seems I'm fine."

Viren was suddenly irritated, at himself as well as at her.

More of jealous honestly.

Abhi hadn't let go of Ayesha's hand even now and was giving Viren a despising look.

"Let's get you home as soon as possible then. Mr. Sinha on the fourth floor is a doctor. I'll have dad call him up. So, he can have a look straightaway."

Viren then moved closer to her and put his arms around Ayesha's shoulders to help her up. In the process, without meaning to, he had pushed Abhi out of his way. Viren heard him let out an audible grunt but was glad he didn't say anything. Probably because Ayesha immediately put her arms around Viren's neck for support as she got up.

Judging by his glowering stare, he would have gladly punched you it seems.

There were only a handful of people inside now. So Viren figured walking out wouldn't be much of a hassle. A short girl wearing a green dress, came up and held Ayesha from the other side. Slowly the three of them made their way out with a limping Ayesha.

"This is Gayatri, by the way, Viren. Gayatri, this is Viren."

They nodded at each other cursorily. Both already knew each other by name. Because of the common source currently hanging on to their shoulders. Viren was glad she understood the urgency of the moment and didn't engage in further pleasantries.

Abhi had followed them out. Another guy wearing a grey waistcoat and white shirt tagged along too. A taxi was hailed right away by the two boys.

As the taxi came to a stop next to them, Abhi immediately opened the door. Viren went in first so that Ayesha wouldn't have to go around or slide in. Ayesha winced in pain as Viren moved and Abhi immediately grabbed the side Viren had let go of. An intense look passed between Abhi and Ayesha, which knocked the wind out of Viren.

Did something happen between him and Ayesha tonight?

As Viren slid in, he noticed Abhi whisper something into Ayesha's ears. She responded with a nod as both he and Gayatri helped her get in. It took a few seconds to get Ayesha into a comfortable position after she sat down. Viren's heart broke a little as he noticed that Ayesha was still holding on to Abhi's hand. He got a little solace when he saw that she was holding Gayatri's hand too.

"I'll call you once I can, okay? Don't worry too much. Thanks for tonight."

Viren was unsure who she said that too because all three people leaning in towards her nodded their heads. Ayesha gave one final squeeze to their hands and let it go as the taxi started moving.

She immediately leaned her head back on the seat and closed her eyes. Though she didn't say it in words, it was obvious to Viren that she was in pain.

There were a thousand things he wanted to talk about, but he chose to remain silent. His heart and mind were a jumble of emotions, ranging from jealousy, to curiosity, and anxiety to anger.

Viren felt a little better when Ayesha reached out to grab his hand. He did his bit to console her by caressingly moving his fingers on her palm.

This ride back home was proving to be the most undesirable one he had with his present company. He could only hope things got better, after they made it home, and later too.

Sadly, the drama had just begun to unfold.

Maurya Re

"Festivals have this aura about them, which makes people want to forgive and forget and just celebrate."

\- Ayesha Banerjee

"Jai Deva Jai Deva Jai Mangalamurti

Darshanamatre Manakamana Purti"[50]

The loud chanting of the Ganesh[51] aarti could be heard clearly. Removing her footwear quickly, Ayesha walked meekly behind Gayatri and Sharad.

They had been invited by Abhi to his residence to be a part of their Ganesh Chaturthi [52]festivities. The minute Ayesha entered their apartment, she was awestruck by its grandeur.

A Ganesh idol had been placed on a small mandapam[53] next to their home temple. At least 50 people were gathered for the aarti. The Agarwal family was right in the front, with Mr and Mrs. Agarwal in the centre, and their two sons on *either side of them.* The couple were moving

---

[50] A religious song/Aarti sung during Ganesh Chaturthi. It is also adapted in the form of a song in the Bollywood movie *Vaastav*

[51] Ganesha, also spelled Ganesh, also called Ganapati, is an elephant-headed Hindu god of beginnings, who is traditionally worshipped before any major enterprise and is the patron of intellectuals, bankers, scribes, and authors. His name means both "Lord of the People" (gana means the common people) and "Lord of the Ganas" (Ganesha is the chief of the ganas, the goblin hosts of Shiva). Shiva lit. 'The Auspicious One' also known as Mahadeva 'The Great God'), is one of the principal deities of Hinduism. He is the Supreme Being in Shaivism, one of the major traditions within Hinduism.

[52] Ganesh Chaturthi, also known as Vinayaka Chaturti, or Vinayaka Chaviti is a Hindu festival celebrating the arrival of Ganesh to earth from Kailash Parvat with his mother Goddess Parvati/Gauri

[53] (in southern India) a temple porch.
As temporary platform set up for weddings and religious ceremonies

a magnificent gold-plated lamp in a circular motion before the idol. On their right, Varun, the elder son, was jingling a small handbell. Abhi was on the left side, banging rhythmically on a golden plate with a small brown stick. All four of them had their eyes glued to the idol in complete reverence.

Ayesha quickly joined in the unanimous clapping. In between, she couldn't help but admire the affluent aura around the Agarwals and their residence. The décor of the hall, their home temple and the mandapam was enough to give her an idea of how classy the rest of the house must be.

A feeling of Déjà vu came over her, as she saw Abhi approaching her with a plate of ladoos.

When did he notice them come in?

She often wondered about his ability to conjure up wherever she and Gayatri were in the college too. He was wearing a navy-blue kurta with golden buttons in the front. A bit of his torso was exposed because a few of the top buttons were undone. Ayesha felt herself flushing at the memory of her hand on that chest. It felt like a lifetime ago. However, the titillations were still there, and she had to look away before her mind made her do something stupid again.

Her eyes fell on Varun, Abhi's elder brother.

Good looks run in the family it seems.

Though not quite as tall as Abhi, Varun still towered over most of the people in the crowd. He was carrying a plate with the lamp so people could take their blessings. The red kurta he wore was like Abhi's, yet it looked so different on him. Where Abhi's looked well-fitted and clung to his biceps and chest, Varun's was a little loose. However, that didn't make him look any less dapper.

Both the brothers reached the trio of Ayesha, Gayatri and Sharad at the same time.

"Glad you guys could make it. This is my brother Varun."

"Hello. Nice to see you again, Sharad. Hi Gayatri. I believe I saw you at the Ram Navami aarti. Hey Ayesha, glad to finally meet you."

The three of them nodded at Abhi and waved a hello to Varun. The brothers quickly moved on because there were other visitors to attend to.

"Varun looks hot!"

Ayesha turned around and punched Gayatri on the shoulder.

"Ouch! Come on. You've already stolen Abhi. Let me have his elder brother at least."

Ayesha rolled her eyes and punched her harder this time as she said, "Will you stop this romcom [54]drama? It's all in your head. There's nothing between us, alright."

"Ahem"

Sharad coughed to make them realize he was there with them.

"Not that it's any of my business. But listening to my sister crushing over two boys, one of whom happens to be my best friend, is really creepy."

"Hey guys, come and meet my parents please."

Abhi interrupted their chatter and Ayesha thanked her stars. Because she was sure Gayatri had a smart mouth response ready for Sharad. It would have led to another bout of teasing directed at Ayesha from both the siblings then.

Ayesha noticed that Abhi was looking at only her as he invited them. He gave her a warm smile which sent butterflies down her stomach. Then he turned and led them towards his parents. They were cleaning up the space around the idol.

"Mom, dad. These are my friends from college. You already know Sharad well. That's Gayatri, his younger sister and this is Ayesha, Gayatri's classmate and our friend too."

Gayatri and Sharad folded their hands in a namaste. Ayesha bent down to touch their feet. There were shocked expressions on the faces of

---

[54] Romantic comedy (also known as romcom or rom-com) is a subgenre of comedy and slice-of-life fiction, focusing on lighthearted, humorous plot lines centered on romantic ideas, such as how true love is able to surmount most obstacles.

Abhi, Sharad and Gayatri. The couple however looked incredibly pleased, put their hand on Ayesha's head lovingly and blessed her.

"Welcome. Nice to see you again, Sharad. All of you please sit for a while and have something before you go.", said Mrs. Agarwal. Her humility was obvious in the manner she spoke.

"Maybe next time, aunty. Because we need to reach home for another Ganesh aarti at a neighbour's house. I keep dropping in frequently."

All three of them started to walk out when Abhi said, "At least you can stay Ayesha. Let these two busy siblings go."

He wants you to stay. He wants to spend more time with you.

Yeah, so?

Gayatri passed on a knowing smile to both. Ayesha immediately knew what was coming so gave her a warning look to shut up.

"Maybe next time. There's an aarti at one of my neighbour's houses too."

A dark look crossed Abhi's face.

Is that disappointment?

He sighed and nodded reluctantly as a way of saying "Okay, fine."

Sharad and Abhi hugged each other before he moved out. He then hugged Gayatri and said, "Thanks for coming, bombshell."

Gayatri chuckled and hit him playfully before exiting. Ayesha didn't like how her body instantly froze whenever Gayatri and Abhi hugged or touched each other in any manner.

It's plain jealousy babe. Just admit it.

Abhi looked at her curiously with raised eyebrows. She was anxious about what would come next. She extended her hand for a handshake, but he pulled her into a hug before she could react. His spicy aroma made her lose her mind right away. A tingling warmth spread over her as she hugged him back. Her hand would have reached into his hair next. But he had the good sense to pull himself back. Their eyes locked for a second before he let her go. He was looking at her with the same longing expression he had during the fresher's day party.

Ayesha broke eye contact and rushed out before things could become awkward for everyone present there. The three of them waved Abhi a final goodbye as they got into the lift.

Ayesha felt Gayatri's sly and Sharad's curious eyes on her. But she was glad they didn't say anything.

"See you guys tomorrow."

Ayesha quickly said her goodbyes as they reached down and walked out the gate. She did not want to give Gayatri a chance to begin another round of teasing. They bid adieu and made their way towards Dadar railway station.

Ayesha walked in the opposite direction making her way back home. She was now familiar with the routes and roads around Dadar and Matunga. So much so that she was accustomed to walking around the neighbourhoods in these two localities, rather than hailing a taxi.

She knew it was hardly a ten-minute walk and she would reach quicker on foot. Her thoughts went back to Abhi and how her equation with him had changed following the fresher's party. After that awkward moment of intimacy, they came to their senses and enjoyed the food as well as dancing. The piercing intense eyes of Abhi hadn't left Ayesha for a moment though. She had felt his lingering gaze following her every move as she danced away to the music.

Things had then taken a turn for the worst. She grimaced as she recalled the moment that had led to ten days of house arrest and bedrest for her. It happened when Sharad had both Gayatri and her dancing on either side of him as he held *their palms*. The girls had first twirled towards him and then away from him while swaying to the beats of the music. While moving away from Sharad Ayesha hadn't realized there wasn't enough space to complete that step. Bang! She had hit one of the tables hard. In the next second, while trying to steady herself with the support of the table, she slipped to the floor. Her right foot had completely twisted and was bent at an awkward angle behind her back. She had tried straightening herself and getting up, but a sharp pain had shot through her leg.

Way to make a sensational climax to an already eventful evening!

Gayatri had rushed forth to help her get up, but it was in vain. Even the combined efforts of Sharad and Gayatri had not worked. In fact, her pain only got worse the more she tried to move. That's when, with a loud exasperation, Abhi had stepped forward and in a single move, scooped her up in his arms as if she were a ragdoll. Anger and apprehension were writ large across his face. The accusing look in his eyes was the nonverbal equivalent of "I knew this would happen". She put his arms around his neck for support as he moved forward while carrying her in his arms. The closeness between their faces almost made her want to touch him and entangle her hands in his hair. His eyes never left hers, and the expression on his face became softer, more concerned as he moved towards the nearest table.

Gently, he helped her sit down on the cushioned seat. That's when she noticed Viren.

Uh oh! How long has he been waiting and how much of this scene did he see?

Viren made his way towards her almost indignantly. The look on his face darkened as his eyes fell upon Abhi's hands, one of which was caressing her back and the other one was holding one of her hands. The way he stared at Abhi made her stomach churn. She had to intervene before he punched Abhi, because it very much looked like he wanted to.

What followed were the most awkward and painful moments. Abhi and Viren had looked like they wanted to have a physical go at each other any moment. She was glad to be on her way home in the next few minutes. Mr. Sinha was already home when Viren helped her in. He had then excused himself quickly.

For the next few days, she was completely focused on getting her foot back to normal. Though in much pain, her body hadn't forgotten the titillations it had felt a few days back. Even now, thinking about the way Abhi's lips felt on her forehead, left her lips parched and her throat dry.

Strangely, Viren had become noticeably distant post that night. She hadn't been able to go for her morning walks and he hadn't texted to ask about her wellbeing.

This is very unlike the caring side of him I've seen so far.

Is he upset about something?

She had re-joined college a couple of weeks back. Since then, Gayatri hadn't left any stone unturned. Every chance she got, there was a sly comment right out of her smart mouth. Tonight, had just been another one of the ever-increasing instances of her leg pulling. There was no awkwardness between her and Abhi though. The only difference between before and now was that they talked to each other in a friendly manner.

As opposed to initially wanting to cut each other's throats, you mean?

Well, that had just been you, Miss Know-it-all.

That is true. He has almost always been nice after the form submission mishap and his snide remark on the first day of college.

Ayesha felt a blush creeping up her face again, as she again recalled how this change had been brought about. Thankfully, attending the lectures and being part of the cultural committee kept both her and Abhi busy. This ensured that their conversations and meetings circled mostly around these topics. So there had been no time to think back on or discuss that moment. Neither, thankfully, had there been a replay.

Life out of college had fallen back into the initial routine too. Her morning walk routine had restarted. But Viren was never there.

"Maybe he changed his timings, or he is probably focusing more on his studies. He did mention that the prelims were nearby.", she mused.

She was hoping to catch him in the aarti tonight. Soon she was inside the Sunrise premises. Lost in her thoughts, she hadn't realized when she reached. She took the lift to Mr. Sinha's floor.

I hope my parents are already there. Mr. Sinha said the aarti will begin at 8.

"May Lord Ganesha give me strength to deal with these guys, and even Gayatri."

She prayed as the lift moved upwards.

The Lord, however, had completely different plans about her coming days with these people.

Do Not Disturb

"When you need to set your priorities right, it's prudent to choose the option where your future seems better."

-Viren Joshi

"Are you sure you don't want to come even for ten minutes? I think it will be a good change. Your mind will be refreshed. Let's pray together that you clear the prelims."

Viren let out an exasperated sigh and mumbled a reluctant 'okay'. It was better to relent to his mother's wishes than explain why he was avoiding the aarti.

The thought of coming face to face with Ayesha discomfited him. Since the past few weeks, he had changed his morning walk time to avoid running into her. He had got updates about her wellbeing from his mother. Both Ayesha's and his mother were now members of what he called 'Active Aunties' group Sunrise.

So, he hadn't called or messaged her directly either.

Like that didn't make you miss her at all.

Go to hell!

It seemed to be working so far. He had his own (in his opinion) valid reasons for going MIA[55] on her. Firstly, the events of her freshers' party coupled with his own distracted thoughts during her time at the party, had left him annoyed at himself. He didn't want to know the details of what unfolded at that goddamn party which had led to her injury. Secondly, his prelims were only two weeks away. He didn't need that kind of drama upsetting his very clear priorities in life at the moment. His goal was to clear UPSC in the first attempt itself and that meant focusing on clearing the prelims. He refused to let a girl, whom

---

[55] Missing In Action

he had only known a few months, hamper his goals, that he had been working on for a year.

The trick had worked. Since he wasn't seeing her at all, the thoughts about her had been abated to the most extent. There were times his mind strayed towards what was going on in her life. Then there were the more uncomfortable questions about what might have transpired between her and Abhi that night.

You could simply ask her.

Yeah, and then let all hell loose.

However, the desire to score well soon overcame the priority of these thoughts.

The prelims had gone fairly well as far as he could tell. However, with UPSC one could be sure about the results, only when they were declared. He had taken a few days of relaxation, wherein he chose to binge on a few movies and web series he had been meaning to watch for a long time. This hadn't gone on for long though because he got bored of sitting and staring at his laptop the whole day, in just two days.

Or is it because all the love scenes made you think of her?

His family had soon intervened in the matter too, insisting he make use of this free time to go out instead of staying home, like most of his other days. Since then, he had been meeting up with old friends and acquaintances, almost every day. In fact, a few of his friends even cajoled him into a weekend trip to Igatpuri. It had done him ample good. Being in the lap of nature, away from the chaos of the city, and the chaos in his mind, had brought him some much-needed peace of mind. The thought of Ayesha did come to his mind occasionally, but it didn't linger for more than a few seconds.

Good on you buddy!

He chuckled at how simple it could be to get over something (*you mean someone, right?*) that has been bothering you. You only need to set your priorities right or keep yourself engaged in something that makes you forget everything else.

"Are you going to wear that to the aarti? Please change and join later. We're leaving because we're ready and it's getting late."

His mother's irritated declaration brought him out of his epiphanic moments. He quickly changed into a kurta, washed his face, and set his hair a bit. Soon he made his way up to Mr. Sinha's place.

Ah! Okay let's pray that we clear the prelims.

And also, that she is not there.

He could already hear the initial lines of the aarti as he removed his chappals and entered their residence. He spotted her right away and bam!

Oh my, you're gone dude.

All his resolutions went out the window. It took all his willpower to turn his face and focus on the idol placed in front. The Sinhas had been bringing home an idol of the same design for many years and they had done so this year as well. Viren quickly took his place in the crowd next to his family. He joined in the clapping and chanting but soon found himself looking at Ayesha. He had deliberately stood at an angle from where she would be visible. Though he had chided himself for forgetting his priorities, currently his mind over matter philosophy had gone into sleep mode.

Why not just look at her and pray to her?

Yeah, right!

She made eye contact with him and passed such a warm smile that his heart melted. He smiled back a little reluctantly and turned his face again. He could feel his gaze on her though. He turned and looked at her questioningly, but she blushed and looked away. She was wearing a light green and yellow salwar kameez [56]with a yellow dupatta. Both her hands were adorned with silver glittery bangles and on her ears, she had put on green colored netted hoop earrings. Viren marvelled at

---

[56] A pair of light, loose, pleated trousers, usually tapering to a tight fit around the ankles, worn by women from South Asia typically with a kameez.
Kameez- A piece of clothing like a long shirt worn by many people from south Asia and the Middle East

how well she could carry off both western and Indian attire. Both Mr and Mrs. Banerjee stood next to her. They noticed him and passed on a warm smile too.

The aarti ended soon and Viren rushed to make a quick exit. He didn't want to engage in conversation because his mind was already wavering back to the thoughts he had been able to avoid over the past weeks. She obviously had other plans though. Because she caught him before he could step into the lift.

"Viren, wait. Can we talk please?"

"Yes, of course."

"Not here. Let's go somewhere quieter."

He noticed Nalini and his mother looking at them suggestively as he and Ayesha got into the lift together. He dreaded the fresh bout of leg pulling which was sure to start as soon as he returned home.

"To the Kings' Circle Garden or do you want to sit in the society garden?"

"The society garden please."

Viren chose the latter because that way they would be cutting off the to and fro walking time. The lesser time he spent with her, the better. She seemed fidgety, which meant she was nervous about whatever conversation she wanted to have with him.

They seated themselves at one of the few benches in the small park. She played with her dupatta for a few minutes, probably gathering the courage to begin talking. Maybe she was waiting for him to start the conversation, Viren mused. He deliberately maintained his silence. There was no way he was going to make this easy for her. She owed him an explanation and a bit of gratitude too, he felt.

"Umm.. so.. I don't know if you have been avoiding me deliberately. If you have, I don't know how to make things right between us. Firstly, let me say thank you. Both for the drop and pick on the party evening, then for getting me home in my damsel in distress state. And also, for ensuring Mr. Sinha's quick check-up."

Viren just nodded. He didn't know how else to contribute.

She went on, "It feels like I have hurt you in some way. I'm not sure what it is but I just want to say sorry. I miss you. Can we go back to being friends please?"

Then she took Viren's hand in hers and looked at him expectantly with the most pleading eyes.

What the hell!

How are we supposed to get out of this?

It was his body that would easily forgive her now. What with the sensations he felt taking over his mind because of that single touch of her hand?

He stayed silent for a long time, trying to come up with the best response. And also, because he was trying to control the urge to embrace her into the fold of his arms.

"Ayesha, I already told you about my prelims. I was busy preparing for that and I needed some space away from the "Kuch Kuch Hota Hai" [57]kind of drama I was getting engulfed in."

She winced slightly at that, but he went on, "I'm sorry but there's no other appropriate or better way to define it."

An awkward silence followed. However, both were comfortable holding on to each other's hand. Viren was glad about that at least. But also, kind of agitated because his body demanded for more.

Go on, hug her.

"I'm sorry from my side as well. But please understand that my priorities are clear."

Ayesha nodded. There was a dejected look about her, so he decided to steer the conversation to safer grounds.

"So, tell me, how's college and more importantly how's your foot now?"

---

[57] Situation where the girl has to choose between two boys. Referring to the Situation where Ayesha has to choose between Abhi and Viren. The reference is drawn from a popular hindi movie with the same name with a love triangle as the major plotline.

She went into a long monologue about how she was loving the course. She had even managed to become the Class Representative and was part of the cultural committee. It felt nice to see her speak about college with such enthusiasm. He was also glad she didn't bring up that dolt's name anywhere in the conversation.

Maybe she is deliberately doing that because there was something to hide?

The thought made him uncomfortable.

"Just today a bunch of us did a small skit. It was to spread awareness about using eco-friendly idols. Me, Gayatri and one other guy from our class teamed up for it. Along with Sharad, Abhi and two girls from their batch. It was fun participating in something without humiliating myself for a change." She chuckled lightly but the light went out from Viren's eyes. He felt his jaw tightening at the mention of the imbecile.

So, they had worked together for a skit?

That means spending a lot of time together.

Probably also just the two of them sometimes.

An uneasy feeling crept up inside him.

Ayesha probably noticed the change in his body language and facial expressions. Because she quickly averted the discussion and asked about what he had been up to and how were his prelims, et al. He answered as briefly as possible. Soon they were out of topics to talk about. There was a comfortable silence for a while, and Viren felt a contentment in his heart. It felt as if a huge weight that had been clawing him from the inside was finally lifted.

"Shall we head back then?"

"Only if you promise to be there for the morning walk tomorrow."

He hesitated, but it was hard to deny.

The dimple on her face isn't helping at all, either

"Yeah, sure. But you must promise to not become a damsel in distress too. If you break your leg or any part of your body again, I'll probably stop talking for a longer period this time."

She chuckled and punched him playfully.

There come the goosebumps again.

Control yourself, Joshi!

He gently let go of his grip on her hand as they made their way back. A few stray dogs suddenly barged towards them barking loudly. The unexpectedness of it scared her probably because she clutched his arm tightly. There it was again! The very thing that had started the distraction. He hated himself for the sensations her touch sent down his spine.

He soothed her by putting his hand over hers and shooed the dogs away. He was thankful she removed her hand from his arm right away.

"It seems I'll have to continue being your knight even if I don't want to."

There is that smile and dimple again.

As they made their way to their respective homes, he was sure of one thing. However hard he tried, with her around, it was going to be mind over matter. At least till he figured out why his heart and body took over his practical mind when it came to her. And how he could deal with it.

All The Best

"A good student attends all the lectures and scores well in the exams. A great student attends a few lectures, engages in co-curricular activities and scores well in the exams."

- Abhi Agarwal

"Time's up. Please keep your pens down."

The invigilator announced loudly. Abhi tried to scribble down the remainder of his answer as quickly as possible. He smiled satisfactorily as he handed in his answer sheets. Examinations always made him feel invigorated. Unlike most people, Abhi never felt nervous or panicky about them. His belief was that if one is prepared well, the confidence to perform well, is a natural outcome.

He fell in step with Sharad as they made their way out of the examination hall.

"I think I messed up the difference between Traditional and Contemporary Political Theory. Otherwise, it was easy. How about you?"

"Mine was great. I , in fact, revised the Introduction to Political Theory right before entering the exam hall. So that's one answer I'm most confident about."

"What's the plan now? Shall we go catch a movie?"

"Yeah, I'm in. We surely deserve a break now that the examinations are done with."

Abhi could do with a day out with friends and some entertainment. The last month had been hectic and harrowing. There were the internals first, including project submissions for each paper. They hardly got some breathing space and then the theory exams had begun. Being a senior had also meant mentoring the juniors. Many of them had come asking for notes and guidance. He had helped as much as he could. After all, just last year, he had been in the same position as them.

He guiltily realized that a particular junior had been helped a little more than others. Ayesha had been behaving hyperactively, wanting to know everything she could. Not a day had passed when she hadn't messaged asking doubts. He had been more than relenting. In fact, he was glad to be finally interacting with her outside the college too. Every morning it had become a ritual to send her a motivating message with an 'All the best' for the next internals or theory paper. The sheer quantity of messages exchanged between them made him smile. The thought of catching a movie with her in the next few minutes, made the smile grow wider.

Coming out of his blissful reverie, Abhi noticed Gayatri and Ayesha standing and talking outside one of the classrooms. His heart skipped a beat as it always did when he saw Ayesha. She was wearing a red round neck t-shirt and a pair of black jeans. There was some text on her t-shirt which he was unable to make out. Currently she was running her hands through her hair in an agitated manner. Gayatri had one hand on Ayesha's left shoulder, trying to placate her.

Is she in trouble again?

The girl had a knack for attracting drama it seemed. But then, what would life be without drama, especially when it involved Ms. Banerjee.

And when it gave you the change to be her Knight in shining armour?

As Sharad and he neared the girls, their eyes fell on the boys. Ayesha immediately straightened up and tried to change her facial expression to a happy one. It was useless though because Abhi knew by now that she couldn't hide her feelings even if she tried. That was one of things he had grown to like about her; whatever she felt, her face mirrored it. Even if it was anger. In fact, especially if it was anger. The flared-up nose had given him quite a few memorable moments. He loved how there were no pretences about her.

"How was your exam?"

It was Sharad who initiated the conversation. Ayesha hesitated a bit, but Gayatri answered right away.

"Mine was good. I am sure Ayesha's was too, but she refuses to believe so. I don't understand how one can be so worked up about a tiny mistake, that too when she's not sure she made one."

Abhi turned his gaze towards Ayesha. She was looking furtively here and there. It was obvious that scoring well in exams meant a lot to her. He could now make out the text on her t-shirt which said **"I'm sorry for how I behaved when I had my exams"**

He chuckled. That made her look at him with questioning eyes. He could already see her nose starting to flare-up. It only amused him further. Her eyes narrowed as she gave him a cold look.

"This might be funny for you. But taking up this course is a step towards my future plans. That means I need to ensure I score well in my exams, every single time."

Oh boy!

That condescending tone he had come to hate in the initial days was back. She was about to turn around and storm off. But he reached out and held her hand.

"I'm sorry for how I behaved when I had my exams.'

The laughter that rang out from her lips felt like music to his ears. She punched him playfully on his chest. It did things to his body he wasn't proud of declaring. He could only pray that the turmoil inside his body wasn't evident on the outside.

However, he felt instantly better. Not only because she was out of her miserable mood. But also, for being the one responsible to bring a smile to her face. Especially, after what had obviously been an unsettling experience for her.

"If you two lovebirds are done. Can we go and chill a little today please? Sharad was suggesting catching a movie. Are you guys in?"

'Yes'

Ayesha and Abhi answered at the same time. Both Sharad and Gayatri rolled their eyes as if to say, 'so cheesy you two'.

After a lot of debate, they finally decided to catch the movie *Pink*. Sharad and Gayatri insisted on *Ae Dil Hai Mushkil*. Though Abhi would have preferred *Pink* too, he refrained from picking any movie. He didn't want to become a target of 'you will obviously side with her' from the Kulkarni siblings.

Finally, they flipped a coin and *Pink* it was. Fortunately, there was a show in just about an hour at *Suncity Cinemas*.

"Knowing Abhi, he is going to suggest that we walk. But since I still have my chivalry intact, I will suggest that we take a rickshaw."

Abhi glowered and said, "I have a better suggestion. Let the girls take a rickshaw. We'll walk. Whoever reaches first can buy the tickets."

He was glad they all agreed to it immediately. They helped the girls hail a rickshaw as they walked out of the campus. They made their way afoot too.

"The girls reached before us. I see them at the ticket counter."

Sharad declared as they were about to reach. The tickets purchased, four of them made their way to the designated screen.

They were all hungry, but since the movie was about to begin soon, they decided to eat inside the hall itself. Abhi and Sharad bought popcorn, sandwiches, and cold drinks. Soon they were at their seats with a bucket load of snacks.

Abhi was seated next to Ayesha. He somehow felt this was conspired by the Kulkarnis. His doubt was confirmed when Sharad whispered "All the best" before moving towards his seat.

This was the first time Abhi would be spending time with Ayesha outside festival gatherings and the college campus. It heightened his already tingling sensations. Though he was enticed into the movie as soon as it began, there were many distractions. Number one being her dewy fragrance, which made him want to get lost within her embrace. The second and harder to ignore was how their hands kept colliding when reaching out for the popcorn.

Their eyes met a few times whenever their hands touched. He was glad to see he wasn't the only one to feel the physical tension between them. Her eyes had the most docile and stimulating look. He suddenly felt thankful that they had picked this movie. God only knows what watching a romantic movie together would have unfolded.

The movie was on a social issue and Abhi couldn't help noticing the range of emotions appearing on Ayesha's face. Every time the female leads were questioned by the men, Ayesha looked enraged. When the women answered back, she almost clapped with approval. It was like watching a movie within a movie for Abhi. Seeing her so charged up, filled his heart with a strange sense of fulfilment. He felt dejected when the movie ended, and they had to return to the world outside the movie hall.

"Should we have dinner together somewhere?", Abhi asked, hoping to spend some more time together.

"We need to go home and pack. We're leaving for Kolhapur the day after. Mom will already be ready for a fight because we haven't reached home straight after the exam."

"I need to rush too. Bye guys. See you after the vacation."

Ayesha declared in a breath, and before any of them replied, she hailed a rickshaw and left. Abhi wondered what the emergency was. An image of the bespectacled guy (*what was his name again?*) and Ayesha laughing together conjured up in his mind. He felt like throwing up.

"When do you leave for Himachal?"

Sharad's question made Abhi stop gazing with a sinking feeling at the retreating rickshaw in which Ayesha had just left.

"We leave in two days."

He wondered if Ayesha had any plans for the vacation. He would miss seeing her every day.But he would also miss the daily texting between them, that he had grown quite accustomed to in the past month.

Would it be desperate and clingy to continue their chats now? Even if he did, what would they talk about now? It was a dilemma that left him anxious.

She might grow closer to him in the meanwhile. So, you better keep in touch.

Thanks Mr. Loveguru.

For the first time, he wished the college didn't close for so many days during Diwali[58].

He at least had the trip to look forward to.

Maybe going up in the hills would bring him the calmness he needed, mind and body, heart, and soul.

Yeah, good luck with that.

Sighing, he made his home and into what he hoped would be 'Ayesha free' days.

---

[58] This is one of the most popular festivals in the Hindu calendar. This festival commemorates Lord Rama's return to his kingdom Ayodhya after completing his 14-year exile. The most beautiful of all Indian festivals, Diwali is a celebration of lights.

Give Me A Break

"Moving to a new city and making new friends, doesn't mean you forget your ties with your old city and friends."

-   Ayesha Banerjee

"When are you leaving for Chandigarh?"

"Tonight. At 11:30 pm from Dadar by the Amritsar Express. It's such an inconvenience that the train doesn't halt at Chandigarh. We're getting down at Ambala and then continuing by road. My uncle will be picking us up. We're staying at his place so thankfully no onward journey or change of transportations after reaching Ambala."

Ayesha and Viren were walking back to their society after their morning walk. Viren was only coming three days a week now. During those too, he had been rushing home quickly.

He had cleared the prelims (Ayesha had muttered an 'obviously' under her breath before congratulating him on that achievement)

That was a great vote of confidence though, right?

But now he was studying harder than ever for the mains. He kept pointing this out to her every time they chatted for more than fifteen minutes. Thanks to his alarm clock type reminders, she knew the prelims were just over a month away now.

Sometimes, she wondered if it had not been for Viren, would she have known so much about UPSC? She felt herself blushing at the obvious answer.

"Let me come to drop you guys. You might need help with the luggage and to find your way to the right platform."

Ayesha was pleasantly surprised.

Why was he offering to help at such a critical time?

He lurvesss you...

She looked at him questioningly, but the predictable statement came soon.

"Let's hurry back now. I can't spare much time because..."

"The mains are only a few days away."

He laughed, "Yeah, okay. Joke's on me and I'm sorry for being so intolerable. Just a few more days, I promise."

"I'll forgive you the day you give me your full attention without UPSC coming up even once in the conversation."

"But currently I should be forgiven for bringing it up twice in a conversation. Because we're here and I need to go. I'll come up to your place at 10:15 pm. See you then."

Ayesha waved him a half-hearted goodbye. Though she would never say it to him lest he get distracted, she missed not talking to him every day. Their five-ten-minute chats that sometimes even went on for half an hour, were one of the highlights of her morning walk. She woke up smiling in the morning, looking forward to seeing him during and after her walk. Her father had spoken to him many times too. In fact, he had seemed most impressed after learning that Viren had cleared the UPSC prelims. Ayesha had informed him at dinner a few days after the results were declared.

"Viren has cleared the UPSC prelims. I asked him to seek your guidance, if needed."

"That's very impressive. Of course, I will be more than happy to guide him."

The next day, to Ayesha's utter surprise, her father had done something she had never seen him do with any of her friends. As Ayesha and Viren were about to exit the garden, he had approached Viren and congratulated him profusely. Viren had looked mighty pleased with himself too.

Huh! Where was this smile when I congratulated him?

Ayesha had been a little put off. But then seeing them talking animatedly about their interspersed prospective professional lives, had given her a strange sense of satisfaction.

"What is your plan if you clear the mains? Have you decided anything?"

"Yes, uncle. My first choice would be IAS[59], but I wouldn't mind IFS[60] either."

"That's wonderful. Have you prepared for the interview yet? I can arrange for you to talk to experienced and in-service IAS officers if you need first-hand help and guidance. In fact, if you'd like, you can speak to them now as well."

Ayesha remembered thinking this was getting a bit much. Agreed that she had offered Viren the same suggestion a few times too. But where was this proactively helpful side of her father when Ayesha had wanted her migration certificate expedited and sent to her college directly? She had got the *'You will get no help from me in excelling in your career'* lecture. Apparently Viren was a worthier candidate. Though filled with envy, she also kind of liked the fact that her father liked Viren so much.

What is this silly daydreaming girl?

She forced herself to concentrate as she heard Viren respond.

"Surely, uncle. I would love that."

Her father had then walked off to where his friends were sitting. Apparently, he told them about him too. Because they all turned to where she and Viren were standing and smiled widely.

So, he is someone to show off to friends too now?

"I don't remember him being this proud when I was in the city top 10 for my board results."

Viren was smart enough to pick on the sarcasm, so he had smiled back briefly at all the uncles and then started walking out. Since that day, her father had spoken to Viren quite a few times, asking specific questions

---

[59] The Indian Administrative Service (IAS) is the administrative arm of the All India Services of Government of India

[60] IFS stands for Indian Foreign Service

about which sections he found challenging, et al. Viren had once come home to speak to one of her father's colleagues over the phone too. Her mother had gushed over Viren, being the most gracious host. Ayesha had never seen them being this forthcoming with any of her friends before.

"Your parents must be so proud. This is a remarkable achievement.'

Ayesha was stunned to hear her mother remark. Before she could stop herself, "Err. You guys do remember my achievements, right?"

Both her parents had given her a cold look which clearly translated to, "This is not about you. Where are your manners?"

That had her shut for the next half an hour as the compliments continued.

"I'm sorry I never asked this before, uncle. But what exactly is your job?"

"I'm a Policy and Intelligence Analyst. I work in liaison with agencies like the CBI[61]. I also serve as a freelance Political Advisor to whoever asks for my services in upcoming elections. I was asked to come to Maharashtra for the upcoming BMC[62] Elections of 2017."

Viren was dumbfounded for a few seconds. Sensing that the information had overwhelmed Viren, Mr. Lalit steered the conversation towards Viren's career again.

Ayesha was envisioning a replay of the same tonight as she had entered her home after returning from the morning walk.

"Are you done with your packing?'

Her mother's question brought her back to the present.

"Yes, just a few small things left."

Her phone buzzed then, and she picked up with a smile on her face.

"Hello, Gayu. Did you guys reach safely? How is it going for you there?"

---

[61] The Central Bureau of Investigation (CBI) is the premier investigating agency of India

[62] BMC stands for Brihanmumbai Municipal Corporation. It is also referred to as Municipal Corporation of Greater Mumbai (MCGM)

Ayesha mouthed 'Gayatri' to her mother's questioning look and went to her room.

An excited Gayatri replied, "It is so peaceful out here Ayu. You should have come with us. I'm still mad you chose your old friends over me."

Ayesha could literally visualize Gayatri sticking her tongue out and scowling. It made her chuckle.

"Come on. You know that's not the case. I have my cousins too. It's not just for my friends that I'm going to Chandigarh."

"Yeah yeah, you can spin it whichever way you want. Sharad says Abhi was asking about you by the way."

She mumbled "Umm hmm" in a nonchalant manner but her heartbeats told a different story. She was glad the siblings couldn't see her or the usual 'no smoke without fire' argument would have begun.

"He's in Himachal. I know you want to ask but won't."

She laughed nervously and said, 'nothing like that' but deep inside she did want to know. She had wondered about it ever since she had rushed back home after the movie that day. How she wished she could stay. But no, her father had been clear that she must be home when Viren came. The thought of choosing Viren over Gayatri made her feel guilty.

Is that really the case? Or are you just guilty about choosing one guy over the other?

She let out an exasperated sigh. This made Gayatri take it in a completely different way.

"Relax, he has gone with the family so there's a very slim chance of him falling in love. Unless some Himachali damsel woos him completely. Then you two would have to fight over him. How thrilling!"

"Shut up! What scenes you conjure up. I wonder why you siblings didn't join a film writing course. Anyway, I have to go now."

"You know, I wonder about that too. We could be the next Farhan and Zoya of Bollywood. Anyway, Jaa Simran Jaa. But don't forget your Raj here[63]. I miss you. Happy Journey and don't you dare forget me."

"Like you would let me forget you, duh! Thanks, miss you too. Bye."

She hung up the phone while still smiling over Gayatri's silly jokes.

So, Mr. Abhi is in Himachal.

Though she had acted indifferent, the thought of him meeting some girl did leave a pang in her heart.

"Well, that's beside the point. So much to do and not much time on hands now'

She shrugged and focused on the remainder of her packing.

The day seemed to just fly by after that. She helped her mother clean out the house because it was going to be locked for so many days. Then they checked each other's bags to ensure nothing important was forgotten to be packed. By the time they got done, it was time for dinner, and then time to leave.

Just as they were clearing out the dishes, the doorbell rang.

"I forgot to tell you. Viren has offered to drop us. He thought we could use some help with the luggage. He also said we might need help in finding our way to the train."

"Such a thoughtful boy." Mrs. Banerjee gushed as Mr. Banerjee opened the door and let him in.

"Hello, Uncle. Are you all ready? I have got the cab already."

Soon they reached the station and then their designated platform without any hassles.

"Thanks to you" as her parents kept telling Viren.

The cab ride was as Ayesha had anticipated; thanking and praising Viren. Him being humble about it had only led to more praises being

---

[63] Gayatri telling Ayesha to go and enjoy back at her place but not to forget her Raj (Abhi). It is in reference to a popular dialogue 'Jaa Simran Jaa, Jee Le Apni Zindagi' taken from popular Bollywood movie *Dilwale Dulhaniya Lee Jaayenge* where the male and female lead are called Simran and Raj

showered on him. Ayesha was now amused and pleased rather than irritated.

Are all parents like this?

Because this was something new for her.

They were all aboard once the train chugged in and they found the compartment. Viren helped place their luggage and stayed with them till the horn blew.

"All the best with your preparations. Feel free to call if you need any kind of guidance. Take my phone number from Ayesha."

"Thanks for all your help, uncle. Enjoy your holiday."

Ayesha felt her heart sinking a bit as the train started to move away and they waved goodbye to Viren. Though she was excited to meet her old friends and her cousins, after so long, she couldn't deny the fact that would miss this city and its people.

People? Or just two of them?

There's Gayatri too!

She wanted to share it all with her old friends; everything about her life in Mumbai and how it was so different from her life in Chandigarh and Agra. She couldn't wait to tell them about her new friends, especially Gayatri. Of course, Sharad, Abhi and Viren too. She felt her cheeks flush as she thought of Viren and Abhi. She really needed to control her emotions from mirroring on her face so easily. How else would she talk about them without embarrassing herself or raising a few questions?

"I am sure he's going to clear the mains as well. He's such a hardworking and sincere boy."

Ayesha nodded absentmindedly, still pink in the face. Her thoughts lingered on two boys in her new life for most of the journey towards her old life.

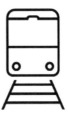

I Can, I Will

"The choice you make when what is right for you and what is the best for you marks the difference between you being good and great."

- Viren Joshi

"Aren't you getting late?"

Trust my mother to state the obvious and escalate the anxiety.

"Yes, I'm leaving now."

"Good luck. You'll be great, don't worry."

Viren smiled and nodded as he waved goodbye and left.

This might be the most nervous I have ever been.

What about the time Ayesha kissed your cheek and you wanted more?

Shut up!

His internal thoughts weren't making this any easier. For the first time in his life, he was glad for the Mumbai hustle and bustle. It helped the turmoil within his mind to take a rest.

Soon, he found himself at the place he was dreading to enter. The nervousness returned but he couldn't mull over it much.

"Hello, is this where the lecture is taking place?"

"Yes, please come in."

There were questioning looks from the students pouring in slowly.

"I hear Mr.Das has gone on leave for a month and someone new is coming in to take lectures from today."

"Oh no! Mr.Das's lectures motivate me to attend college regularly. I hope the new professor is as good as Mr. Das."

Two girls walked in casually into the classroom, talking loudly. They halted in their steps and panicked as they realized the new lecturer was already there. The shocked expressions on their faces also conveyed something else. That they didn't expect *the lecturer* to be *Viren*.

One of them was bemused and the other one had turned white. Her eyes clearly conveyed, "Why didn't you tell me?"

"Please take your seats."

Viren had expected this reaction from Ayesha. He tried to act as cool as possible as he began taking their attendance. Though he avoided looking up, his heart skipped a beat when he called out Ayesha's name. Her voice sounded timid as well as angry. How could one have such contrasting emotions in a simple "Yes, sir". But then, that had always been her specialty.

"Good morning, everyone. I'm Viren Joshi and I will be taking your lectures on Changing Nature of the Federal System till Mr. Das rejoins."

There were whispered murmurs and curious glances. Gayatri waved at him flirtatiously, which made him blush. Ayesha however, continued to glower.

Handle with care.

Not now!

As he began and went on with the lecture, explaining about Fiscal and Emergency Powers in the Federal System, he felt himself relaxing. He became confident as he delved into a subject close to his heart. He slowly began to appreciate his decision to take up a job like this while he awaited the results of UPSC finals. Besides making some money, he would also be doing something he was sure he would enjoy.

Though the subject was more theoretical, he made it interesting by popping in questions every now and then. All the while, the accusing and cold brown eyes of Ayesha bore into him. He also noted with some disappointment that she wasn't participating in the lecture.

You could have said no.

But I can't let an opportunity like this go just because…

What, because you love her?

I do not love her!

He was glad these silly thoughts did not hamper with what came out of his mouth. He was about to wrap up the lecture when, "Excuse me sir, when is Mr. Das coming back?"

Viren would be able to identify that voice even with his eyes closed. However, the accusatory tone was what surprised and hurt him.

"Trust me, I would miss him too if I were in your place. I was his student not so long ago, so I understand your disappointment. However, let's cut him some slack. He has some personal matters to attend to and will rejoin from February. So, you won't have to tolerate me for long."

There was silence for a few seconds.

"Really, am I that bad? I promise I won't badmouth you all in front of Mr. Das. Also, I'm much cooler than this on your side of the class. If it helps, I'll wear jeans and a t-shirt from the next lecture. Though I'm pretty sure I may end up losing the job if I do that."

There was muffled laughter and a few "No sir, we like you" and similar responses.

He turned his eyes towards Ayesha directly and said, "I know some of you are heartbroken, but you'll have to make do with this double for some time."

Ayesha blushed and shook her head as if to say, 'I didn't mean that'. The hurtful expressions on her face persisted though. He felt like closing the distance between them right there and then by enveloping her in his arms.

Get a grip! You're her professor now.

"Sir, the lecture timings are over. Can we leave now?"

He nodded at Gayatri. He was sure she had deliberately done that. One by one, the students started to walk out. Gayatri hung around at the door as Ayesha walked towards him.

Uh oh! She still looks angry.

"What the hell, Viren? How can you not tell me such an important thing?"

"Look, I am sorry, okay. But right now, I must rush because I need to meet the HOD[64]. Can we meet in the canteen after?"

"Yeah, sure. But this discussion is not over."

"Is any discussion ever over till you have the last word?"

She punched him playfully but quite hard.

Yikes! She's really angry.

"Ouch! You seem to forget that I'm your teacher here, Miss Banerjee."

"Okay then, Professor Joshi. I shall see you in the canteen. Good day."

She walked over haughtily to Gayatri, and they made their way out. Gayatri winked at him as she came back and peaked at him from the door.

Viren found himself blushing as he chuckled and waved at her.

"What are you doing? Let's go!"

Ayesha's irritated voice floated in as a hand appeared in the doorway and pulled Gayatri.

Was that jealousy in her undertone?

You wish!

Viren walked out of the classroom soon and made his way to the HOD's cabin. He still had two lectures for the day. He was dreading one of them more than the one he had just completed.

Don't punch him during the lecture.

Maybe outside the college then?

What is wrong with you?

Ayesha had seemed different ever since her return from the Chandigarh trip. But he contemplated that the whole thing might just be in his head. He had been so involved in studies and consumed by books in the past two months, that any human contact had seemed weird.

---

[64] Head of the Department

Ayesha and Viren had only met a handful of times, but she had stayed in touch on text. That had been pleasantly surprising. It began with a casual 'Happy Dhanteras[65]' during the Diwali days and then it became a regular thing.

He still felt jittery thinking about how he awaited her 'Good luck' texts during his exams. His mind (more his heart) had been somehow convinced that if she didn't wish him, he wouldn't fare well.

I'll put things right between us now that I have time.

Right, as in romantically?

Viren focused on the present as he neared the HOD's cabin. It felt weird entering a teaching authority's space as an employee rather than as a student.

Gulping down his nervousness, he entered.

He could only hope that the reception here would be warmer than the one he had received in the classroom.

It was warm enough, but you only felt cold because of those brown eyes.

Piercing brown eyes, please.

---

65 Dhanteras, also known as Dhanatrayodashi, is the first day that marks the festival of Diwali in India

No Stone Unturned

"If there is competition, even in personal life, you have got to treat it like a test, and give your best."

-    Abhi Agarwal

"Will you stop it please? I'm already angry and you're not helping at all!"

"But that's what my duty as a friend is."

Why is she angry though?

Ayesha and Gayatri walked into the canteen, obviously not realizing how loudly they were talking. They made their way in, slightly embarrassed about suddenly being in the spot. The canteen was almost empty, and the few people in there had turned to look at the girls, staring curiously at them.

Gayatri spotted Sharad and Abhi at one of the tables and hurried forward, with Ayesha in tow. Abhi couldn't help chuckling as he noted how Ayesha had gone red in the face. She was wearing a sleeveless white top with black polka dots. He noted appreciatively how the slim fit black jeans brought out her curves. This was further enhanced, as she had tucked in her blouse. A stylish brown belt with a butterfly buckle, held the jeans and blouse in place on her waist.

28 inches max

Would you like to measure it with your own hands around that waist?

Sigh!

She had tied up her hair in a high ponytail which bounced as she walked. The clickety click of her black boots and the jingling of the few bangles on her right arm, made everyone continue to stare at her.

Are you sure they're staring because of that?

His heart refused to accept the fact that people were checking her out.

"Stop behaving like you two are in a movie."

Sharad was looking at his sister accusingly. Gayatri bounced her hair back in style as she scowled at him and took her seat.

"Being best friends with this girl surely makes me feel like I'm in one."

Abhi's ears immediately perked up. He had been giving a challenging look to the few boys still staring unashamedly at Ayesha. He had to remind himself that it could very well be Gayatri they were staring at. She looked equally suave in a peach-coloured knee length floral dress. But it made Abhi want to get up and punch them in the face anyway.

"'an you stop exaggerating please?"

Ayesha's irritated reply made him turn to her with a questioning look. She shrugged her shoulders but didn't answer.

"Argh! Why isn't there seating arrangement at the outside stalls? I like their food more than what's available here."

The lane outside their college had more than a dozen food stalls lined on each side of the street. These offered a wide variety of delectable street food. The stalls were all equally popular, with neither being better or best than the others. The only downside of eating there instead of in the canteen was that there were always throngs of students present on every stall. Add this to the fact that one had to stand and eat. It was no wonder the four of them chose the canteen for their breaks between the lectures to relax and chit chat.

Abhi was amused more than concerned about Ayesha's outburst now. He had never seen her annoyed at someone else. Not being the reason behind that flared-up nose was a refreshing change.

"Mademoiselle, would you like something from outside? We can ask for it. You underestimate the influence we hold around here."

That brought a smile to her face. She nodded gratefully at Sharad who beckoned one of the waiters. Once they had all listed out their desired food items, the waiter walked away with an incredulous look. It was clear he couldn't believe that four people could eat so much.

"So, tell us what unleashed the angry young woman again?"

Ayesha chuckled and hit Sharad on his palm playfully. That made Abhi frown a bit. She seemed in a better mood and was about to answer when the grim expression returned. She was staring at something behind them with narrowed eyes. Before Abhi could turn and look at the source, Gayatri blurted out.

"Here comes the reason.'

Abhi already had a foreboding about this when he heard from behind.

"Can I have a word with you privately please?"

Though Ayesha still looked mad, there was a softness in her eyes.

"Professor Joshi. How kind of you to join us. Would you not like to meet your students first before we talk?"

Though Abhi kind of enjoyed her sarcastic side, the feeling of envy overpowered it.

"This is Gayatri. That's her elder brother Sharad Kulkarni and that's Abhi Agarwal. Sharad and Abhi are in the fourth semester."

A few seconds of awkward hellos followed. Abhi too waved dishearteningly, wishing he could use the hand to do something else.

Like what, punch him?

Yes!

Right, like you would do that to a professor!

"Hello, Gayatri and Sharad. So, Abhi Agarwal? Is Abhi your full name? Will you be Abhi only now and be Kal [66]Agarwal tomorrow?"

A loud laughter rang out from Gayatri and Sharad. Gayatri went into a laughing fit. Abhi maintained a passive expression and gave an imperceptible nod. Internally he was cursing the idiot with cuss words that would've shamed a roadside thug.

Relax, you will probably be attending his lecture in a bit.

Like you could do something with Ayesha around anyway.

---

[66] Tomorrow

Abhi noted with some relief that Ayesha was fuming too. His fists turned into a ball. But he controlled his rage and faked a laugh. Gayatri was still laughing. Ayesha gave Abhi an apologetic look and stood up.

His fury turned worse as Ayesha grabbed Viren's elbow and dragged him to another table.

He heard her say, "What the hell was that?"

"So, he can crack a joke about his name, and I can't?"

They sat down two tables away from them. Abhi couldn't hear their conversation completely. But phrases like "but I wasn't sure till last night" and "I have nothing to do till February" were decipherable.

"Err, the food is here, lover boy. Or will you be going on dharna outside the college gate?"

He scowled at Sharad. Yes, he had lost his appetite. But he didn't want Sharad's point proven right. He was affected by this new and unwanted presence.

That's only for you, Gayatri seems to love him

Great. Another female admirer.

But he wasn't going to make his displeasure obvious. And he would not let *Mr. I-Crack-Jokes-That-Make-Girls-Laugh* win either. So, he dug into his idli sambhar just to distract himself.

He avoided looking at their table, but it was proving difficult. Thankfully, Viren got up to leave in some time. However, Ayesha was looking much calmer. What was worse was that she was smiling at him in the most endearing way. As Viren made to turn away and walk out, Ayesha grabbed his hand and pulled him into a side hug.

Abhi felt like somebody had punched him in the stomach. He felt better as Viren walked out and Ayesha made her way back to the table.

He wasn't sure what his feelings for Ayesha were. Heck! He wasn't even sure if this was love, just a passing crush, or maybe just possessiveness as a friend.

But he was sure of one thing. He was not going to leave any stone unturned.

In doing what?

Well, for starters, topping Professor Joshi's class.

Atta boy!

He smiled widely as Ayesha sat down and began to munch on her food. It gave him a strange satisfaction just observing her. Maybe it was more because he had a plan in mind now. Soon it was time for Abhi's and Sharad's lecture to begin. They bid the girls a quick goodbye and made their way to the college.

Let's get the ball rolling.

Abhi mentally Hi5ed himself as he walked into the lecture.

Mr. Funny was already there. He was talking casually to the few students seated in class. He nodded in an indifferent manner towards Abhi and Sharad too. Sharad mumbled a 'Good morning, sir' as the two of them sat down. Abhi felt like punching him already. But he acted cool.

When Abhi's name came up in the roll call, an imperceptible cold stare passed his way. It must've gone unnoticed by most, but Abhi saw it. Sharad however received a warm smile.

So, is the special treatment reserved for me?

As the lecture began and went on, Abhi couldn't help being impressed. Mr. Specs obviously knew his stuff. Abhi found himself getting immersed in the lecture. To his own surprise he also participated in the Q&A. Abhi did note that Viren avoided asking any direct questions to him though. It didn't matter, because Abhi kept his questions pouring in.

Whenever Abhi popped a question, Viren would answer without looking at him. Or worse, he would look at Sharad and answer. It annoyed Abhi only a wee bit. Because being a teacher's pet wasn't on his agenda this semester. His aim was to top the subject now. And for that he would need to focus on what was being taught. Even if it meant getting ignored by Mr. Know-it-all.

"That's it from my end today. As I was telling the first years, Mr. Das will rejoin in February. So, till then you'll have to make do with this double."

He pointed towards himself in mock disbelief. A muffled laughter followed. Abhi noted with some annoyance that the girls laughed a little louder. Some even giggled and looked at Viren admiringly.

So, it's not just Ayesha and Gayatri. This guy seems to be popular with the ladies everywhere.

Abhi repeated "No stone unturned" to himself as Viren waved and walked out. A few girls rushed out after him.

"May the best man win", Abhi muttered under his breath.

"He seems like a good replacement."

Sharad immediately shut his mouth. The dark expression and annoyed look on Abhi's face were enough indication for him to take the hint.

Sophie's Choice

"You can empathize with someone all you want. But you won't understand their dilemma till you are in a similar situation yourself."

-   Ayesha Banerjee

"You know what this means, right?"

"Not really."

Ayesha was with Ketaki and Sneha. The three had been friends for as long as they could remember. They had been nicknamed 'The Golden Girls Trio' by the teachers and 'The Nerdy Beauties' by the students in their school. After coming to Chandigarh, Ayesha had only stayed at her uncle's place as courtesy. She had hopped on to her cousin's moped and barged into Ketaki's house in barely half an hour of entering Chandigarh.

"OMG!! Is it really you? You vamp, why didn't you tell us you're coming? Wait, does Sneha know?"

That had led to them barging into Sneha's house next.

Currently, the three girls were seated (sprawled out rather) in the cutesy balcony of Sneha's bedroom.

Ah! How I missed this peaceful abandon.

This had been their spot for talking out all matters under the sun, right from important questions in a subject to who was more likely to get married first (yes, even nerds discuss these things!)

Ayesha continued to sip on her delicious tea.

Nothing beats the taste of homemade tea with your closest friends.

She was oblivious to the other two exchanging a "What do we do with this idiot?" look.

"Sooner or later, I'm guessing sooner rather than later, though. But you're gonna have to pick one of them."

Sneha's rather annoyed voice brought Ayesha back to the discussion.

"Huh? What are you talking about?"

"It is obvious you have a crush on both Viren and Abhi. From what you have told us so far, the fire is equal on both sides. So, one of them is going to pop the question soon. What are you going to do then?"

Ketaki was right of course. Though she wouldn't admit it to them, Ayesha knew this to be true in her heart. She had avoided thinking about it because of two reasons.

a. She wasn't sure about her feelings for either Viren and Abhi, and,

b. Why walk down a lane whose destination you don't want to reach?

Look at you all go nerdy in matters of the heart too. Bulleted list and all.

Ayesha rolled her eyes and forced her mind shut.

"I somehow feel you are more attracted to Abhi."

"Oh please, she clearly likes Viren more."

"C'mon, she would have obviously kissed Abhi at the fresher's party if not for Sharad's intervention."

"Really? And what about how she runs into Viren's arms every time she feels vulnerable?"

Ayesha had to throw a pillow at them both, to make them stop.

"Thanks for your help, you bloodsuckers. Also, in case you didn't notice. I'm right here."

The discussion had stopped then. But it hadn't stopped popping up every time they met. The more they dissected her apparently obvious feelings for Viren and Abhi, the more it left her anxious and confused.

In a fit to figure it out herself, she had begun texting both the guys every day. She had the perfect excuse too. It was Diwali! She had to wish them. If nothing but courtesy dictated that.

What had begun as a 'Happy Dhanteras' soon became regular texting.

You're a player, you know! Toying with the feelings of two boys.

Buzz off!

She thought she had Ketaki and Sneha under her thumb more or less. How wrong and premature in her relief she had been. During one of their meetups the two girls had casually made a video call to Gayatri. God only knows how they managed to get hold of her number from Ayesha's phone. Before she could voice out her disbelief and anger over it, the situation became worse than anticipated.

"Wait, did she tell you girls about the skit we did during Ganesh Chaturthi? Sharad told me I was only included because Abhi insisted on it. He apparently wanted to make Ayesha feel comfortable with the seniors."

Okay, what?

"Oooh! Fresh piece of gossip. Twenty points to team Abhi."

Wait, they have teams now?

"Okay, but let's not forget that Viren is a family favourite. I think uncle and aunty already see him as Jamai Raja[67]."

Ayesha gritted her teeth in disbelief and frustration. She tried everything from shouting out in anger, to begging. But ultimately what made the three stop the charade was when she threatened to walk out.

Ayesha had been looking forward to the Diwali vacation for some peace of mind. What they had ended up bringing was turmoil in her mind and a silly giddiness in her heart and stomach. The daily reminders by the trio of Gayatri, Ketaki and Sneha only made it worse. Surprisingly, the only solace were her daily chats with Viren and Abhi. Though the boys were busy, they always managed to respond to her texts right away. It instantly brought on a megawatt smile to her face. Anyone who happened to be with her at that moment, was sure to give her a questioning look or ask, "Is everything okay?"

Luckily, it was the festive season and there was much activity around her. Right from delectable food to beautiful décor and stylish clothes, there was so much to keep her happily engrossed. Add socializing with friends, family and neighbours to the mix and she became blissfully

---

[67] Son-In-Law

oblivious to the turmoil of her mind and heart, at least for a few hours. Hence, there was enough to keep herself and much to her relief, the 'Gangster Girls' (what else would a girl call her supposed best friends out for her blood?) busy too.

She didn't even realize when it was time to leave. On the departure day, Ketaki and Sneha offered to drop Ayesha.

"Let your parents come in another car with your uncle and aunty. This way we get to spend a few more hours with you and some alone time too."

"Yeah, it will only be a couple of hours for us."

Ayesha loved the idea and agreed right away. Her parents and relatives didn't mind either. Because it was obvious that one car would become too cramped up for everyone. But nobody had pointed it out earlier, lest it seem rude. So, this was a convenient way out.

What Ayesha hadn't anticipated was the 'no escape' option. This had been her bait whenever the girls brought up the topic of her supposedly entangled non-existent love life.

The first few minutes passed comfortably in chatting about Diwali celebrations and other stuff.

"So, have you thought about what you're going to do about your lover boys?"

Ayesha scoffed and gave a threatening look to Sneha. But that hadn't stopped Ketaki from teaming up with her.

"At some point you'll have to make a choice, Ayu. You can't roll your eyes and expect it to be alright."

She couldn't answer. How could she when she didn't know who to choose? And more importantly, did she want to choose one of them at all?

"Do you still write?"

The unexpected question from Sneha brought her out of the chaos in her mind.

"Yes, I do. In fact, since I'm a part of the cultural committee now, I encourage others to write too. We make it a point to have a writing activity every week or once every few weeks."

"By 'we' you mean you and Abhi?"

She should've seen that coming but she nodded, "Not just the two of us. There are ten of us in the committee. Including Gayatri and Sharad."

"Do you see my point though?"

When Ayesha shook her head, Sneha went on. "You have more in common with Abhi. He helps you excel in the things you love. Academics, writing, debates, etc."

Ayesha remained silent. There was much to mull over, in her oncoming journey and then when she faced Abhi and Viren again.

"Here we are."

Ayesha breathed a sigh of relief. She could not bear another round of questions and suggestions from these two. Agreed that they were only looking out for her. But Ayesha had realized that some things needed to be figured out on one's own.

"Gosh, I am already exhausted. I wish they would start a direct train from Chandigarh to Mumbai soon. This back and forth will be tiring for each visit you make."

Ayesha rolled her eyes at Ketaki and chuckled, "Darling, I travel this much every day, to and fro from home to college and back. So, I'm okay."

A look was exchanged between Sneha and Ketaki. Ayesha clearly understood it to mean 'There she goes again with Mumbai vs Chandigarh'. Ayesha somehow felt proud of herself though.

Viren and Abhi would be proud of you too.

How is that relevant here?

It always is.

They boarded the train soon and before they knew it, the horn blew.

Ayesha felt sad that she was leaving two of her 'Gangster Girls' behind. But she was looking forward to seeing the third one again soon.

Admit it, you're more excited about seeing your lover boys again.

Oh, so we're calling them 'lover boys' too now?

Go to hell.

"Pick me, pick me, pick me."

Ayesha couldn't help laughing. Ketaki and Sneha had begun a chorus and danced to a tune of their own. As ridiculous as it looked, this was their parting gift and something they obviously thought was good advice. She waved a goodbye feeling more confused rather than sad.

Once back to Mumbai, she couldn't wait to resume her routine. It was amazing how the city that had once made her nervous, now excited her.

As expected, Viren had stopped coming for the morning walks completely. She was however glad that they had continued their daily texting. His replies though had become limited to just once a day. They would come at the oddest times, sometimes in the middle of the night, to when she would be in college. Whatever the hour though, they never failed to bring butterflies to her stomach. It could be a simple 'Hey, what's up?' or a longer one where he would tell her how his exam went. Irrespective of the length of the messages, the width of her smile remained ear to ear. As did the depth of the blush on her cheeks.

It was while absently reading one of these messages that it happened. She was strolling in the hallway, waiting for Gayatri. She hadn't realized where she was headed.

Bam!

She had bumped right into something strong and heavy muscled. While trying to balance herself, she was about to fall backwards. She closed her eyes in anticipation of the pain to follow the fall. But strong arms enveloped her back tightly as a spicy aroma made her dizzy with desire. It was then that her eyes flew open, and she gazed right into those dreamy hazel eyes. His grip on her became tighter as did the intensity of his stare. Her heart was beating so loudly, she feared it echoed around the entire hallway. One of her hands was on the top of his shirt which exposed a bit of his chest. The bare skin felt hot to her touch. She heard him gasp as one of his hands went to her cheeks too. He moved his thumb across her cheek in the most gentle and endearing way. It sent titillations down to the tip of her toes. She closed her eyes, basking in the pleasure that her body felt.

She could feel his breath on her mouth as the distance between them made it impossible for even a gust of wind to pass. Her breaths had become shallow too.

Kiss him now!

Her lustful inner self screamed loudly to make the most of this moment. One of her hands found its way into his wavy hair as she pulled him closer, while the other one circled around his exposed torso, making him breathe harder with each second. As the distance between their lips grew closer, a mild shocking look crossed his hazel eyes which was gone in a second as his lips found hers. It sent shockwaves down her entire being as she got lost in his embrace completely. His lips were gentle at first, and then became demanding as he probed further with his tongue. She found herself responding as her tongue began to explore his mouth just as greedily.

A heatwave passed through her entire being as her body craved for more. She arched herself closer to him and tugged at his shirt buttons wanting to explore more of his taut body.

"Ahem"

Oh, damn damn damn!

It took her a second to steady herself as he pulled her up. She couldn't help noticing that he was extremely gentle as he did so. For a few seconds Ayesha had to jog her memory a bit to remember where she was.

Dear lord! We're in college. What was I thinking?

You believe you were thinking? How cute.

Thankfully, it was just Gayatri. But she was looking at them with the most wicked expression on her face.

Oh, this is not looking good.

Abhi quickly adjusted his shirt and apologized to both the girls. His gaze however was directed only at Ayesha. She could still see the hints of desire dancing in there. It made her blush once again. She could also see a hint of her lipstick on his lips. She had to shake her head to pull herself together not to think about what those lips had made her feel only seconds ago.

"Is that how we're welcoming each other now?"

Abhi sneered at Gayatri and punched her on the shoulder playfully. Ayesha was still reeling from the feel of Abhi's lips on hers. Her face felt hot as she quickly adjusted her hair and then her clothes.

Abhi sensed her awkwardness and excused himself to make way to his lecture. He did turn around to ensure she was okay and smiled in the sweetest manner. Ayesha's heart melted as she realized she was in deep trouble.

After that episode, Ayesha did not have the courage to talk it out with Abhi about what had happened. She felt embarrassed about her slip. After all, it was she who had encouraged it. But Abhi did become more relaxed around her. Occasionally he would put his arms around her shoulders and hug her every now and then too. Ayesha did not mind either, but she didn't let herself go rogue again, despite her mind and especially her body, demanding otherwise.

Let yourself go girl.

Like I'll listen to you after what happened that day.

This would have gone on and Ayesha might have forgotten it soon too. He did not bring it up much either, except that one time. The two of them were alone in the canteen. Gayatri was talking to one of the seniors and Sharad had not come to college that day.

"Do we need to talk about what happened in the hallway the other day?"

"Listen, Abhi. I'm embarrassed about it okay. It was a slip in judgement. Please don't take it to mean anything else. I'm not sure about any romantic engagements in my life right now."

He had given an imperceptible but understanding nod. Other than a little resistance from Abhi from then on, life on campus had seemed undisturbed.

She was getting impervious to Gayatri's jibes too. She simply ignored it and managed to bring the topic back to their studies or projects in a matter of minutes.

But then, *plot twist*. Viren joined as a lecturer. It was a rude shock for her.

Yes, she was annoyed of course. But she was also worried about being in the middle of a Sophie's Choice [68]kind of a situation now. The way Viren and Abhi glowered at each other, ready to beat each other to bits, was no solace.

She knew she had to have a talk with both. Unfortunately (or fortunately?), the talk never happened, and her choice was made without much effort.

---

[68] Used in reference to a difficult situation in which a person must choose between two equally deserving alternatives

Taken

"Tried and failed is overrated. Sometimes letting things be is a wiser step."

- Abhi Agarwal

"YOU DID WHAT?"

Okay, Sharad needs to chill.

"Yes, I did."

Abhi felt himself flushing as Sharad gave him an incredulous look. He was also annoyed that Sharad wasn't offering any emotional support. He could do with some 'It's okay." or "It'll be fine."

Well, you were quite impulsive and ludicrous.

Abhi was about to justify his action to Sharad. But he was suddenly yanked around. A hand gripping his elbow had made him pirouette and face the intruder. He could only register the pools of fire radiating the rage in those dark brown eyes.

Whoosh!

There was a ringing in his ears and a sharp tingling on his right cheek. He stumbled back a few steps with the impact of the slap. For a few seconds he could only hear jumbled words that were angrily pouring out of Ayesha's mouth.

"You…. No right…tell him…How could you?"

She was pointing an accusing finger at him while rambling on. Strangely, he didn't regret his action that had led to this. And to an extent, he was even aroused at her reaction to it. He was faintly aware of Gayatri trying to pull her away from him. Sharad put a hand on Abhi's shoulder in a consoling manner, but he jerked it away.

She's even more sexy when she's angry.

But you knew that already.

She was turning away when he grabbed her hand and pulled her to
him. She resisted initially. Her hands were on his chest trying to push
him away with all her strength. This only made him tighten his grip
around her waist. He continued to keep looking straight into her eyes.
Her facial features changed from anger to disbelief and abandon in a
few seconds.

Tears threatened to run down her cheeks at any moment, but she
continued to look at him disbelievingly. Her dewy fragrance enveloped
his physical and mental senses, as he wrapped her in a tight hug. She
lifted her face to look up at him and he cupped her chin gently. His
heart demanded a repeat performance of what they had done in the
hallway a few weeks back. His mind however had the good sense to
realize they were not alone. So, he made do with simply kissing both
her cheeks. Her skin felt soft, almost like silk. He found himself being
drawn to her lips instinctively but managed to control his
overwhelming and at that moment, inappropriate desire. With each
kiss he planted on her cheeks, he also gently brushed away the tears
that had rolled down. He noticed her shudder as his lips touched her
bare skin. Her hands that had been limp on her sides after abandoning
to push him away, enveloped around his neck and shoulders, as she
looked down shyly.

"About time."

Abhi heard Sharad say as Gayatri did a loud 'wohoo' and then
enveloped both Abhi and Ayesha in a bear hug. There was a round of
applause. Ayesha continued to stare at the floor, but Abhi noticed that
they had quite an audience. There were about 30 people scattered
across the hallway, most of whom cheered and clapped at the scene
they had just witnessed.

Some of the boys thumped Abhi on the back as they continued on
their way to class or out of the college campus. A few of them even
congratulated him.

"May I remind you that you are in an academic institution?"

He could easily identify the voice he had come to dislike more and
more over the past few months. Though he didn't want to, he let go
of his hold on Ayesha as she pushed away from him. A look was
exchanged between Viren and Ayesha. It spoke volumes even though

no words were exchanged. There was hurt and disappointment in one, embarrassment and apology in the other.

Why does she look sorry?

Do you have to be bothered about that now?

"I need to speak to both of you in private. Please come with me now!"

Ayesha followed almost too eagerly, yet sheepishly. Abhi shrugged at Gayatri and Sharad as he rushed to fall in step with her too.

As they walked behind Viren, Abhi looked sideways at Ayesha. She blushed and looked away.

Now what does that mean?

Well, she is obviously embarrassed, you idiot.

He found himself smiling slyly as he recalled what had brought on the little spectacle they had just put on. For over a month now, Abhi had been trying to build up the courage to talk to Ayesha privately. None of them had discussed the little *kissing* debacle. Ayesha also seemed to be avoiding being alone with him. Either Sharad or Gayatri, sometimes both, were always there with Abhi and Ayesha. When on one occasion when they were finally alone, and he had broached the subject, she had made her dissent quite clear.

Though it had been hard, he had forced himself to stop thinking about how her soft lips had felt on his. He was coping well with the remnants of that memory. Till today that is. He had seen Mr. I-Am-Still-Your-Competitor and Ayesha walk into the college campus together.

Oh, so they travel together now?

Well, they're neighbours. So, it does make sense.

Stop being so obvious and logical, will you?

The thought of them sitting together, side by side, in a local train compartment, with their hands and legs touching each other, accidentally or otherwise, had haunted him all throughout the day. He had become so overcome with rage, jealousy, and possessiveness that he had done something impulsive and stupid.

After their lecture with Mr. Joshi today, he had hung back under pretence of clearing a doubt. While making small chatter about

Theories of Democracy, Abhi had slipped in a chit in amidst his stuff on the teacher's desk. He wasn't proud of the contents of the chit. Sharad's reaction and Ayesha's outburst on finding out about it, had only made his self-disdain go up a notch. However, what happened between him, and Ayesha later had been forgiving enough.

"In here please."

Viren's demanding voice brought Abhi back to the soup he had landed himself in. Both Ayesha and Abhi followed Viren skeptically inside an empty classroom.

He had always figured Viren to be a tolerant guy. However, his demeanour and face belied everything he had presumed about his personality so far. Agreed, Abhi had been insolent, but he had expected a far greater explosion than the calm suppressed way Viren was handling the situation.

"Firstly, Mr. Agarwal.."

"Just Abhi is fine….Sir…"

Ayesha flinched and gave him a warning look. Viren however simply shrugged and went on.

"Okay, Abhi. I know it was you who left that chit on the desk. You could have simply told me rather than going through all that trouble. And Ayesha, what you do outside class and in the time you spend without me is none of my business. However, I do advise you two to be careful about keeping your relationship a bit…umm.. for lack of a better phrase.. under the covers.."

Ayesha gasped and Abhi suppressed a chuckle.

You gotta admit. The guy is funny.

Oh, so now that he's no longer a competitor, you're suddenly an admirer, huh?

I'll deal with you later.

Though Viren spoke calmly, the suppressed rage was not missed by either Abhi or Ayesha. Without waiting for them to respond, he turned to walk out. Before leaving, he turned and handed something to Ayesha. She looked at him pleadingly, but he shook his head nonchalantly and walked out.

There was a minute of strained silence in which Ayesha looked at the piece of paper in her hand.

"I'm still mad at you for doing this. Also, what a crude pictorial representation and words. At least you could have done that with some sophistication."

Abhi smiled sheepishly as he looked at the chit that had unfolded today's events. He couldn't believe he had done such a thing with a professor. But, now that the deed was done, he was glad that for once he had let his heart overpower his mind.

"But do you agree with the statement there?"

In response, she merely melted into his arms. He hugged her back right away, letting his hands explore her body, right from her nape and neck to her back and even the little exposed bit of her back waist. Her hands explored his body just as hungrily. They paused only to look into each other's eyes. All four eyes looked equally pooled with an aching desire. As their lips met again, it was like the days between their first kiss and now had never happened. They continued right where they had left off, blissfully ignoring Viren's word of advice.

The ringing of the bell acted like a warning bell. They jerked away from each other as if just realizing where they were.

Abhi gave a sly smile as Ayesha tucked her hand in his and they walked out together.

Greener Pastures

"Moving on, sometimes takes just one tiny moment of clarity."

- Viren Joshi

"Hey, when are you leaving?"

Despite the change in their relationship equation, Viren found himself smiling. He still wondered how he had got through being Ayesha and Abhi's professor. Especially after that day when Mr. Possessive made it amply clear that there was no competition.

How understanding of you.

Umm, like I could do anything else? She chose him too.

And you just accepted it?

Cut it out.

Despite his initial scepticism on taking up the job, and then a little discomfort while teaching Ayesha and Abhi, he had enjoyed his short-term as a lecturer. In fact, going by the farewell he had received, the students had enjoyed having him as a professor too. He couldn't believe it when Professor Das had called him up and said, "I am finding it hard to fill in your shoes, Viren. The students keep asking for you. They even compare our teaching methods now."

That had been a humbling and proud-worthy moment. In fact, if truth be told, that had been the eureka moment. It was then that he had decided on his next plan of action.

"I leave tomorrow evening."

He quickly typed a reply as he refocused on the mammoth task at hand.

"Are you sure that's enough? I can make some more snacks for you to take."

His mom's question made him smile. He went over to her and hugged her tightly.

"Are you ever going to feel it's enough? I will manage. Don't worry so much."

"I still can't believe you have actually cleared it. I mean yeah, I saw you working hard. But I had my doubts."

"Thanks for the vote of confidence."

Viren replied with mock hurt. But there was some truth in what his mom said. He had given it his best, but there was always a doubt in his mind.

When he read the 'RECOMMENDED'in bold letters at the bottom of his digital UPSC scorecard, he had triple checked. He entered his roll number multiple times. When it had stayed the same, he had done a victory lap up and down the apartment, jumping in joy. A few months back, Ayesha would have been one of the first people he informed. But this time he called the father instead of the daughter.

"I never had a doubt, dear. Congratulations. Please come home tonight so we can celebrate properly."

He hung up saying that he would try. But deep down he knew he wouldn't be going.

You're avoiding her.

No, I don't want to make things awkward.

Suit yourself.

Of course, he had to face her wrath the next morning. Despite his many attempts to avoid running into her (*pun intended?*), Ayesha had managed to crack down his morning jog schedule. So, there she was, hands on hips, at the garden gate. Her eyes fiery and her face, a ball of rage.

Why is she so hot?

You mean angry hot or sexy hot?

What followed as he neared her, were a blow of physical and verbal punches he was sure to remember for a long time.

Which ones though?

Of course, the physical ones, duh!

Her soft hands had felt arou…

She's taken for God's sake!

It was then that he knew he had to get away. Then Mr. Das's phone call came and he got his answer on how he could do it. The very next day, he had applied for the post of a UPSC trainer. In a week he had received the joining letter. And now, he was just a few hours away from getting away. He had chosen Sriram's Coaching because not only were they among the best, but they had a vacancy too. Not to mention a friend had readily agreed to share his flat where Viren would get an entire room to himself. What's more, the said flat was in the same neighborhood as the coaching class. It was like things were meant to be.

But you chose it because it's Sriram and that reminds you of her. Jai Shree Ram!

No, it's a great career opportunity and I have my interview there in April anyway.

You can mould this however you want; it's still called running away.

I'll deal with you later.

"Let me come to drop you off this time. Return the favor so to say⬜ ".

Why is she winking?

She's still flirting with you duh.

Ayesha's reply had him blushing. Even though a little hesitant and a tad bit guilty, he found himself replying with "Sure, but there's no need. I have my family coming with me too. And things are sure to become filmy with my mom and sister around."

"You can't push me away this time. Plus, my parents are insisting I do this too. Mom is also inviting you to dinner tonight."

So, the evening had been spent at the Banerjee residence. It was a pleasant couple of hours. Ayesha seemed a little less put off and more welcoming than his previous visits. He chuckled remembering the first one.

As he made to leave, he couldn't stop himself.

"Thanks for keeping the music down. See where it led me."

All three Banerjees burst out laughing. He touched Mr. and Mrs. Banerjee's feet. Mr. Banerjee hugged him warmly and said, "Please keep in touch and don't hesitate to ask for help. I have friends in Delhi too."

The next evening, tables turned, as Ayesha came to his house this time. Thankfully, his mother and Nalini behaved. Though their sly smiles showed up from time to time, they didn't embarrass him (or themselves) through words.

Things seemed cheerful but everybody was aware of the underlying grief. Viren knew it would be difficult staying away from his family. But it was a compromise he was willing to make for his career. The career he had slogged his ass off on for the past few years. The career he refused to not focus on just because...

Because of her.

Will you be making an exit too now, please?

As he boarded the Rajdhani Express, Ayesha chuckled. When he looked at her questioningly, she shrugged and said, "Well, of course you had to choose an express train too. Everything has to be in the fast lane for you."

He couldn't help guffawing at her cheekiness. He waved a final goodbye to them as the train signalled its departure. They too waved back, smiling with slightly tearful eyes.

He looked on towards them till the train would allow him to. Nalini was already exchanging numbers with Ayesha. His mother was looking at Ayesha with endearment too. The scene filled his heart with mixed feelings of longing and regret. And of course, incredulousness.

"Green pastures await."

He mumbled to himself as he made his way towards his seat and a changing life.

Testing Times

"Sometimes what may feel right, may not be right for you."

- Abhi Agarwal

"It gives me immense pleasure and no surprise at all to declare the college topper and University top 10 rank holder. Please give a round of applause to Abhi Agarwal."

Mr. Das announced with admiration and immense joy. Abhi made his way to the stage with a mixture of pride and humility. Choosing this course had led to a lot of convincing and cajoling. Thankfully, his father had relented in the end. Today his father's claps echoed among the loudest ones in the gathered audience. In that moment he knew they both were pleased with what had been an ugly confrontation a few years back.

It felt weird to be on the other side of the stage. Being part of the audience and not of the organizing committee was surreal. He looked at Ayesha waving at him cheerfully from behind the stage. Gayatri winked and gave him a thumbs up too. He was sure they had rushed forth just for this moment.

"Thank you, Professor Das. Receiving this felicitation from you is an honour. You were someone I always looked up to. No sorry, you still are someone I look up to. It was thanks to teachers like you and the way you taught that I was able to achieve this feat."

He bowed down to the faculties and the audience as they continued to clap loudly. He couldn't believe it had been almost a year since he passed out from college. A lot had transpired within that time. Not only did he now have a kickass job as a Junior Political Correspondent. But he and Ayesha were going strong for just over two years now.

He felt his heart flutter as he looked at her retreating figure behind stage and made his way back to his seat. The rest of his batchmates were handed out their degrees one after another too. He clapped the loudest when Sharad's name was called out. Gayatri and Ayesha made an appearance again as well. He couldn't stop beaming at the pride on both their faces. Looking at Ayesha still made his stomach do somersaults. The way her skin felt against his, could only be best described as fireworks.

Still can't believe she's yours huh?

Yeah, I mean just look at her.

How are you going to live without her then?

Trust you to spoil a happy moment.

"Do you want to stay back with your friends for a while?"

The surprisingly gentle tone of his father brought him out of his daydreaming. Abhi hadn't even realized when the ceremony ended.

"I know you would rather come home by train. So, we'll take the car."

He is full of surprises today, isn't he?

Abhi could only nod because apparently, he had lost his ability to speak. How else would a son who had never easily got his way, react? His father pulled him into a hug before leaving the hall. Radha Agarwal left teary eyed too.

"So, Varun is coming in a bit. Shall we go out for dinner?"

"Of course, you would know his schedule better than me now, Gayu."

Abhi laughed and pulled Gayatri into a hug as she stuck out her tongue. Though she pretended to be offended, he didn't miss the blush that had spread on her cheeks. Varun and Gayatri's relationship had been a pleasant surprise for Abhi. But not so much for Ayesha, who had played cupid to get the two together.

"So, shall I go home then? This seems more like a couple's date to me now."

Three pairs of raised eyebrows and incredulous looks shut Sharad down.

"Let me invite Nalini too." Ayesha said, winking slyly at him. Sharad said a nonchalant 'okay' but nobody missed the twinkle in his eyes.

"When are you leaving?"

The mood turned sombre in an instant. Though the question seemed casual, Abhi easily sensed the suppressed melancholy within. Ayesha was never good at hiding what she felt.

"I'll stay as long as you want me to."

"Aww" went the Kulkarni siblings as if on cue.

Ayesha laughed, as tears threatened to roll down her eyes. Abhi enveloped her in his arms. Her dewy fragrance only made it harder for him to console her rather than kiss her.

"Don't do this, Ayesha. I don't want to remember you crying on our last day together."

This only made her break down. The tears that she had been holding in, broke out relentlessly. It was as if someone had opened the floodgates of a dam. He kissed the top of her head and kept patting her back constantly 'sushhing' her in a soothing manner.

"This is just a coma, not a full-stop. C'mon, let's enjoy. There's a lot we need to celebrate. I hear Gayatri has finally beaten you to top the class this semester."

That brought out a laugh from Ayesha.

Phew!

"Excuse me. What do you mean finally? I was always just a few marks behind her. I guess I have you to thank for making her lose focus."

That made them all laugh as finally the mood lightened.

"So, how excited are you to join Columbia?" asked Sharad as the four of them made their way out.

"Not as excited as I was when this one finally said yes."

Ayesha laughed and punched him playfully. He was relieved to see the change in her mood.

"Really though. I still can't believe I got in."

"But why do you need to go now? The semester begins in April, right?"

Abhi looked at Ayesha before answering. He was sure she had the same question again in her mind. He had already had the conversation with her more than a couple of times. The result had always been the grumpy expression Ayesha currently had on her face. He sighed as he looked at Gayatri and answered her this time.

"I need time to settle down. Besides finding myself a convenient accommodation I also need to find a suitable part-time job."

Gayatri turned to look at Ayesha. The girls exchanged a 'he's an idiot' look. This amused Abhi rather than annoying him. He was glad Ayesha had Gayatri to lean on while he was gone.

Sure, a long-distance relationship seemed tough to work out. But getting into an Ivy League college for his master's degree had been an ambition. An ambition he had worked hard for since he was sure of a career in Political Science.

The four of them walked into the college canteen to wait for Varun and Nalini.

"So would you like to order something from the stalls outside?"

Ayesha challenged Sharad and the four of them burst out laughing. They reminisced that moment and many others spent in this very spot. Abhi's heart was suddenly filled with contentment and grief.

"Testing times await but let's taste this time to its fullest first."

He mumbled to himself as he dug into his idlis.

I Do

"Learning from your mistakes and getting inspired from other's success is the way to growth."

      -   Ayesha Agarwal

"Oh my God! You look freaking amazing Ayesha."

Ayesha blushed crimson.

You're already blushed with rouge today, darling.

Ah you. I won't let you ruin my happiness today.

She winked at Nalini while admiring herself in the mirror. It had taken a lot of trails and shopping rounds and an increasingly agitated mother to get here.

"I know right. But my my, look who's dressed to kill today."

Dressed in a maroon sequin Ghagra[69], paired with a netted green halter choli[70] and a maroon-green sequin dupatta, Nalini would make any guy's head turn today. With a pang, Ayesha realized how much she looked like her brother.

Especially the nose and the wavy hair.

The eyes too.

Without the specs though.

Focus!

"Are they here yet?"

"Are who here, what's going on here?"

---

[69] (in South Asia) A long full skirt, often decorated with embroidery, mirrors, or bells.

[70] a short-sleeved bodice worn under a sari by Indian women. (Sari-A garment that consists of a long piece of cloth that women, particularly in the Indian subcontinent, wear draped around their bodies)

Trust these two to make a dramatic entry.

Ayesha got up from her mirror facing chair. Ketaki and Sneha, who had just barged in, gaped loudly. Then all the three girls came forward to envelop Ayesha in a bear hug.

"Ayu, I always knew you were the best looking among us. That made me a little jealous too sometimes. But looking at you today is only filling me with admiration and happiness. I can't believe we're here for this big day."

"Of course, you are here Sneha. You think we would miss having you two here on such an important day?"

"Delhi agrees with you, Ayu. JNU[71][72] must've been exciting. But you must be thrilled to be back in Mumbai. You look gorgeous in this blue by the way. Whose choice was it?"

"Ahem"

The girls turned in unison at the loud interruption. Nalini blushed, but the rest of them turned to Sharad with hands on their hips.

"If you girls are done admiring each other, we need to get on with the event please."

"Oh, come here you dweeb."

Ayesha pulled him in amidst the four of them as the girls surrounded him from all sides.

"You look nice too, don't worry."

"Definitely very dapper."

"A lot of hearts will be broken today."

There was a loud wohoo when Nalini kissed him on both the cheeks as a way of complimenting him.

Ayesha's heart was so full of gratification that she felt it might burst out of her body.

"They're here. Please let Sharad go. He's needed at the entrance."

---

71 Jawaharlal Nehru University (New Delhi)
72

The stern yet endearing voice of Mrs. Kulkarni broke them apart. The girls giggled as Sharad walked out, still blushing.

"Ayesha, Gayu is…."

"Oops, yes I know…"

Ayesha picked up a dupatta from the bed.

"Okay, time to get to our duties. Nalini, go check the stage and music. Sneha, you go with her. Ketaki, you come with me."

All four of them rushed out of the room. Two of them ran towards the big stage on the open ground. While Ayesha and Ketaki ran to the opposite room.

They gaped and then shrieked in delight at the sight that awaited them.

I have never seen a more beautiful bride.

I agree for once.

Ayesha ran forward and hugged Gayatri tightly. She felt overwhelming emotions as Ketaki joined her in the group hug.

"You're choking me. This lehenga[73] is killing me with its weight already. Now you two fatsos are adding to it."

Gayatri was trying to be funny and stern. But her voice sounded choked too. She was a sight to behold in her white and red Ghagra and green choli with mirror work. The red and green dupatta draped around her head had tiny golden and white balls on its border. Anyone who looked at her would be left stunned for a few seconds.

"Shut up. Stop being a bridezilla for a few seconds.", Ketaki chuckled and replied.

Ayesha laughed as she let go of Gayatri. Ketaki did so too, but rather reluctantly. They couldn't stop admiring her though.

"Ayu, you look amazing. See I told you, orange and blue would look great on you."

"You're the focus today babe. Here is the dupatta. Shall we go then?"

---

[73] A full ankle-length skirt worn by Indian women, usually on formal or ceremonial occasions.

Ayesha and Ketaki stood on either side of Gayatri. Ayesha passed on one side of the dupatta to Ketaki and the two of them held it above Gayatri's head. Rushing into the room, and almost breathless, Nalini and Sneha joined behind Ayesha and Ketaki in holding the dupatta too. They slowly walked out of the room towards their destination. With the golden kaleeras[74] hanging from the dupatta and the LED lights now turned on, nobody would miss looking at Gayatri. The five of them walked slowly to the mandapa while *Shubh Aarambh* [75]started playing in the background. Of course, Gayatri had to make a statement entry, so as soon as the female lyrics came on, she broke into an impromptu dance. Ayesha couldn't stop beaming as she led her best friend towards her new life.

"Varun looks hot."

Gayatri whispered to Ayesha before taking her seat opposite her husband-to-be. Ayesha laughed out loud recalling the very statement which had led to this.

Ayesha's eyes teared up as she read the "Gayatri weds Varun" banner at the entrance of the ground.

"Can you get some water for me please?", Gayatri pleaded.

Ayesha's bridesmaid's duties called again as she sprung to action.

"You three stay with her, okay? I'll be right back."

She instructed Ketaki, Sneha and Nalini who were seated near the mandapa as she walked towards the water counter. She turned around holding two glasses of water when,

Bang!

A familiar spicy aroma enveloped her before she could look at the culprit. The water had spilled over her choli, and she was about to lose her balance. The glasses fell out of her hands, as she placed one of her hands on the countertop to balance herself. Her other hand reached out to his chest instinctively, as strong hands gripped both her arms.

---

[74] Kalira is a silver or gold embellished, umbrella shaped ornament that is attached to the bride's bangle, which is a set of traditional white and red colored bangles worn on each arm.

[75] A Hindi song from the Bollywood movie *Kai Po Che*

Well, there are those eyes with the specs now.

Banging into guys while fetching water seems to be your thing.

No improvement there since 2016 I see.

Go away!

"Are you okay?"

His concerned question brought her back to reality.

What is he doing here?

"Yes, I'm fine. Sorry about that."

She replied, fumbling. She felt his gaze lingering on her as he let go of his grip on her arms slowly, as if still not sure if she could stand on firm ground.

Say something!

"Hi."

"I didn't expect you here."

They spoke out together and burst into nervous laughter. Ayesha looked towards the mandapa and remembered why she was there. That's when she noticed Gayatri, Ketaki, Sneha and Nalini huddled together and giggling while looking at her.

So, this was their plan.

"Varun is an old friend. We were classmates in school. We lost touch for a bit in between but were able to reconnect because of Nalini."

Of course!

"Ahem"

Their attention turned towards the intrusion. Abhi, holding two glasses of water, was looking at them with a curious expression. He looked dapper as always in a maroon kurta with golden embroidery. It seemed like he wanted to say something. Thinking otherwise, he simply shrugged and smiled nervously. Then shaking his head, he turned and made his way to the mandapa.

"He looks…"

"We are not together. We were mature enough to be clear about our ambitions. But unfortunately, also naïve enough to believe we could make long-distance work despite our varied career choices."

"Well, I was going to say he looks different from what I remember. But okay, that works too."

He has got the sense of humour intact.

But he's got better in the looks department. Look at those well-toned biceps!

Go away, will you?

Clearing her throat, she declared, "I'm coming to Kolkata soon for my PhD. Professor Das was kind enough to write a lovely recommendation. Thanks to that, I've been able to get into Rabindra Bharati University. I hear you're posted in West Bengal too."

"That's great. Yes, I'm the Subdivisional Magistrate of Baranagar. You have my number. So, call me maybe[76]?"

"You remember that?" Ayesha laughed and asked.

"I do."

His eyes looked at her most intensely as she blushed under his bespectacled scrutiny.

She soon excused herself and made her way back to the mandapa.

The girls broke into a chorus of *Kuch toh hai tujhse raabta* as she sat down next to Gayatri.

"Can we focus on getting one of us married first please?" she had to remind them with a warning tone.

However, as she looked out at the ground, her eyes immediately searched for and landed on him. Her heart filled with hope as the girls continued their signing and she blushed.

Who knows what Kolkata has in store?

But with him around it'll be easier, right?

Just the way it was in Mumbai.

---

[76] A reference to Carly Rae Jespen's popular English song *Call Me Maybe*

We'll see about that. Let's not get ahead of ourselves, girl.

March 2024

Epilogue

"You'll move on and make progress the way you aimed to. But what you really want is never found at your job, however good it might be."

\-   Viren Joshi

Her character became a label based on what she wore,

The girl in the mini skirt soon began to be called a whore.

Even her habits and liberal thinking added fuel to this,

Smoking, drinking, fighting for women's rights only made people, with her attitude, pissed.

Unlike her was another who was far away from such croon,

Burqa clad, shy, and timid she stayed in her own cocoon.

People hardly noticed her when she was around

Even when they did, they turned their faces away with a frown.

Some self-proclaimed well-wishers of the society,

Took it upon themselves to bring some sobriety.

Unable to see a woman being so rebellious and outspoken,

They defamed her, threatened her, and did everything they could to leave her spirit broken.

Using religion to evoke violence,

The Politician plotted his win by manipulating people's emotions.

Ruthlessly the people took out on each other their wrath,

All over the city in the name of religion there was a bloodbath.

One girl was fearless, another fearful,

One continued in her ways, another locked in the house worried and tearful.

Both met the same fate though in different situations,

When both were tied, gaged, hit, and raped for hours by so called protectors of religion and the nation.

This situation brings to the fore an important question,

Are women always going to be the victim of religious and cultural obsession?

Irrespective of what the girl does, wears and whether she speaks or stays mum,

Is she bound to face the same rage and outcome?

The tumultuous applause that broke out didn't do justice. The poem was powerful for sure. But what made it compelling was the narration.

"May I have a photograph too along with the autograph?"

"Hey, what a surprise. What are you doing here?"

Viren had deliberately waited till the crowd dispersed. He knew she was popular. But he hadn't expected a long line of admirers to be buzzing around her. It had taken a while to catch her alone.

"Well, for starters. I've been meaning to get my copy of *Angst, Anger & Adulting*, signed by the author herself, since forever now. I do believe that this event was 'talk of the town' for the past few weeks. Hence, I was drawn to it the way most of Kolkata was. Also, I wanted to see Ms. Banerjee in action. I remember the first time someone showed me a video of you. It was during my second training phase in Dehradun. When I told them I know you personally, my popularity hit the roof. Everyone started referring to me as 'the one who knows Bandit Banerjee'. It was tough answering the questions they had for me. Let me tell you, some of them were outright invasive."

She laughed with a twinkle in her eyes. Although, she did look a little embarrassed.

There's that dimple again.

She's humble about her success too. That's kind of admirable.

What about the way she looks? Isn't that more admirable?

Well….

"Here. Let me sign that for you. As for the photograph, let's go somewhere we can capture a really good one. How about we head out for dinner? I believe there's a lot of catching up to do."

"Yes. I do believe I owe you a conversation without UPSC coming up even once."

She chuckled as they walked out of the venue together.

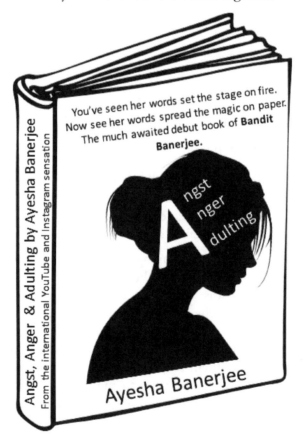

The *Love (Try) Angle* playlist

SONG NAME	MOVIE/ALBUM	REFERENCE
Maahi Ve	Kaante	Chapter-*Slow and Furious* Abhi listens to this song after leaving the parking lot at the station and thinking about Ayesha, who he had met for the first time.
Neha Kakkar Version of Maahi Ve	Maahi Ve Unplugged	Chapter-*A Musical Meeting* When Ayesha is mocked by Viren for singing too loud and disturbing him in his studies.
Waah Waah RamJi	Hum Aapke Hain Kaun	Chapter-*Temple Run* Song heard by Abhi as he enters his house
Heartbeat (Instrumental)	Kal Ho Na Ho	Chapter-*My Dream is To Fly* When Ayesha recites a poem on stage on her first day of the college
Diva	Single Track	Chapter-*My Dream is To Fly* When Gayatri performs on stage on the first day of the college
Party All Night	Boss	Chapter-*Party All Night* When Abhi enters the venue after Ayesha ignores him and enters the party hall without looking at him.

Do You Wanna Partner	Partner	Chapter-*Do You Wanna Partner?* The name of the game that Abhi announces in the Fresher's party.
Bang Bang	Bang Bang	Chapter-*Do You Wanna Partner?* The song to which Abhi and Gayatri dance to after winning the game
Ang Laga De	Goliyon Ki Rasleela Ram-Leela	Chapter-*Do You Wanna Partner?* The song to which Sharad and Ayesha dance to after winning their game
Sajna Hai Mujhe Sajna Ke Liye	Saudagar	Chapter-*The Way You Look Tonight* When Viren's Mother teases him for dressing up to pick up Ayesha.
The Way You Look Tonight	Swing Time	Chapter-*The Way You Look Tonight* The song that Viren heard in the background while dreaming that Ayesha and Abhi were dancing with each other
Pyaara Bhaiya Mera Dulha Raja Banke Aa Gaya	Kya Kehna	Chapter-*The Way You Look Tonight* The song that Viren's Sister sings when he is about to leave the house to go and pick up Ayesha from the dance party.
Jai Deva Jai Deva Mangal Murti	Vaastav	Chapter-*Maurya Re*

		Ganesh Aarti that Ayesha could hear while entering Abhi's home on Ganesh Chaturthi.
I Gotta Feeling	I Gotta Feeling	Chapter-*Do You Wanna Partner?* Abhi sings this song to himself while entering the Fresher's Party venue after witnessing the scene between Ayesha and Viren
Call Me Maybe	Kiss	Chapter- *Call Me Maybe and I Do* Viren uses this song line to crack a joke about how Ayesha could now call him since they had just exchanged numbers. Later in the chapter I Do he cracks the same joke recalling their initial meeting when they had exchanged numbers.
All The Best	All The Best	Inspiration for the chapter titled *All The Best*
Maurya Re	Don (2006)	Inspiration for the chapter titled *Maurya Re*

Listen to these songs via the **Love (Try) Angle** special playlist on Spotify – Scan the QR code below,

Glossary of Terms

TERM	MEANING
Union Public Service Commission (UPSC)	The Union Public Service Commission (ISO: Saṅgh Lōk Sēvā Āyōg), commonly abbreviated as UPSC, is India's premier central recruiting agency. It is responsible for appointments to and examinations for All India services and group A & group B of Central services.
Mumbaikar	a native or inhabitant of the city of Mumbai
VT Station	Chhatrapati Shivaji Terminus (CST), formerly known as Victoria Terminus (VT), is a UNESCO World Heritage Site and a historic railway station located in the heart of Mumbai.
Ram Navami	Rama Navami is a spring Hindu festival that celebrates the birthday of the Hindu God Lord Rama. The festival celebrates the descent of Vishnu as shri Rama avatar, through his birth to King Dasharatha and Queen Kausalya in Ayodhya
Aarti	A Hindu ceremony in which lights with wicks soaked in ghee are lit and offered up to one or more deities.
Kurta	a long, loose shirt worn by men and women in south Asia
Ayodhya	An ancient town in North India, in Uttar Pradesh State. As the birthplace of Rama, it is sacred to Hindus.
Prasad	A devotional offering made to a god, typically consisting of food that is later shared among devotees.
Mecca	a place that many people wish to visit because of a particular interest
kaali peeli	a kaali peeli is a black and yellow taxi that runs on the streets of Mumbai

Vada Pav	Vada pav, alternatively spelt wada pao, is a vegetarian fast food dish native to the state of Maharashtra. The dish consists of a deep-fried potato dumpling placed inside a bread bun (*pav*) sliced almost in half through the middle.
Aamchi Mumbai	It means Our Mumbai. "Aamchi Mumbai" is the loving phrase used by Maharashtrians in general, and Mumbaikars in particular, to refer to their beloved city, the economic capital of the country, Mumbai.
Ram (Rama)	A deity or deified hero of later Hinduism worshipped as an avatar of Vishnu
Mandir wahi banega	A slogan to build "Ram Mandir" in Ayodhya as a place of birth of Lord Ram. Mandir: Temple
boondi ladoos	Boondi laddu or bundiar laddu is made from bengal gram flour based boondi
besan ladoos	Besan laddu is a popular Indian sweet dish made of besan (chickpea flour or gram flour), sugar, and ghee
Sai Jayanti	Birthday of Shirdi Sai baba in India
temple	a building where people pray to a god or gods
earthen lamps	A diya, diyo, deya, divaa, deepa, deepam, or deepak is an oil lamp usually made from clay, with a cotton wick dipped in ghee or vegetable oils. Diyas are native to the Indian subcontinent often used in Hindu, Sikh, Jain and Zoroastrian religious festivals such as Diwali or the Kushti ceremony.
Rangoli	Rangoli is an art form, originating in the Indian subcontinent, in which patterns are created on the floor or the ground using materials such as coloured rice, coloured sand, quartz powder, flower petals, and coloured rocks
Ramayana	Rāmāyana is one of the two major Sanskrit epics of ancient India and an important text of Hinduism, the other being the Mahābhārata. The epic, traditionally ascribed to the Maharishi Valmiki, narrates the life of

	Rama, a legendary prince of Ayodhya city in the kingdom of Kosala
Annam Vlilaku lamps	The Nachiarkoil lamp, also called Annam lamp or Nachiarkoil Kuthuvilakku, is an ornamental brass lamp made of series of diyas, a handicraft product which is exclusively made by Pather (Kammalar) community in Nachiyar Koil town in Tamil Nadu, India.
Thali	Thali (meaning "plate") or Bhojanam (meaning "full meal") is a round platter used to serve food in South Asia and Southeast Asia. Thali is also used to refer to an Indian-style meal made up of a selection of various dishes which are served on a platter.
Brass Diya	Diya is an oil lamp with a cotton wick dipped in ghee or vegetable oils. Brass is a hard yellow metal that is a mixture of two other metals (copper and zinc).
Conch	The shell of a sea creature. In India certain kind of conches are played by blowing into them on auspicious occasions
Dupatta	A dupatta is a scarf worn by people in India
Bangle	a circular metal band that is worn around the arm or wrist for decoration
Beta	A person's son
Mithibhai	Mithibai College of Arts, Chauhan Institute of Science & Amruthben Jivanlal College of Commerce and Economics is a college affiliated to the University of Mumbai
Rickshaw	A small light vehicle with two wheels used in some Asian countries to carry people over short distances. The rickshaw is pulled by a person walking or riding a bicycle
bade baap ki bigdi aulaad	Aimless kids with too much money to spend from their filthy rich parents' bank accounts.
HSC	The Higher Secondary Certificate (HSC/INTERMEDIATE) is a public examination in Bangladesh, India, Nepal and

	Pakistan. HSC is equivalent to GCE A Level in England and 3rd and 4th year of high Schools in the United States
Dabeli	Dabeli, kutchi dabeli or double roti is a popular snack food of India, originating in the Kutch or Kachchh region of Gujarat. It is a sweet snack made by mixing boiled potatoes with a special dabeli masala, putting the mixture in a ladi pav (burger bun), and serving it with chutneys made from tamarind, date, garlic, red chilies and other ingredients
Jaa Ayesha Jaa, lee le aaj ki raat	Go and enjoy the time of your life tonight. Inspired from an iconic dialogue 'Jaa Simran Jaa, Jee Le Apni Zindagi' from a popular Bollywood movie *Dilwale Dulhaniya Le Jaayenge* where this dialogue is said by the female protagonist's father to encourage her to chase a life of her dreams.
Ganesh Chaturthi	Ganesh Chaturthi, also known as Vinayaka Chaturti, or Vinayaka Chaviti is a Hindu festival celebrating the arrival of Ganesh to earth from Kailash Parvat with his mother Goddess Parvati/Gauri
Ganesh	Ganesha, also spelled Ganesh, also called Ganapati, is an elephant-headed Hindu god of beginnings, who is traditionally worshipped before any major enterprise and is the patron of intellectuals, bankers, scribes, and authors. His name means both "Lord of the People" (gana means the common people) and "Lord of the Ganas" (Ganesha is the chief of the ganas, the goblin hosts of Shiva). Shiva lit. 'The Auspicious One' also known as Mahadeva 'The Great God'), is one of the principal deities of Hinduism. He is the Supreme Being in Shaivism, one of the major traditions within Hinduism.
Mandapam	(in southern India) a temple porch. As temporary platform set up for weddings and religious ceremonies
Romcom	Romantic comedy (also known as romcom or rom-com) is a subgenre of comedy and slice-of-life

	fiction, focusing on lighthearted, humorous plot lines centered on romantic ideas, such as how true love is able to surmount most obstacles.
MIA	Missing In Action
Salwar Kameez	A pair of light, loose, pleated trousers, usually tapering to a tight fit around the ankles, worn by women from South Asia typically with a kameez. Kameez- A piece of clothing like a long shirt worn by many people from south Asia and the Middle East
"Kuch Kuch Hota Hai" kind of drama	Situation where the girl has to choose between two boys. Referring to the Situation where Ayesha has to choose between Abhi and Viren. The reference is drawn from a popular hindi movie with the same name with a love triangle as the major plotline.
IAS	The Indian Administrative Service (IAS) is the administrative arm of the All India Services of Government of India.
IFS	IFS stands for Indian Foreign Service
CBI	The Central Bureau of Investigation (CBI) is the premier investigating agency of India
BMC	BMC stands for Brihanmumbai Municipal Corporation. It is also referred to as Municipal Corporation of Greater Mumbai (MCGM)
Jaa Simran Jaa, don't forget your Raj here but	Gayatri tells Ayesha to go and enjoy back at her place but not to forget her Raj (Abhi). It is in reference to a popular dialogue 'Jaa Simran Jaa, Jee Le Apni Zindagi' taken from popular Bollywood movie *Dilwale Dulhaniya Lee Jaayenge* where the male and female lead are called Simran and Raj
HOD	Head of the Department
Diwali	This is one of the most popular festivals in the Hindu calendar. This festival commemorates Lord Rama's return to his kingdom Ayodhya after completing his 14-year exile. The most beautiful of all Indian festivals, Diwali is a celebration of lights.

Dhanteras	Dhanteras, also known as Dhanatrayodashi, is the first day that marks the festival of Diwali in India
Kal	Tomorrow
Jamai Raja	Son-In-Law
Sophie's Choice	Used in reference to a difficult situation in which a person must choose between two equally deserving alternatives
Ghaghara	(in South Asia) A long full skirt, often decorated with embroidery, mirrors, or bells.
Choli	a short-sleeved bodice worn under a sari by Indian women. (Sari-A garment that consists of a long piece of cloth that women, particularly in the Indian subcontinent, wear draped around their bodies)
JNU	Jawaharlal Nehru University (New Delhi)
Lehenga	A full ankle-length skirt worn by Indian women, usually on formal or ceremonial occasions.
Kaleera	Kalira is a silver or gold embellished, umbrella shaped ornament that is attached to the bride's bangle, which is a set of traditional white and red colored bangles worn on each arm.

About the Author

Manali is a full-time freelance writer and editor cum blogger. Though that sounds fancy, it came after a few years of working in various fields like Marketing, Teaching and Content Writing. Currently, apart from her ad hoc writing and editing assignments, Manali runs her blog _arusticmind.com_ on which she shares book reviews, travel experiences, life anecdotes, inspiring human stories, poetry, and flash fiction. Manali has been a two times bestselling author via her books **_The Untold Stories_** and **_The Art of Being Grateful & Other Stories_**. Her short story **_'The Walls Have Ears'_** helped her bag the Best Short Story Award in 2020. **_Love (Try) Angle_** is her debut novel and first foray into long form creative writing. It has already helped her bag the **Best Author: Fiction** award by **Cherry Book Awards.**

If not writing, you can find Manali either reading, travelling, listening to music, binge-watching a series she might be currently hooked to, catching up on her movies watchlist, or more than one of these at the same time, in no particular order.

Follow Manali on all social media platforms under her pen name **A Rustic Mind.**

Books by this Author

The Art of Being Grateful & Other Stories

Aashna receives a mysterious phone call in the middle of the night. The caller is a girl who says she has been kidnapped and will die if Aashna doesn't help her. Before Aashna can get details about the girl and her whereabouts, the phone gets cut off. Who was she and why did her voice sound eerily familiar? Will Aashna be able to help her?

Maanvi's life has always been about making everyone around realize that she is worthy too. From her test grades to her body type, everyone always had a piece of advice to give or some judgement to pass. How does Maanvi get affected by these?

Does she manage to prove her worth to the world?

These and six other stories in this collection, cover a range of genres including romance, mystery, horror, thriller and much more. Delve in for a delightful reading journey!

The Untold Stories

Have you wondered about the events that happen around us? Do you think about the kind of lives people we come across everyday lead, and how they came to be what they are today? Our life is our story, but what about those little everyday incidents which create the anecdotes filling up the chapters of our life story? 'The Untold Stories' shares tiny anecdotes from people's everyday routines which go on to make remarkable chapters in their life stories. These anecdotes range from incidents around contemporary social issues and events such as terrorism and environmental imbalance to those circling around relationships.

A Rustic Mind

"We never think about the effects or repercussions of our everyday actions or even the things we come across on a daily basis. Through 'A Rustic Mind' I aim to provide a thoughtful take on such actions and incidents. Poetic in its expression, these words will strike a chord which is not only deep but relatable on many levels. "

Ten Tales

This is a collection of short stories by authors across the world. The stories have been handpicked and selected based on their quality. The stories cover all genres in fiction.

Manali's story in this book is titled 'I'm Glad I'm Not Beautiful'. It spins a story around the much needed to be curbed issue and social stigma of acid attacks. The story circles around two school going teenage girls, Abha and Vidhya, who are best friends, but are opposite in nature and appearance and how a few incidents on a particular day turns their lives upside down.

Zista

"Zista represents Culture, the hub of which lies in India."

This title holds in its pages the very essence of India, its people and its culture, conveyed through a selection of short stories by few of the best authors of India.

Manali's story in this book is titled 'The Walls Have Ears'. This story helped her bag the Best Short Story award. It talks about a young girl's day out in the infamous Kamathipura aka The Red-Light District of Mumbai.

Praise for the Author

The Art of Being Grateful and Other Stories gave me an opportunity to know Manali Desai as a person.

Her modesty and pure commitment to her work is undoubtedly evident with the way she has put forward a book which will stay in your bookshelf as a cherished possession.

(Review for Manali's book *The Art of Being Grateful & Other Stories*)

-   **Kevin Missal**

(bestselling author of multiple books)

I love Manali's fluid poetry. A beautiful mix of different emotions expressed in the form of poetic lines.

I could relate to most of them on a personal note which made this all the more a delightful read.

(Review for Manali's book *A Rustic Mind)*

-   **Anusha Sridharan**

(Author of *Conversations with Coherent Worlds*)

The tales have been written in simple words which I find is the most efficient when it comes to microtales.

Because while reading them, readers are also compelled to think about the past and present associated with it.

The stories show us that even the mundane things that we consider part and parcel of life, are significant for the person who is living the situation at that moment.

(Review for Manali's book *The Untold Stories*)

-   **Ankita Khataniar**

(PhD Scholar, Literary Critic and Author)

Contents

Preface

Over our 10 combined years of experience in preventive and rehabilitative programs in both university and corporate environments, we have come to realize that motivational problems present
a major challenge for fitness personnel. Often clients simply do not
comply with their programs, forcing exercise leaders to behave like
drill sergeants to achieve desired ends. If unresolved, these problems are destructive to both programs and participants. For
example, programs may face economic strains from a high dropout rate or may present an unattractive image to the community.
Even clients who do stick with the program may fail to make desirable performance gains or may view exercise as self-imposed
punishment.

How do we deal effectively with motivational problems? Are there
ways to make exercise more enjoyable? Is objective exercise prescription based on heart rate the correct formula? Should we better
prepare our clients for exercise? The purpose of this text is to provide answers to these and similar questions. Although this book's
content is soundly based on research and theory, we also rely
heavily on our own practical experiences and those of our colleagues. Exercise leaders and program directors will find this information most useful, but it is also invaluable for administrators
of health clubs, for those involved in the development, operation,

and evaluation of corporate wellness programs, and for others concerned about making the most of fitness activities.

For readers with little knowledge of psychology, we have transformed complex concepts into easily understood terminology. This organizational structure does not imply the lack of a systematic approach to the problem of motivation. Rather, the plan of the text is logically consistent with state-of-the-art methods used in modifying health behaviors.

We begin in chapter 1 by taking an in-depth look at what motivates exercise behavior. Why is it so complex, and what type of intervention is most likely to yield success? We stress the importance of an individualized approach to motivation and emphasize the roles of thought and reinforcement structures. To implant a motive for exercise behavior, your methods have to be systematic. We list 10 major components that are part of any sound motivational program. Your first challenge is to learn what you need to know about clients and how, with minimal effort, such information can be acquired.

In chapter 2 we take on the challenge of getting to know clients. How do past history and present physical condition influence reactions to exercise? What has brought each client to your program? What turns individuals on to fitness? Where are clients' priorities, and what do they hope to gain from their exercise experience? These and similar questions form the basis for programming that targets the individual. This foundation allows you to determine where to take specific clients, how to get them there, and what interventions may be useful in the process. Instituting such a practice will also further your understanding of human behavior and will provide an excellent means of evaluating program offerings. For example, perhaps you will discover you should consider different forms of feedback or alternative modes of orienting clients.

Chapter 3 logically follows assessment by asking the all-important question, How does one prescribe exercise? If there is a single point to learn in the third chapter, it should be this: The prescription of exercise must be specific to the individual. What end have you achieved if after 3 weeks of a physiologically sound aerobic workout schedule the client quits? We are not downplaying the need for a proper physiological basis to prescription. In fact, it plays a critical role in meeting clients' personal needs. However, you must keep in mind that, above all else, prescription involves behavior. Information acquired from the interview process described in chapter 2 enables you to tailor exercise prescription from a subjective perspective.

The next step in the motivational process—building and repairing commitment—is presented in chapter 4. Although commitment requires continual reevaluation, it is particularly important prior to the onset of exercise. Do clients understand the nature of their prescriptions? What can they realistically expect from them? How do the payoffs rank in an individual's priorities? What reactions to exercise pose a threat to commitment? Contrary to what many believe, you have to be prepared to both build and repair commitment. The exciting news is that there are several methods to accomplish this that can be easily integrated into a properly designed setting.

Chapter 5 explains how to use goal setting and feedback. Why does goal setting work? How can you incorporate goals into the prescription process? In the motivational system we present, goals are important not only as evidence of achievement, but also as a mechanism for building self-confidence and personal esteem. Goal setting is used as an intervention technique to encourage desirable thought patterns in clients. With your knowledge of behavior, you will understand why goal setting may fail at times and what to do when it does. Feedback is an obvious component in goal setting, but it also functions independent of structured goals. This chapter also discusses how and when to present feedback. We provide a case study as a model and consider the art of communication, contrasting weak and strong approaches to the feedback process.

As a final target for intervention, chapter 6 critiques specific elements of the exercise setting. What type of exercise leader behaviors are constructive? How are reinforcements used? Are motivational props worthy of consideration? Is the physical setting important? As we see it, the exercise setting provides the bridge between thought and action. Intervention at this level often determines compliance and dropout rates 3 or 6 months after entry.

We feel that as you use the suggestions and ideas we present, you will be able to make your professional dedication really pay off. We hope you will be inspired to generate new ideas appropriate to your clients and situations. We wish for you and your clients the adherence and compliance results we have enjoyed by following planned yet flexible approaches.

Acknowledgments

Space does not permit acknowledgment of the numerous scholars, personal friends, and clients who contributed in various ways to this text. There are, however, those who deserve special mention. The first author would like to thank Julian Rotter for sharing his wisdom on social behavior. Although not formally associated with social psychology, he is a master of that subdiscipline, an eminent scholar who bridged the often obscure arena of theory to clinical practice. Similarly, the theoretical contributions of Icez Ajzen and Martin Fishbein merit recognition, for it is their work which stimulated our interest in the role of social influence on exercise behavior.

No less important are our families and friends. In particular, the wife of the first author, Luanne, for her humorous editorial remarks and support that went far beyond the realm of technical assistance. To Jared and Alexis for their constant reminders of what really counts in life, and to Steve for his patience and friendship. And finally, a special note of thanks is in order to Paul Ribisl and the patients of the Wake Forest University Cardiac Rehabilitation Program for sharing with us their personal experiences. Unknown to them, their input has contributed immeasurably to what we know about exercise compliance.

Chapter
1

A System for Understanding Fitness Behavior

Having chosen fitness as a career, you face one of its greatest challenges—motivating people. It is a challenge that won't pass with time or change of location. No other single task compares in difficulty; it requires a willingness to understand the complexity of human behavior. Failure to accept your role in creating client enthusiasm for fitness will spell serious trouble in your professional development. It will restrict participants' achievements, reduce your own job satisfaction, and hinder career advancement. Unlike most challenges, however, mere persistence on your part may have little or no effect on clients' exercise behavior. In fact, sometimes your enthusiasm to help may actually encourage noncompliance!

Techniques for dealing with noncompliant behavior and the skill for generating enthusiasm are not inborn traits; rather, motivating people is a learned process. It takes a lot of long hours and hard work to learn the ins and outs of exercise testing and training. Effectively delivering what you know requires as much of an investment, and perhaps more. The bottom line is that getting people started in fitness-related activity and maintaining their interest is as much *your* challenge as it is *theirs*. Ignoring that noncompliance exists, or worse, placing the blame for it on the participant, only accelerates an already destructive process.

Why is it so difficult to get people to adopt and maintain a physically active lifestyle? After all, a growing body of research evidence

1

Ignoring noncompliance will only accelerate an already destructive process.

indicates that a consistent program of exercise can have many positive side effects, including controlling weight, countering illness and disease, and renewing one's vigor for life. You may be familiar with the research literature or have personally experienced these effects; perhaps they were even instrumental in your commitment to pursue a profession in exercise or wellness. Is the problem, therefore, lack of knowledge or experience? If your clients really understood the benefits of exercise, would the lack of motivation suddenly disappear? In an attempt to illustrate this situation, we would like you to consider an experience of ours with a patient in cardiac rehabilitation.

Client Inconsistencies and Contradictions

In 1984, P.K. had a heart attack. Six months after this event, he swore that exercise had been responsible for the speedy recovery of his physical condition. He attended nearly every single exercise session for 3 months and gave his best effort to the program. What a powerful incentive for changing from a previously inactive lifestyle to an active one. Yet, 6 months later, P.K. complained of a lack of enthusiasm. He began missing exercise sessions and gaining weight, and once again became obsessively involved with work goals. What had gone wrong? He obviously knew what exercise meant to his life, or did he?

The following sections examine a number of factors that help to untangle such apparent contradictions. More important, it will become obvious that client behavior is often inconsistent with how you think clients should behave. This paradox may be due to an ineffective intervention or perhaps competing behaviors. By way of example, recall TV commercials that try to change your attitude about the use of some product yet lack a convincing approach. You don't get up from the couch with a strong urge to use a product more frequently or to switch brands. And then there have been those times when you knew from past experience that something was not healthful to begin with, but you indulged anyway. Perhaps it just didn't seem that bad or there was a better reason to ignore what you did know. Behavioral scientists have plenty of evidence indicating that there is more to human behavior than logic. The point here is that a combination of factors explains your clients' actions. By seeing these factors as a whole, you can understand why people behave as they do and develop a very effective approach to motivation. In this chapter, we will discuss the 10 components of a sound motivational program.

Learning to motivate people is a process of understanding what triggers human behavior. It involves much more than the hyped-up sales pitch and goes beyond the pat on the back or the lettered T-shirt. These strategies have their purpose, but unless you understand why, when, how, and with whom they are to be used, their effectiveness is substantially diminished and you will lack the necessary skills to promote compliant behavior.

Understanding the Value of Reinforcement

To understand why people lack motivation, you first have to acknowledge a simple, yet important, characteristic of exercise; that is, unlike many behaviors, such as paying your income tax or going to work, exercise is voluntary. Would you elect to do something if it didn't have some form of meaningful payoff? We doubt it. For many people, exercise has little positive value; it simply isn't reinforcing. As a matter of fact, at times, exercise can be punishing. Let us give you some real-life examples of what we mean.

Mary began her daily exercise program because of annoying increases in weight. She chose exercise rather than some other behavioral option for two reasons. First, she was struck by the convincing words of Richard Simmons, a popular fitness advocate: Exercise would not only help her control weight, but give her a much needed zest for daily living. Second, and possibly more important to her, Mary felt that with exercise she could still eat a few choice desserts! Initially, Mary was excited and enthusiastic. She purchased a slick new running suit and had no problem waking up an hour earlier each day. Mornings were kicked off by a half-hour of aerobics followed by a 1-mi jog. Like so many other people, however, Mary's workouts were short-lived. Exercise hadn't given her the zest for daily living that she expected. Quite the opposite, Mary experienced increased general fatigue. She found it more and more difficult to get those early morning starts and complained of an inability to manage work and family demands. She just lacked the necessary energy.

The outcome in this scenario is not all that surprising. Contrary to original expectations, Mary experienced decreased rather than increased vitality. Exercise had become a form of self-inflicted punishment. But what about her concern for weight loss? To Mary, there had to be a better way.

Chuck remained faithful to Nautilus for nearly 3 months at the YMCA before he quit. Chuck's real downfall was that he began Nautilus in order to develop a sleek muscular appearance, but it never materialized! His quitting seemed to have had very little to do with lack of desire. But after 3 months he rationalized, "Hey, come on, apparently I just don't have the right genes. Why knock my head against the wall? I have better things to do." Quite simply then, for Chuck, dropping out was a function of unreinforced behavior.

Tom was in our aerobics program for almost 6 months before he quit. Those early morning workout sessions just became too costly. Because of them, he had already missed too many entertaining breakfast get-togethers with his buddies. How long can you expect someone to sacrifice life's little pleasures? In short, for Tom, exercise sessions competed with other reinforcing events, which he valued more.

Tom's predicament actually deserves more attention than we have given it. He certainly appeared committed to exercise and made some respectable gains while he was involved in the program. During that first 6 months, he was rarely absent and always seemed to enjoy himself. Quite frankly, his behavior was a total surprise to program personnel. Yet, everyone sets priorities in life. People choose not to do some things they enjoy, because doing them would mean losing something of greater value. Mindful of this process of setting priorities, you need to evaluate fitness activities in relation to other interests and/or responsibilities (Rotter, 1954). This evaluation is indispensable in the development of your system of motivation. Competition of needs explains a great deal of noncompliance. This is reflected in the first component of a sound plan for client motivation.

Component 1.   Clients will begin and maintain exercise only if the outcomes of the behavior are valued. For each individual, it is important to consider how exercise might compete with other interests and/or responsibilities of daily life.

Making Outcomes Consistent With Client Needs

Consistent with a focus on the reinforcing properties of exercise are three related issues. First, people vary in the degree to which they find events meaningful. For example, recently we worked with a cardiac patient who had been a collegiate athlete. Can you imagine learning to get excited about graduating from 15 to 20 laps in a 1/10-mi gymnasium having once weathered the rugged demands of collegiate football practice? It is easy to see why it would be unnatural for such an achievement to have been meaningful to this person. By contrast, suppose our client had no athletic history. Wouldn't a 5-lap increase carry more significance? We have met a number of people who suffer from what we call the *big gain syndrome*. They experience little or no satisfaction unless their achievements are monumental. This poses a real problem for people who are deconditioned because it may be weeks or months before they feel rewarded for their efforts.

Second, consider how the prescribed fitness activity ties into the client's reinforcement system. As you will see in a forthcoming chapter, one cause of dissatisfaction in fitness settings is the failure of programs to meet clients' needs (Oldridge, 1984). Imagine you went to a fitness center anticipating expanding biceps and well-defined abdominals. Brief workouts on a rowing machine or 20 min of Nautilus three times a week won't yield such results. Or, what if you exercise to rehabilitate yourself after open heart surgery or to improve respiratory function only to find that exercise brings on the very symptoms that you feared in the first place. Would you continue? In other words, you need to make sure that the exercise behavior you prescribe will yield the desired result. Recall the example of Chuck; the Nautilus program he followed could not possibly have fulfilled his personal need. In 3 months' time, no program could have.

And third, a frustrating characteristic of fitness is that results are not immediate. It takes months and often years to achieve what people have in mind. In many respects, it can be compared to setting aside money for retirement. If you have not already faced this financial decision, ask a friend who has. It is not an easy one. Most of us are very "now" oriented and find it painful to delay gratification of needs to some future point in time (Rotter, 1954). And if you think it is difficult to delay rewards, think of the added difficulty in asking someone to suffer a bit for some future gain! The discomfort of exercise is not easily offset by eventual changes in physical or mental health. Confronting and developing strategies to alleviate the potential problems associated with delayed gratification is a sizable task for the fitness professional. In chapter 5, you will learn how to employ goal setting to accomplish just such an objective. For now, however, let's examine the second component of the plan for motivation, keeping in mind its relevance to setting goals.

Component 2.   You should analyze whether probable outcomes of an exercise prescription are consistent with clients' personal needs. It is also important to establish realistic levels of goal attainment for each client, to question whether these are in fact reinforcing, and to counter problems associated with the delayed rewards of physical conditioning.

Balancing Intrinsic and Extrinsic Rewards

In recent years, a lot of attention has been paid to the distinction between intrinsic and extrinsic reward structures (Deci, 1975). An *intrinsic* reward is inherent to the person's experience. Thus clients may exercise either for the sheer enjoyment of an activity or because it provides feedback relative to their personal competence. An *extrinsic* reward denotes something outside of the person. Clients exercise to get cash back from their health insurance programs or to acquire a plaque for achieving a designated amount of mileage in a specified period of time. How do these different reward structures relate to compliance?

There is little question that both intrinsically and extrinsically structured rewards can motivate behavior. The love of the sport (an intrinsic reward) has been sufficient to keep many diehards playing tennis, whereas dollar signs (an extrinsic reward) have been a significant contributing factor in motivating collegiate football players to risk their health with anabolic steroids. The problem, however, arises when behavior becomes driven by an extrinsic motive and suddenly the reward is no longer available. Under such circumstances, you will usually see a decrease in the frequency of the behavior.

Psychologists have identified what they believe to be an even more important problem with extrinsic reward structures. Extrinsic rewards leave people feeling manipulated and take away personal control. Imagine, for example, that a client in your program was extremely disappointed in her performance. Unaware of her feelings, you come along with the good news that, because of her achievement, she is being given a free week of access to the whirlpool and sauna. What is apt to be going through her mind? Very likely one of two possibilities: either you are trying to keep her business or you want her to expand her membership.

A quite different consequence would have followed if, in fact, the client had felt that her behavior deserved recognition. In this context, access to the whirlpool and sauna would have been viewed as a just reward for having done something well. The extrinsic reward now has informational value. Subtle differences in the way extrinsic rewards are used can profoundly affect subsequent behavior. This difference also makes it very clear that a great deal of thought must go into the motivational process.

Often intrinsic and extrinsic rewards are used jointly in the motivational process. For example, when exercise has no initial intrinsic value, you might consider extrinsic rewards as a means of getting clients started. In fact, even when individuals are intrinsically motivated, you should not ignore the potential value of extrinsic rewards. The point here is that motivation is a planned process. If it is left to chance, you will probably lose more battles than you will win. More practical suggestions in this area can be found in chapter 5. The value of extrinsic reward figures into the third component of the motivational plan.

Component 3. You should establish and reinforce the proper balance of intrinsic and extrinsic rewards. A potential danger of extrinsic reward structures is that they will lead to noncompliance when the reward is no longer available. The real problem occurs when clients believe that extrinsic rewards are being used to control them rather than to inform them that they are doing well.

Recognizing Clients' Common Needs

In the first part of this chapter, you learned about the important role played by the reinforcing properties of exercise and several key features of reward structures. Without exception, a necessary requirement for making exercise a part of people's lives is that it will satisfy one or more of their personal needs. At this point, the question you might reasonably ask is whether people have common needs. If they do, then it seems reasonable that there are certain strategies that would work for everyone.

People do share certain needs, and exercise can satisfy several of these. The ones that we have identified in exercise settings include needs for mastery, attention, recognition, social approval, security of health, and social interaction. The catch is that clients differ in the priority they give to these various needs. Also, specific needs are satisfied by a variety of behaviors. For example, your job may provide all the mastery experience you want, and the primary reason you exercise is to secure good health. Suppose you joined a fitness program only to hear repeatedly that exercise will provide you with a new sense of self. If your job already provides this mastery value, then this could get pretty monotonous. You might get to the point where you feel that the fitness center and you just don't hit it off.

Knowing that people have common needs will allow you to develop a variety of strategies in your motivational system. This suggests that there are several potential targets to consider in getting clients successfully involved in physical activity. What it does not suggest is that you ought to lead all individuals down the same path. Doing so will turn off a lot of people.

To this point we have presented the first major factor in a system for understanding fitness behavior—reinforcement value. If you expect clients to exercise on a regular basis, they must feel that some personal need is being met through their behavior. This need may involve something intrinsic (e.g., improved well-being), or the reinforcing value of exercise may be created by some external agent (e.g., a corporation's offer of reduced health care costs to those who meet certain criteria in wellness programming).

To make the most of reinforcement value, however, there are several important considerations. First, exercise behavior does not exist in isolation. There are many other personal needs that are not satisfied by exercise and may have greater priority. Personal needs exist in a hierarchical structure. In our experience, conflict of needs explains a great deal of noncompliance. Second, there will be some clients who have irrational personal needs. They will expect too much, too quickly. Third, the reinforcement value of exercise may require a long-term investment on the part of the client. Yet, people dislike delaying the gratification of needs. Fourth, we may fail to listen to clients' stated needs and consequently involve them in a prescription that misses the mark. The result is that needs continue to be unmet. And fifth, when extrinsic rewards are operative, the danger is that they become controlling. In general, the use of extrinsic rewards should be viewed as a short-term strategy or, at the very least, should be integrated with intrinsic rewards. A summary of these points can be found in Figure 1.1.

Being Aware of Clients' Thoughts and Attitudes

For the past 7 years, we have talked with hundreds of clients entering preventive and rehabilitative programs. One of the major observations from this experience is that a large number of people

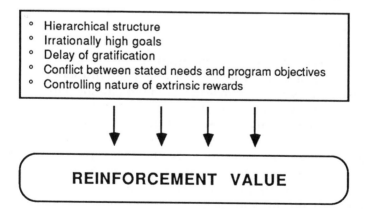

Figure 1.1   Factors influencing reinforcement value.

initiate fitness activities without adequately appraising what it is they are doing or why. Perhaps it will be a spouse, a friend, a convincing physician, loneliness, or just spontaneous consumption with the fitness craze that drives clients to your doorsteps. A number will remain, but many more will be casualties of an ill-prepared beginning. You can prevent this problem, and in subsequent chapters you will find specific strategies to achieve this end. But an important first step is to understand, in greater detail, how what people think and know relates to the way they behave.

Thoughts and Action

Given the opportunity, clients will act in ways that satisfy their needs. Placed in a fitness context, you would predict that if the activity you offer is consistent with clients' needs, and these needs are strong enough, then clients should behave as desired. Unfortunately, it is not this simple. Suppose, for example, you went to a wellness center 20 lb overweight. Chances are you would be advised to make some alterations in your diet and exercise at an intensity and frequency sufficient to yield changes in aerobic power. Although on the surface this seems like a reasonable intervention, 6 weeks later you may be back to your former self—sedentary, disappointed, and growing larger with each passing day. Changes in the intervention or the manner in which it was initiated could have made a difference in this situation.

First, exercising according to commonly prescribed schedules is no picnic if your last significant athletic endeavor was playing frisbee 10 years ago. Your self-confidence will be torn to shreds in a matter of two or three sessions. As you walk vigorously or jog, you may say to yourself, "A physically active lifestyle, are you kidding? I'll be lucky if I make it until the end of the week! This just isn't my cup of tea." Psychologists have shown that, given a choice, people engage in behaviors that they believe they can realistically perform. When people are forced to do things that they lack confidence in, their effort is half-hearted, an approach that almost always guarantees failure. Think back to your high school or college days: When you or a friend felt inadequate in a subject, it is likely that the quality and quantity of study time differed from that of more successful courses. You remained involved, but only because this was required of you. Negative feedback in the form of grades or instructor interactions confirmed your original position—you were not meant to excel in this area. This same dynamic operates in fitness settings. A large number of individuals believe they are not cut out to be the exercise type. Their clumsy attempts to work out, if they occur, confirm this belief.

Second, an issue closely related to self-confidence is whether clients believe exercise will lead to outcomes that they value, a concept we will call *outcome expectancy*. It is risky to assume that people will automatically buy into the belief that exercise will have some stated effect. Outcome expectancy differs from self-confidence because it has nothing to do with whether you thought you were capable of using exercise as a means of losing weight. It involves a more basic question of whether you think exercise is an effective behavior in controlling weight (Bandura, 1977). To clarify this distinction, consider the following. You might believe that exercise can reduce weight, yet have very low confidence that it will work for you—high outcome expectancy, but low self-confidence. In contrast, you may have confidence in your ability to exercise, but feel deep down that exercise will not help control weight—high self-confidence but a low outcome expectancy. Component 4 of the motivational plan addresses this issue.

Component 4.   You should insure that clients believe that the prescribed fitness activities will produce the desired effects and that they have confidence that these effects can be produced if they behave as directed.

A good example of this is a former patient in our rehabilitation program who manifested significant depression. He had been told by his physician that no better prescription existed for depression than exercise. The patient did exercise but continually would make comments like, "Medication didn't work, why should exercise?" or "I've never heard of anything so ridiculous! How is exercise going to change my marriage?" He did not believe his physician to begin with, and all this negative thinking did not help the problem. In effect, he had self-confidence in his ability to exercise but low expectancy that exercise would produce the desired effect. The patient wasn't motivated to secure his physical condition because his depression consumed every thought and stood out as his single most important personal need. He came to the program because, as he expressed it, "I don't have anything else to do right now." But this purpose soon wore thin and he quit. Noncompliance was no mystery in his case. He had a totally inappropriate mind-set prior to getting involved in the program.

Beliefs and Specificity

If outcome expectancies are so critical to performing behavior, as fitness professionals, it would make sense for you to systematically strengthen and broaden these. One example would be reinforcing

the role of exercise in disease prevention. In addition, you could educate participants about other benefits associated with a lifestyle that
includes vigorous physical activity. Assuming that clients are already tuned into this knowledge is a major error. Remember, people
are often extremely naive when first entering fitness programs. If
they remain so, psychological theory suggests that these individuals
will become prime candidates for your dropout pool.

After working with clients in practical settings, you soon realize
that there are some simple, yet often overlooked, strategies for
enhancing the impact of knowledge on behavior. For instance,
knowing that exercise can accelerate the rate at which a person
burns calories has a much stronger impact on someone who has
a desire to control weight. Thus compliance is optimized when beliefs are consistent with personal needs or when special attempts
are made to charge beliefs with emotion. As a result, general programs of instruction will be less successful than personalized interactions that address the individual's needs. In fact, our observation
is that mandatory segments of health education, which are general
by design, are a deterrent to compliant behavior. The reason for
this seems to be that people view such information as a waste of
their time. *Remember, clients have made the choice to exercise.*
Thus, in the time they have allotted for this activity, they will not
want to engage in what they view as irrelevant behaviors.

Later we will give suggestions for broadening a client's belief
structure without creating an overbearing atmosphere. There are
subtle tricks to selling information and implanting incentives that
have a history of success. For now, it is only important that you
understand the potential power of beliefs and why at times your
efforts in this direction may fail. Perhaps you can begin to see now
why it is so critical to have a system for motivation and why much
of motivating people is learned rather than innate.

The second dimension of beliefs that is critical to behavior is that
their content may be negative. It is rare that all beliefs associated
with a specific behavior are positive. Thus, although you can list
several desirable outcomes of exercise or a specific program, no
doubt you also can think of undesirable ones. Additionally, it is not
surprising that negative beliefs play a greater role in noncompliance
as the value of their content becomes more central to the person.
This concept builds on, and is directly related to, the idea that individuals rank their personal needs. In Tom's case, for example,
we previously noted that breakfast with his buddies eventually took
precedence over morning workouts. Giving up this social interaction was simply too costly. But do not be surprised by or underestimate the power of what you think are minor points. We have

seen clients who are unable to tolerate what you may consider minimal discomfort or sacrifice. Sweat, embarrassment over appearance, and other personal inconveniences often imply significant costs. Do not impose your own values on the beliefs and needs of others. If you do, your own behavior will become the real culprit in noncompliance. Component 5 describes how a cost-benefit analysis of a fitness program depends on your *client's* values.

Component 5.   Always consider the role of outcome expectancies and self-confidence in determining behavior. A client's decision to participate in a fitness program can be compared to a cost-benefit analysis. Beliefs in specific costs and benefits become more influential depending on their worth to the individual.

The third and final characteristic of beliefs is their *specificity* (Ajzen & Fishbein, 1980). To understand what we mean by specificity of beliefs, consider the following scenario.

Bob entered the preventive fitness program with several preconceptions of exercise. One was that without some pain there would be no gain. He worked compulsively most of the time, staying in the upper ranges of his exercise prescription. He was often rewarded by fitness personnel because of his special fortitude. Like so many other dropouts, however, Bob eventually got tired of running in high gear and he quit.

What went wrong? For Bob, backing off from his usual driven self would have meant no gain—there was no outcome expectancy under conditions of low-level exercise. In addition, the client was being reinforced for his intense behavior by the accolades of exercise professionals. Do you think he could risk ruining his image? Although Bob held a potentially constructive outcome expectation for exercise, the specific elements were destructive. It does not require pain to make gain. It was too late to attempt to right this wrong by the time he was prepared to quit. He should never have been allowed to initiate this behavior in the first place. It is difficult to interrupt what appears to be correct behavior. We have learned the hard way that clients often have some unusual beliefs about physical activity and that far too often they are vague beliefs. General statements, like "Yes, I feel very positive about beginning exercise," should be interpreted cautiously. Many individuals will verbalize this, yet are overwhelmed at the end of their first workout, "I had no idea this is what they meant!" This awareness of client belief or expectation versus the actual planned goal is the subject of component 6.

Component 6.   You should closely examine what clients believe they have to do to attain desired goals. It is important to shape these beliefs and subsequent behaviors so they are consistent with constructive exercise prescriptions.

The second major factor in a system for understanding fitness is the clients' beliefs. Specifically, these involve the outcomes that they expect from participating in a particular program of exercise and self-confidence concerning their ability to perform the target behavior. As was true of the section on reinforcement value, clients' beliefs require a very thorough analysis. The major reasons are as follows.

First, some clients may hold outcome expectations that are weak or low on their list of priorities. In such cases, it is important to strengthen existing beliefs and/or develop additional outcome expectations that are central to the person. Second, you will want to insure that perceived outcomes are in fact consistent with clients' needs. For example, if clients are exercising primarily for reasons related to health, it is important that they understand the role of exercise in increasing high-density lipoproteins (HDL), an effect that reduces cardiovascular risk. Third, exercise often has negative side effects. There are certain costs of exercising, most obvious of which are the perceived loss of valuable time and/or physical discomfort. When possible, clients must be shown how such effects can be alleviated or managed. And fourth, you will want to clearly understand clients' interpretation of various fitness behaviors. What do they think they have to do to achieve desired goals? These points are illustrated in Figure 1.2.

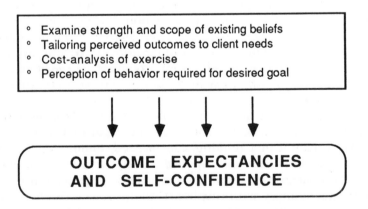

Figure 1.2   Factors influencing beliefs.

Social Influence as a Key Factor in Behavior

In our discussion of beliefs, we placed the spotlight on the individual; that is, we considered the client as independent of other people. A parallel force that either impedes or enhances a client's decision to participate in exercise programs is social influence (Ajzen & Fishbein, 1980). None of us lives in isolation. Peers, colleagues, family, and even TV personalities influence how we behave. A classic example of this latter category is Richard Simmons' influence on people's decisions to adapt their lifestyle to include physical activity.

Sometimes, however, the actual source of social influence is obscure. Recently, we spoke with a former student who currently directs a wellness program for a major corporation. She said her greatest challenge was getting mill workers interested in the concept of wellness, particularly fitness. Compliance in this group was very poor. Quite accurate is her observation that these people have a totally different outlook on life. As a group, they have not been influenced by the fitness craze. Thus there is no reason to get all excited about the program just because their company now offers it to them. In this situation there is a reason for noncompliance. Perhaps you can recall a time when someone whom you considered outside your social group made an attempt to sell you on some point. Regardless of the quality of the message, you probably resisted the appeal.

The same may be true of these mill workers. Why should they be attracted to what they perceive to be a predominantly white-collar interest? It is difficult, however, to identify any one person or event responsible for this phenomenon; rather, it is a function of subcultural dynamics. For you the dynamics are somewhat different. Whether or not you are aware of it, there are very subtle social cues related to fitness in your daily environment. These have probably played a major role in determining where you are and what you're doing.

If social influence is potentially so powerful, how does it operate? Actually, by suggesting that social influence parallels personal beliefs, we were not just making a farfetched analogy. On the one hand, if you think that your spouse, family, or a reference group would like you to participate in our fitness program and you are motivated to comply with this belief, then social influence will be a positive factor in getting you to do what we want. On the other hand, it is possible that you want to do the opposite of what your family, spouse, or some faction of society thinks is good for you. In this case, we are probably in trouble (Ajzen & Fishbein, 1980)! Before closing our discussion on social influence, we would like to add one final comment. A large number of clients never stop to consider how their spouse feels or whether their close friend has any opinion about their involvement in a formal exercise program. And of those who do have an opinion, a fairly high percentage seem to be neutral about such involvement. Furthermore, you will find a number of clients who verbalize nonsupport when the opposite is true. Rather than implying that, in general, social support is weak, we suggest that the realm of social influence has been inadequately tapped as an integral part of motivating people in exercise settings. One of our objectives, therefore, will be to demonstrate how social influence can be made to work for you. This objective is described in component 7.

Component 7.   You should learn how to build on positive and to counter negative social influence. Consideration must be given to significant others (e.g., the family), as well as subcultural factors.

Understanding the Role of Life Stages

Thus far, we have shown how beliefs and the reinforcement of personal needs interact to determine fitness behavior. We will build on these concepts by introducing two additional factors that have direct bearing on them. First, both the causes of noncompliance and the strategies used in decreasing this behavior need to be considered in light of the stage of a client's involvement (Dishman, 1982). This is not a major revelation. There is a big difference between those who drop out in the first week of exercise and those who quit after 6 months or a year. From a motivational perspective, putting these people into the same category is like adding apples and oranges.

Second, in our experience, a client's stage of human development plays a key role in understanding both belief structures and personal needs. At age 28, a person's thoughts and needs are quite different from what they are at 58 or 65. It makes good sense to acknowledge these differences in motivating people. Ignoring a client's individual developmental needs reduces your effectiveness as a fitness professional. In the following sections, we will consider these two factors independently. Notice, however, how nicely they fit in with what you already know about behavior. Perhaps now you can begin to see why motivation is a process that needs to be treated as a system rather than as a collection of fragmented parts.

The Timing of Noncompliance

At some point in your life you have probably had the experience of being really excited about a program or event only to find out after direct experience that it wasn't what you had expected. The general consequence of such disappointment is either to quit the program or to lose interest in the specific event. With fitness programs, clients perhaps just didn't feel as good as they had anticipated or didn't make the kind of gains they thought they would. Perhaps doing the vigorous exercise was too punishing or losing those pounds really wasn't as important as they first thought. They had no idea it would require such commitment. Whereas the reasons for disappointment will be as varied as the people who enter your programs, underlying the reasons is a straightforward and critical stage of the motivational process: *the point at which thought becomes transferred into action.* Traditionally, no formal attention is given to circumventing this type of problem. This is unfortunate because these problems are predictable and many times can be prevented. Component 8 provides the means for prevention.

Component 8.   You should address the potential conflict between what clients think or feel about exercise prior to a fitness program and reactions following adoption of the behavior.

Motivating clients to continue with programs 3, 6, or perhaps 12 months after they have been initiated becomes more complex, but strategies must remain focused on thoughts and reinforcement values (needs). Without question, during these latter stages, the fact that perceived needs have been satisfied is a factor in the dropout phenomenon. For example, suppose you went to a fitness center to learn about aerobics or how to rehabilitate your heart. If after 3 months you felt you had a handle on the problem, would you continue? Or suppose you lost the unwanted 10 lb. Why drag yourself to exercise three times a week? After all, your shape is now back to where you want it. The rest is discipline in diet to keep you trim.

Notice in this last instance how a particular style of thinking can be so powerful in determining action. Perhaps in some cases this style of thinking is very accurate. Maybe a client really does not need to continue structured exercise per se. This must be acknowledged and planned for in the design of programs. At the same time, there are often many inaccuracies. The failure to see exercise as a permanent lifestyle change rather than as a temporary fix ranks high on the list. Moreover, as a client moves through your program you may want to broaden the perceived reinforcement structure of exercise. In other words, although initially a client may exercise to lose weight, with careful attention to the client's attainment of that goal, you can implant other virtues of structured fitness.

Recall the cardiac patient who, 6 months after a heart attack, gave a great deal of credit to the role of exercise in rehabilitating his physical condition. Yet, 1 year after the event, he complained of a declining lifestyle—he had become a noncomplier. You would think suffering a heart attack would serve as a constant reminder of one's vulnerability. A significant problem in noncompliance is that the priority of personal needs changes with time. When patients first have a heart attack, more often than not they become consumed by the event. Suddenly, restoration of health is the number-one priority, and whatever the cost, they are willing to make the sacrifice. But 6 months or a year later the pain and threat that the heart attack once caused are often forgotten or the challenge of a new project at work has greater motivational power, so they quit formal rehabilitation. "I'll fit it into my own schedule," they proclaim. A challenge that confronts you is not only to keep the reinforcement value of exercise alive but also to insure that it is not extinguished by alternate goals. The passage of time makes reinforcement more challenging. This is discussed in component 9.

Component 9.   You should be aware that the passage of time is always a threat to the value of a given behavior or to established priorities.

Stages of the Life Cycle

Each of us passes through different periods of life in which our personal needs and beliefs change, sometimes drastically. Your own conception of what you expect from being physically fit, the confidence that you have in your abilities to perform various behaviors, and your specific personal needs are determined in part by your age and experience. To ignore this facet of human behavior in the context of fitness programming is a serious oversight. Naturally, it is very easy and tempting to assume that other people operate from the same framework as ourselves.

It is equally naive to assume that all people affected by disease or the threat of disease will be driven by common motives. If you operate under such assumptions, you probably will administer a prescription for exercise that is inappropriate. If you offer educational programs, they will likely hit some of the people some of the time. You will increase the chance of a gap between the impact of the experiences the clients actually have in your program and their perception of what they were buying into originally. The clients will develop a feeling that your program is run like a factory, and the end result will be very poor compliance rates.

So, what are these stages of the life cycle and when do they occur? From our experience in fitness settings, there are three critical stages of the life cycle. Each stage has a bearing on how people think and what they value, as well as the respective priorities they place on these. First, when clients are in their 20s or early 30s most are preoccupied with establishing themselves as individuals separate from their families and friends. During this period, exercise strengthens the ego and serves as a buffer against stress. Strength and endurance acquired physically transfer to a sort of mental toughness. Because they focus on developing personal relationships during this stage, these clients see exercise as a means of controlling weight and improving physical attractiveness.

Second, from the mid-30s to 50s, many clients are involved in raising a family and/or serving as key personnel in business and industry. They may view exercise as a technique for managing stress, but for different reasons than in the previous stage. With a concern for the future of the family, health beliefs become potentially powerful levers. This is particularly true when someone is hypertensive or has a significant weight problem. However, an interesting paradox is that wealth often takes precedence over health. Thus occupational conflicts are common, and lack of family support often short-circuits attempts to secure a physically active lifestyle.

Third, in the clients' 60s and 70s, exercise offers a means of maintaining a declining physical self. Many will have ample time for structured fitness and will look forward to this activity as a means of enhancing their social experience as well. Physical self-confidence may well be on the decline. Physical symptoms are more frequent and are quickly recognized not only because of their potential medical threat, but also due to diminished family commitment and fewer occupational concerns. In general, this is a very attentive client population and, as such, has tremendous potential from a business perspective. We cannot overemphasize the value of directing programs and motivational processes specific to client needs and thinking. Details of this procedure are outlined in subsequent chapters. One aspect of this is to be aware of the stages of the life cycle's impact on activity as discussed in component 10.

Component 10. You should program activities to match stages of the life cycle. What people think and their personal needs change with age and experience.

Summary

The contents of this chapter describe the meaning of motivation and the reasons for noncompliant behavior. This framework provides direction for the remainder of the text. As illustrated in Figure 1.3, fitness behavior is best viewed as a dynamic, interactive outcome that has two main factors: reinforcement value and clients'

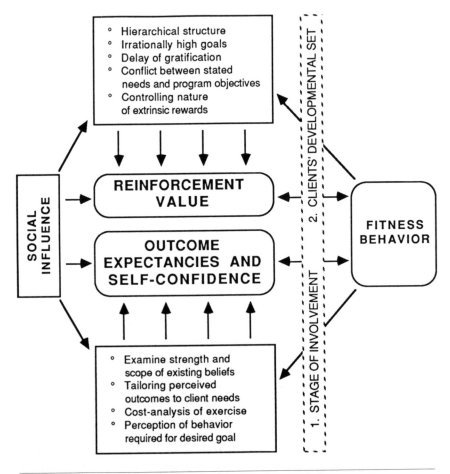

Figure 1.3 A system for understanding fitness behavior.

beliefs concerning outcome expectancies and self-confidence. Social influence has a significant impact on these two general areas. Moreover, the system is dynamic because the actual fitness experience may modify clients' originally stated reinforcement values and beliefs. What is also clear in the system is that stage of involvement and clients' developmental set are important in understanding what drives fitness behavior and the subsequent impact of this behavior on reinforcement values and beliefs.

Because the system is central to understanding the logic of how and why certain techniques improve compliant behavior, we strongly encourage you to recall this common thread as you read subsequent chapters. It is instrumental in your ability to apply what you learn in the following pages to new situations. Although we have attempted to make clear throughout the book the importance of a systems approach and have constantly reintroduced components of the system, you may find it useful to reread sections of this first chapter. Additionally, we would encourage you to apply this system to problems that you may have encountered or to the development of individualized programming for your clients. The more it is reinforced in your own thinking and practice, the quicker you will begin to see the value and ease of its operation in daily interaction with clients.

Suggested Readings

Ajzen, I., & Fishbein, M. (1980). *Understanding attitudes and predicting social behavior*. Englewood Cliffs, NJ: Prentice-Hall.

Bandura, A. (1977). Self-efficacy: Toward a unifying theory of behavioral change. *Psychological Review*, **84**, 191-215.

Rotter, J.B. (1954). *Social learning and clinical psychology*. Englewood Cliffs, NJ: Prentice-Hall.

Chapter
2

What You Need to Know About Your Client and How to Ask

Before you can begin to consider exercise prescriptions or implement motivational strategies, your first task is to learn something about the people you intend to serve. The single point we drove home in chapter 1 was that each client is unique. One individual may want to exercise to lose weight, another to tone the thighs or build a stronger heart. There are those who will enjoy the feelings and behavioral consequences of physical exertion, whereas others will despise sweat and fatigue. Unless you are committed to designing programs around these individual needs and preferences, you will not be successful in helping those who enlist your aid.

You and Each Client

We are probably not telling you anything new. You know individualized care is essential. This fact is repeated constantly by management personnel. Unfortunately, no one ever really explains what constitutes individualized care. Your effectiveness in this area will usually be assessed simply by the frequency of client complaints. Also, your personal charisma will carry a lot of weight. But individualized care is far more than simply striking up occasional conversations with clients, being personable, or establishing a goal or two. This chapter initiates the process of individualized care by explaining what to ask clients and how to ask it. These steps are just as critical as understanding how to implement goal setting or how to design suitable forms of feedback. If done systematically, this process will yield several important results. First, clients will be impressed by the fact that personnel in your organization are well trained and knowledgeable. Second, it will be apparent to the membership that you not only acknowledge but are capable of responding to a variety of personal needs. And third, clients will know exactly what to expect of both themselves and others. The power of this simple procedure in enhancing both compliance and program satisfaction is remarkable; without it, there is little hope of changing the status quo.

We are going to lead you through the evaluation process in a very structured manner. Initially, you will be asked to consider the physical setting you will use for the assessment process and to engage in a little self-examination. Just how effective are you in conducting client interviews? What are major stumbling blocks? Do not overestimate your own abilities and ignore these issues. We can all improve on the interview process no matter how extensive our backgrounds. Once the setting and a proper style of client interaction are established, you will then be introduced to a method for clinical assessment that includes both physical and psychological components. When appropriate, we will reinforce why given information is so critical, but remember, what you learn in this section is basically dependent upon your understanding of chapter 1. Finally, a brief section will be presented on feedback, the final stage of the orientation process. The details of feedback are covered in subsequent chapters.

Physical Setting Makes a Difference

Too often, little or no priority is given to the physical setting in which clients are evaluated and interviewed. This is a major oversight for two reasons. First, clients value privacy, and there is no doubt that client isolation is indispensable to sound evaluation. You will run across quite a few individuals who, for one reason or another, are anxious over some aspect of their physique. It is particularly demeaning to these individuals to have their body fat evaluated while others look on, even at a distance. In addition, most people are reluctant to share information about themselves without the promise of confidentiality. Second, you want to standardize the environment for clients' fitness evaluations and feedback sessions. If you vary the setting in which people are tested, you can expect error in measurement. Similarly, the lack of a formal setting for evaluation feedback will detract from its potential impact on clients.

Some of our own experience may serve to emphasize these points. Reevaluation of clients in our fitness program occurs at 3-month intervals. Several years ago the setting we used to share this information with clients was on a sofa located at the entrance to our testing lab. This interaction was very informal and was often disrupted by nearby activity on the bicycle or treadmill. Quite frankly, the information had little impact on the clients. After a structured evaluation of the program and some reflection, our program director decided to make the feedback process more formal. Now clients are met in private, progress data are plotted on a computer, and the overall process is more professional. The change in reaction on the part of clients has been dramatic. They often talk about "meeting with the man," and there is little doubt in our minds that these

Clients value privacy.

program modifications have made a significant difference in compliance and participant satisfaction.

The setting also contributes immeasurably to an essential element of your program: that clients view personnel as warm and caring people. Your ability to convey such an impression will be sacrificed if your interaction with clients is plagued by interruptions or if it appears that you are trying to converse with them and perform another task simultaneously. Psychologists have found that the environment in which interactions occur can greatly enhance or detract from what is being said. Make a point to have a designated area for client interviews and pay some attention to decor. A room with bright lights and cold metal chairs isn't conducive to self-disclosure. We are not suggesting that you need elaborate facilities; a small pleasant room with a couple of comfortable chairs and a lamp will suffice. Incidentally, this area can serve to enhance clients' perceptions of your professional competence. Display your certifications and degrees. You will have much more success at modifying beliefs and imparting knowledge if you are perceived to be an expert.

How About Your Own Behavior?

One of the fascinating characteristics of health and fitness settings is that when people don't do what we ask, we wonder what is wrong with them. Regardless of the situation, there is a strong tendency in all of us to look to others for the source of a problem. Yet, research on compliance in medical settings has found that those who deliver health services have a profound effect on client adherence to prescriptions. Think of what this implies. You know that professional experiences are disappointing when clients don't meet your expectations. The reason, of course, is that your own needs are unmet. Thus, in a very significant way, we are all the masters of our own fate. Granted, improving your attitude toward the client will not remedy all compliance problems, but it will influence some, and the increased quality of clients' reactions to you will provide more than adequate reinforcement.

Six Secrets of Successful Interaction

What can you do in your interactions with clients to help turn them on? Although there are no hard-and-fast rules, clearly the number one skill for successful interactions is the ability to project concern, sensitivity, and trust. Whereas an appropriate physical setting sets the stage for inducing these perceptions, your body language and style of interaction will eventually determine success or failure. Of course, you must realize that what makes one client feel confidence may strike another as arrogant. Despite individual differences, however, some excellent general strategies have proven effective for a wide variety of clients.

Take advantage of first impressions. Exchange names and be sure to shake clients' hands. Make an effort to address clients in a way that will make them the most comfortable. Perhaps nicknames are their preference, or it may be that clients want to be more formal with something like "Mr. Smith." We recall being informed by one gentleman who was in a retirement community that he was to be addressed as "Dr. Jones" even though the other participants were called by their first names. When questioned about this request, he simply indicated that for him a first name basis in initial interactions had a connotation of disrespect. Interestingly, however, once he was with the program for a short period of time, he chose to switch to his first name.

You can continue to make clients feel cared for if, when escorting them into the interview room, you step aside and place your hand on their shoulder or back as if you were guiding them into the room. Human touch is very powerful, but beware, it can be overdone. Remember, you are a relative stranger to your clients at this point. Keep your touch light and casual.

Give clients an opportunity to tell their story. A very effective lead-in question is to ask clients to describe why they are getting involved in your program—what would they really like to achieve? Remember to listen carefully to what they say. In addition, you must be prepared to deal with clients who are reluctant to talk. For these individuals it may be necessary to ask very pointed questions. How did they hear about your program? Is there a particular body part they are unhappy with and would like to see changed? Perhaps relating a short anecdote about your own experience will open things up a little. For example, one client we had was particularly closemouthed about her reason for joining the program. In an effort to stimulate discussion, one of the interviewers recounted her success in losing inches from her hips and thighs solely through a regular running program. In turn, the client expressed her disgust with her own hips and legs. By carefully listening to everything clients say, you will gain insight into their goals and recognize areas that require special attention.

Manage your interaction.   In the interview, adjust your physical distance from the client to a point where it is apparent that he or she is comfortable. This will vary with different clients, but in general, you want to be relatively close (e.g., 3-5 ft). Keep your arms opened as opposed to folded, smile on occasion in response to statements made by the client, use hand gestures when speaking, nod your head to indicate that you understand, and try leaning forward in your chair a little from time to time. These simple techniques will vastly improve your communication skills. Remember, however, although practice makes perfect, perfect can be artificial. Relax, be comfortable, and you will find that clients do the same.

Choose your words carefully.   Avoid emphasizing sophisticated medical or physiological terminology, but don't ignore it altogether. The best strategy is to pick out three or four important terms and to provide a little education. For example, you may decide with a particular client that it is appropriate to talk about aerobic fitness and how this differs from muscle tone. In taking an educational approach, you won't confuse clients with specialized terms, yet it will be clear to them that you welcome questioning and that you obviously possess the appropriate technical knowledge. This will further reinforce the image that you are an expert.

Don't control responses.   If you really want to know what people think, do not ask questions in a manner that controls the response. For instance, notice the sharp contrast between the two following styles of introducing a question:

"You know we deal with people who have a lot of different reasons for wanting to exercise and all are very legitimate. What do you see yourself getting out this experience?"

"It's obvious that you have a concern for your health or you would not be here in the first place. Oftentimes, however, people have misconceptions of what exercise can do for them. What are your goals in the program? That is, what do you expect to change as a result of your involvement in exercise?"

In the first example, there is a clear statement that you do not intend to be judgmental; in fact, you are not looking for a specific response. By contrast, in the second example, you put clients in a position to fear their response will be judged a misconception, and you risk making them feel odd if health isn't a driving force in their decision to exercise.

Emphasize personal responsibility.   During conversation with clients it is important that you support their ability to control the exercise setting, providing positive feedback for individual responsibility. You want to come across as an *informational source* rather than a *controlling force*. Also, show great enthusiasm about statements that even hint at an intrinsic interest in physical activity. You may recall from chapter 1 that one of your goals should be to foster intrinsic motives and to cut down on the controlling nature of extrinsic rewards. What better way is there to initiate this objective than through that all important initial interaction?

Mutual Participation

These suggestions constitute the basis for sound interpersonal interaction. If practiced, they will encourage an attitude of mutual participation and provide the cornerstone for the development of trusting and satisfying relationships. By mutual participation, we are suggesting that you become established as a concerned expert who will provide guidance, while emphasizing the critical role of self-responsibility on the part of the client. In the following section we will discuss the type of information that is critical for effective programming and elaborate on the concept of mutual participation and, in particular, the issue of self-responsibility.

The Medical History Form and Beyond

When you begin the client evaluation process, it is important to have a systematic plan. For example, what questions would you want to have answered, and is the order in which they are asked important? When clients leave this session, what should they know about the exercise program? It is most effective to begin with medical history and fitness-related evaluations. This gives you an opportunity to break the ice and learn a little about clients' dispositions. Are they easily embarrassed or cynical in their attitudes about other people? Following this evaluation period, we suggest a semistructured interview designed to explore the motivational structure behind clients' exercise behavior (chapter 1). Finally, the session should conclude with feedback that is client specific.

Special Health Needs

A review of medical history is standard practice in orienting new clients to their exercise program. This is an important first step. The following boxed checklist of past and present physical problems can reveal some very important information about client motivation.

Health Appraisal Checklist

Part I

1. When was the last time you had a physical exam? _____

2. If you have been told that you have any disease or illness please list
   these. _____

   _____

   _____

3. Are you presently taking any prescribed medications? If yes, please
   list these and the purpose for taking them. _____

   _____

   _____

4. Have you ever been hospitalized? If yes, when and for what purpose?

   _____

   _____

   _____

Part II

5. During the past 12 months have you

	Yes	No
had a weight change of more than 5 lb?	_____	_____
exercised or dieted to lose weight?	_____	_____
fainted, felt lightheaded, or blacked out?	_____	_____
had problems sleeping?	_____	_____
experienced blurred vision?	_____	_____
had severe headaches?	_____	_____
had a chronic morning cough?	_____	_____
had temporary change in speech patterns?	_____	_____
had unusual heartbeats (e.g., skips/palpitations)?	_____	_____
felt your heart racing for no apparent reason?	_____	_____

Part III

6. At present, do you   Yes   No
   have shortness of breath during light
   work?   _____   _____
   experience swelling in your feet or ankles?   _____   _____
   get pains or cramps in your legs?   _____   _____
   experience pain or discomfort in your
   chest?   _____   _____
   experience pressure/heaviness in your
   chest?   _____   _____
   have high blood pressure?   _____   _____
   know if your cholesterol level is high?   _____   _____
   have diabetes?   _____   _____
   If so, how is it controlled?
   _____ diet   _____ insulin injections
   _____ oral medications   _____ uncontrolled

7. How often do you experience high levels of stress?
   _____ never _____ occasionally _____ frequently

8. Have you been told that you have any of the following medical
   conditions?
   _____ Myocardial infarction   _____ Arteriosclerosis
   _____ Coronary thrombosis   _____ Heart disease
   _____ Heart block   _____ Claudication
   _____ Aneurysm   _____ Heart murmur
   _____ Angina   _____ Rheumatic heart
   _____ Heart failure   _____ Coronary occlusion
                                                 Yes   No
9. Do you smoke?   _____   _____
   If yes, indicate which method and the number per day.
   _____ Cigarettes _____ Cigars _____ Pipe # per day _____
                                                 Yes   No
   If no, were you ever a smoker?   _____   _____

Part IV

10. Has any member of your immediate family been treated for or sus-
    pected to have any of the following conditions? If so, please identify
    their relationship to you (e.g., father, mother, brother, sister, etc.).
    A. Diabetes _____
    B. Heart disease _____
    C. Stroke _____
    D. High blood pressure _____

Take Mike, for example. He was a successful businessman with a history of back problems, which had recently prevented him from doing any exercise. Because of his promotion to an executive position requiring a lot of desk work, Mike wasn't as active on the job as he used to be. Consequently, he put on weight and developed a potbelly. At this point, Mike came to to our fitness program to lose weight. However, he presumed it was going to be easy and he wanted results within a month, just in time for a weekend at the beach. Although his program was expertly designed to prevent further back trouble, because of his sedentary lifestyle, Mike experienced overall muscle soreness including discomfort in his back. Though he agreed that the soreness he felt was very different from pain due to injury, Mike decided he needed to rest for a week or so. His exercise leader called him weekly to inquire how he was feeling. He consistently cited "back discomfort" as the reason for not returning to exercise. Long after any back injury should have subsided, Mike still refused to return out of "fear of hurting his back." He never exercised at our facility again.

In retrospect, Mike's case made us realize the necessity of informing those with a history of orthopedic problems that a certain amount of discomfort is normal when first exercising. More important, however, clients need to accept an adapted exercise prescription, one which will imply slower progress. There is no way Mike should have begun to exercise with the belief that he could lose his potbelly in a month. Even a person without back problems could not achieve such a goal. Additionally, it is important to follow these clients closely for the first few weeks and to check on any discomfort they may experience. Informing them that you would like to consult their physician will remove anxiety about exercise.

Groups with special needs. Whereas individuals with orthopedic problems constitute a large percentage of those requiring special attention, there are other groups with special needs. These include those suffering from, or who are at high risk for, heart disease; the obese; and diabetics. Like Mike, individuals falling into these categories require adapted exercise prescriptions. In addition, these groups will have certain characteristics *from within* their particular situation that play a critical role in their motivation. For example, for recent cardiac victims there may be a powerful motivation to exercise. Yet, as the memory of the heart attack or surgery begins to fade, they are very likely to return to their old ways, which may include a sedentary lifestyle! Also, you should not disregard the possibility that symptomatic patients will interpret changes experienced during exercise as complications rather than harmless sensations. If left unassuaged, this belief would clearly create compliance problems. The important point to realize is that, although heart disease can be a powerful motivator of health behavior, it can also sensitize the individual to physical symptoms.

In the case of obese persons, particular care must be taken to insure they are not embarrassed while exercising and to include only those exercises that they can perform comfortably. You will have to work hard to make exercise fun and socially reinforcing, because more often than not these individuals find exercise stressful. Although it is logical to use non-weight-bearing activity such as biking with the obese, their exercise program ought to be run concurrently with restrictions on caloric intake. The idea here is to maximize the possibility of weight loss.

A third group, diabetics, is often encouraged to exercise to decrease blood sugars and increase HDL, the lipoprotein that helps to discourage cholesterol from building up in the arteries. However, there are risks for the exercising diabetic that can decrease motivation. For example, a diabetic may become hypoglycemic (low blood sugar) during or following a workout, whereas those diabetics who are poorly controlled may actually experience hyperglycemia (high blood sugar). It is essential to consult with physicians in planning exercise programs for diabetics, so that insulin levels and time of exercise can be coordinated to insure safety. Similarly, instilling client self-responsibility is of utmost importance. This is necessary to insure that diabetics comply with the schedule of insulin use and that they closely monitor blood sugar levels in case adjustments are required.

Level of Fitness

Another vital consideration in the discussion of medical history is clients' current level of fitness. This information is valuable from two perspectives. First, exercise prescription is based, in part, on the point at which individuals begin. That is, an aerobically fit person can tolerate a higher exercise demand than someone who is unfit. And second, the unfit client requires a good deal of care. Some of these individuals may never have participated in a consistent program of exercise. If so, chances are they have misconceptions about what exercise involves and why it works. Remember, physiological changes experienced both during and after exercise are going to be novel; clients should be told what to expect. Additionally, unfit clients who were former athletes or fitness buffs present a unique challenge. Initially, these people may forget that they ever stopped exercising, a mind-set that can lead to injury and/or disappointment.

Exercise Testing

According to the American College of Sports Medicine guidelines for exercise testing, a graded exercise test is required of anyone over the age of 35 who is planning to begin vigorous exercise (American College of Sports Medicine, 1986). As many fitness facilities do not have the capacity to perform these tests, they are done elsewhere. Often the only feedback is a prescribed training heart rate range. In an effort to assess fitness level, a submaximal exercise test should be conducted in the fitness facility. The information gained from this test not only helps in the initial development of an exercise program, but also serves as a baseline measure for subsequent feedback sessions. Because most people begin exercise with the anticipation that they will become more fit, an update on changes in aerobic power can be very reinforcing.

Initial measures of body fat serve a similar function. By taking skinfolds at baseline and again at regular feedback intervals, you have an objective means of monitoring body composition. Relying on weight alone can be problematic because exercise can increase the amount of lean tissue. Thus someone can get heavier yet actually lose fat! One word of caution: Make sure you are very competent in measuring skinfolds before you use them. If possible, have the same person take the skinfold measures each time a client is retested and be sure to document precise anatomical sites. Also, we suggest using six or eight sites, giving feedback in millimeter change per site. This provides a more comprehensive profile of the individual and increases your chances of documenting any change that is taking place. Feedback on body composition is sensitive and can create problems, so be careful. We had one client who felt she had worked very hard for 6 months and actually did experience change in aerobic fitness; however, her skinfolds and weight remained stable across this period. She was very angry about this, demanding an explanation. Not wanting to degrade the accuracy of skinfolds or risk insulting her by suggesting that perhaps her diet was part of the explanation, we could not offer what she considered a satisfactory explanation. She quit soon after!

The Semistructured Interview

As the literature would suggest, knowing that someone smokes, has diabetes, or is not fit may help to predict complications with compliance, but this type of information provides limited guidance to you. Thus, after securing an appropriate medical history and evaluating current level of fitness, the next step is to explore individuals' motivational systems. Consistent with chapter 1, we begin by examining what has brought the clients to your program; what do they expect and value? Second, consideration will be given to exercise-related beliefs. Just what do they think about exercise and how confident are they in their ability to achieve stated objectives? Third, attention is given to social support structures. Are clients socially isolated in their quest to become fit? And fourth, you will want to know how clients are apt to respond to physical stress and frustration. Not everyone finds physical effort pleasurable, and there are several clues that can help you identify these individuals.

Clients' Needs: What Do They Expect and Value

Without question, the most important facet of treating individuals is learning about the value they attach to exercise. What do they want and expect from involvement in exercise? How does exercise fit into their day? Everyone sets priorities in life. Undoubtedly, you have been forced to give up a few things yourself for personal experiences of greater value. The same is true of your clients. Thus,

Find out what your clients really think about exercise.

a critical step in the client interview is to evaluate where fitness activities are ranked in relation to their other interests and/or responsibilities. By asking them when they intend to exercise, you can get an idea as to what sort of priority exercise has been given.

Those who plan exercise at the start of their day are usually realistic and committed. They recognize that, if they don't exercise early, there are going to be days when events interrupt their fitness program. Other positive signs are clients who travel but go out of their way to insure that they are able to exercise by booking hotels with fitness facilities or executives who turn down invitations to business lunches in order to work out. An easy way to get a handle on this type of information is to ask clients what they would do in particular situations. In contrast, those individuals who plan to exercise on a "when I have time" basis are prime candidates for non-compliance. Hesitation about support from the boss or family are equally threatening clues. There is no question that with these individuals your very first challenge is to strengthen commitment. Strategies for accomplishing this are discussed in chapter 4.

A second component involves an understanding of what clients want to get out of your program. There are many different reasons why people exercise, and there is evidence that having access to this information may be useful in tailoring exercise prescriptions. A very effective procedure is to have clients list needs that they would like to have satisfied by virtue of involvement in your fitness program. For example, we have directed patients in cardiac rehabilitation in the following way:

> When people choose to participate in cardiac rehabilitation, they often have specific objectives in mind. In other words, there are certain needs that they would like to have met. The number is not important; you may only have one purpose in mind or there may be six or eight. List below, *by priority*, what you hope to achieve by participating in this program.

It is best if this needs assessment is completed prior to the interview. Then you can take time during your interaction with clients to discuss whether it is possible to meet these objectives and, if so, how this will be accomplished. You have to be very careful about promising to do things you cannot do. Suppose, for example, that someone was exercising primarily to reduce stress. There is no guarantee that exercise is an effective remedy for stress-related disorders, particularly when clients' business or family lives remain unchanged. You will find it helpful in these situations to suggest stress management training in conjunction with exercise. Offering yoga, relaxation programs, time management seminars, and even affiliated stress management workshops will augment your success with this type of client. From the very beginning clients should have a clear understanding of what they can expect from your program and what their responsibilities are to realize specific goals.

A related problem is that underlying most clients' needs is the prerequisite that exercise be enjoyable. Research conducted in Australia as part of the "Life Be In It" project divided exercisers into several groups based on their attitude toward exercise and their extent of participation (Becker, 1977). The largest group, labeled "Drifters," consisted of people who generally had positive views toward fitness activities, but were not motivated sufficiently to participate on a regular basis. As it turns out, these individuals exercised when activities were *fun*. It is safe to say that a similar group exists in the United States; yet, what do we do to make exercise a fun experience? Many exercise prescriptions are dull and possibly displeasing, requiring a lot of patience and hard work. There are many things you can do to inject an element of fun into fitness. Aerobic dance is a classic response to this need. However, you will find that not all the fun has to occur during the running or calisthenics program. The warm-up and cool-down periods offer equal opportunity to make fitness enjoyable. In chapter 6, we will cover this topic in detail.

Exercise-Related Beliefs and Self-Confidence

It may be that a large percentage of your clientele has very limited knowledge of exercise. The danger in this is that they may possess misconceptions of how exercise works or its potential side effects. Additionally, clients may begin to question their ability to achieve what is being asked of them or they may respond with overconfidence. If a prescription is too difficult, overconfident clients will be embarrassed to admit it and probably will try to tough it out—an experience that leads to disappointment and displeasure.

Rather than challenge clients' misconceptions, a much more constructive approach is to provide some basic education on physical training—how it works and what are realistic consequences. An effective technique to enhance retention is to instruct from diagrams and charts located in the exercise areas. Encourage clients to question exercise personnel at any time about these or related issues. Above all, keep it simple.

With regard to clients' self-confidence, it is important that they are encouraged not to compare their reactions to exercise or their progress to that of their peers. Don't overwhelm beginners with excessive mileage targets or other potentially threatening workout regimens. It is useful to prescribe an initial adjustment phase in fitness programs during which there is little or no focus on productivity. If clients project an aura of overconfidence, wanting to get into the thick of things right away, ask that they spend at least a couple of weeks learning about the center and the programs offered before becoming too intense. Judgments about what they can or ought to do are best made after some experience with the exercise behaviors in question.

Social Support

The realm of social influence has not been adequately considered as a tool for motivating people in exercise settings. This is disappointing given that many clinicians feel it is probably the single most powerful determinant of compliance. The orientation process for new clients gives you the perfect opportunity to explore just how much support clients really feel they have from significant others. Two things are important to keep in mind, however. First, significant others may include the family, supervisors at work, and even close friends. The importance of any one person will vary for any given client, and in some cases the family or work environment may be irrelevant. And second, we are concerned with *perceived* support. A spouse can manifest supportive behaviors; however, if they are not viewed as such by the client, then no support exists.

You will find that the best way to assess social influence is to ask clients if a boss, spouse, or friend has ever commented on their becoming involved in a formal fitness program. If the answer is yes, then you want to know what they said. If the answer is no, then you follow with, "Well, how do you think they feel?" A number of clients have no concrete evidence to justify lack of support; they just assume it exists. Also, spouses, supervisors, or friends may make comments in jest that leave clients feeling as if they really were displeasing others. Although initially clients may not appreciate the role of social influence in their exercise programs, eventually its impact will surface. As we noted previously, exercise often requires backing off from some commitment or extending the day; it competes with other events or personal responsibilities. It is easy for others not to understand such a choice, and bitterness can result unless precautions are taken to prevent it.

Predicting Reactions to the Stress of a Physical Training Program

In dealing with reasons for clients' participation, we discussed the importance of creating a pleasurable fitness experience. Thus one final area that deserves attention in the interview is assessing how clients will respond to the added stress of a physical training program. Two different types of information will help you to make this assessment: (a) probable reactions to the symptoms associated with physical work, and (b) an evaluation of clients' reactions to daily hassles.

Asking clients to describe their exercise history can indicate probable reactions to the symptoms associated with physical work. This is because past experience is a powerful predictor of future responses. For example, research on inactive fitness groups has shown that a previously negative experience with exercise (i.e., frustration, being made to feel like a failure) is a major deterrent to further involvement in exercise. The development of a negative attitude toward exercise leaves clients believing that exercise is not going to work for them. When you do encounter someone who has failed at exercise, but who is willing to try again, be cautious. Despite what they say, there is bound to be an element of pessimism. We distinctly remember a client who fell into this category.

The pessimist.   Patty had previously belonged to a small local club where she was given a standard aerobic program appropriate for her age and estimated fitness level. However, because Patty had never exercised before, she had more difficulty than others in meeting the goals set for her. After several weeks of trying to meet goals she became frustrated, decided she was wasting her time, and dropped out. Six months later, deciding she had to lose 10 lb without starving herself in the process, Patty came to our fitness center. She was not convinced we could help her stick to an exercise program, but she was at least willing to try. By considering Patty's personal exercise preferences and consulting her in setting exercise goals (a process described in chapter 5), we were able to encourage her. Slowly Patty gained confidence in her ability to succeed. She began to lose weight and take charge of her own program. Predictably, her attitude toward exercise changed as well. Generally, people cope better with adverse events when they perceive some control over the stressors. Because we allowed Patty to have an active role in the progression of her exercise program, she enjoyed it more and was willing to stick with it, making a change in her weight and gaining confidence in her ability to exercise.

The first-time participant.   Another category of clients includes those individuals who have never before participated in or have had very limited experience in any organized exercise. Research in our laboratory has shown that initially these individuals have a tendency to overreact to physical exertion. This is particularly true of both female clients who throughout their childhood were told that

exercise wasn't very feminine, and male clients who never identified with the physical prowess of masculinity (Rejeski, 1985). With
these individuals, you need to emphasize the fact that fitness can
be fun and meaningful for everyone—it is no longer the exclusive
activity of jocks. The slogan "no pain, no gain" does not apply to
the way their program will operate. You will have to work especially
hard to set the initial hook, but once you do these people will probably become some of your most dedicated participants. It is valuable to discover what these individuals do in their leisure time. A
good strategy is to explain how their fitness program could enhance
their leisure interests. For example, perhaps you have a golfer. By
incorporating into the exercise program a few good stretches and
some strength training for the muscles used in golf, you create an
intrinsic motive to train.

The happy achiever.   On the flip side, you will also encounter
people who have had very positive experience with exercise. Such
individuals will be those who find they are able to achieve certain
goals with exercise and enjoy the challenge and feelings associated
with a good workout. Our only warning with these clients is that
due to their self-motivation they may be ignored by exercise leaders.
Don't overestimate their dedication. Take the same care and detail
in the interview process that you would with a novice. Also, make
an effort to touch base with these clients periodically to make sure
they aren't pushing too hard or just to tell them "Good work!".
Simple compliments mean more than you may think.

In addition to exploring probable reactions to the symptoms of
physical stress, you should make a brief assessment of clients' reactions to daily hassles. The reason for this is twofold. First, it will
give you an idea of how burdened your clients are with other life
stress and will serve as a warning to fitness personnel. If they are
angry and impatient in the business world or with their families,
you can expect more of the same when things don't go as planned
with their exercise. And second, you may be surprised at how well
reactions to daily stress generalize to exercise-related stress.

Harry is a successful executive who commutes into New York City
from New Jersey. He joined a corporate fitness facility because he
acknowledged the importance of regular exercise. To this particular busy executive, however, membership in a health club at a
considerable financial investment meant that exercise was just
another time commitment in an already packed day—another
appointment to keep! The added stress inevitably caused a rise in
Harry's blood pressure and even brought on headaches. Harry's
inclination wasn't to exercise but to lie down! Originally Harry had
planned to leave work a little early and exercise before catching his

regular train home, but with all the hassles this just did not work. In attempting to change things and adapt his exercise schedule to his busy day, Harry's exercise leader suggested that he consider exercising before work. Then he could roll out of bed, catch an earlier train and a little shut-eye on the way in. After exercising, he could shower, shave, and go to work, enjoying the feeling of having already accomplished something useful. That did the trick for Harry! Instead of worrying all day about fitting exercise in, he did it first and enjoyed it without the headache or rise in blood pressure.

Perhaps you may feel a little hesitant about discussing life stress. It is very personal, and clients can be made to feel as if it is an invasion of privacy. The key, however, is to keep the questions very nonthreatening. Tell clients that because you are in the business of health you simply want to get a handle on what their typical day is like. Sample questions include the following: Does your job carry a lot of responsibility? Do you ever feel rushed or pressured? When you get angry or upset are people around you likely to know about it or do you keep it inside? How do you feel about waiting for someone to show up for an appointment? Do your children often try your patience?

Physical Evaluation and Interview Outline

We find ourselves reviewing the basics frequently. We have included this outline as a quick refresher for your future use.

I. Medical history
 A. Are there factors that complicate responses to exercise?
 B. What is the individual's current level of fitness?
 C. What is the individual's percent fat?

II. Personal needs
 A. How is exercise ranked in the client's list of priorities?
 B. What are the reasons for the client's participation in exercise?

III. Beliefs
 A. Does the client have misconceptions about exercise?
 B. What does the client think exercise will do for him or her?
 C. What are the client's confidence levels?

IV. Social support
  A. Does the client perceive support from friends, family, and boss?
  B. Has the client correctly read communication dealing with support?

V. Reactions to exercise and life stress
  A. Has the client ever exercised regularly before?
    1. What kind of exercise?
    2. Was it structured or not?
  B. What type of experience was it?
    1. Positive?
    2. Negative?
  C. If the client has never exercised before, what are his or her leisure activities?
  D. How does the client react to daily hassles?

Feedback

After you have gathered all the pertinent information, your final objective will be to introduce the exercise prescription and discuss client-specific goals. Chapter 3 presents, in detail, the critical issues involved in prescription, and chapter 5 covers goal setting and the details of feedback. In addition, if it is clear that a client is at risk for noncompliance, this is the appropriate time to initiate intervention. As you will see in chapter 4, many of the strategies for dealing with noncompliant behavior require little time from either yourself or the client. In fact, several techniques really involve standard operating procedures that apply to all clients.

Feedback is a critical component of the orientation process, and clients need to have a clear understanding of their own goals and responsibilities. Furthermore, it is important that clients understand your role in their fitness programs. When will they get subsequent feedback, and what sort of checks insure that everything is going as planned?

Summary

And there you have it—what you need to know about your clients and how to ask! If you are serious about motivation, there is no substitute for conducting this formal session. Without it, clients will be misinformed and improperly treated. Conducted in a professional manner, the physical evaluation and semistructured interview are your best first steps to insure client satisfaction and encourage compliant behavior.

Suggested Readings

Baumgartner, T.A., & Jackson, A.S. (1982). *Measurement for evaluation in physical education* (2nd ed.). Dubuque, IA: Wm. C. Brown Co.

Dishman, R.K. (1982). Compliance/adherence in health-related exercise. *Health Psychology*, **1**(3), 237-267.

Zimbardo, P.G., Ebbesen, E.B., & Maslach, C. (1977). *Influencing attitudes and changing behavior* (2nd ed.). Reading, MA: Addison-Wesley.

Chapter 3

The Prescription Process and Motivation

It may seem odd to find an overview of exercise prescription in a book dealing with motivation. For two reasons, however, it not only makes good sense, but is necessary. First, recall that a significant determinant of behavior rests on the belief that acting in a particular manner will produce some desired effect—outcome expectancy. You probably have felt the disappointment and anger of investing time in some venture only to find weeks or months later that your efforts yielded little in tangible returns. You do not want to err in exercise prescription, and with a little care you won't. Second, consistent with our system of treating clients, exercise prescription is best viewed as an interactive process. You serve no purpose if a prescription is inherently punitive or at odds with a patient's physical or psychological limitations.

We begin the chapter by reviewing the current status of physiological principles underlying exercise prescription. Whereas your first temptation may be to scan or completely ignore this section, we ask that you take time to refresh your memory. Perhaps reviewing this material once more may draw your attention to information that has become clouded. More important, there are recent developments that have led to changes in basic procedures. Following the physiology of prescription, we explore the merits of using ratings of perceived exertion (RPE) in the prescription process. If you are not familiar with this concept, you will find this chapter to be very intriguing. Quite simply, clients' perceptions of how hard they are working correspond quite well with metabolic changes experienced during exercise. Thus, RPEs offer a valuable nontechnical means of regulating workloads.

In addition, we will introduce the concept of evaluating clients' emotional reactions to exercise during the activity itself. As a result of our own laboratory and clinical studies, we have reason to believe that attending to emotional responses during exercise allows you to short-circuit many potential problems. Finally, we summarize the stages of exercise prescription, a process that requires exchange between clients and exercise leaders. In chapter 2, you learned about the type of information required to implement this interactive prescriptive system.

Physiology of Aerobic Conditioning

Aerobics is the major focus of the current fitness craze in the United States. Whether it is running, dancing, cycling, swimming, or skipping rope, a large percentage of people involved in fitness training do so to reap the rewards of cardiovascular activity. The components of a sound aerobic program involve workout intensity and type of activity, duration and frequency, and progression and specificity. Our intent in this section is to examine these components and then to explore the possible motives behind clients' involvement in such training. This is an important step because it is very possible that the general population has been misled as to the effects of aerobics. Although they are into jogging, individuals may well desire effects that are actually produced by other forms of exercise.

Although we realize that the type of activity is the first consideration in an exercise prescription, intensity of training is the most important component of any activity if it is to provide an effective aerobic training stimulus (Ribisl, 1984). Thus our first consideration is training intensity. We will discuss four basic guidelines for setting training intensity in the next several pages. Mode of exercise is a topic that is dealt with later in this chapter.

Recognizing Levels of Training Intensity

If the clients you serve have an explicit desire to enhance their cardiorespiratory function, the most important consideration is that the activity they perform must create an overload on these systems. It is a simple principle of adaptation. Unless the heart and muscles are stressed beyond the normal range of activity for a given individual, there is no stimulus for their efficiency or capacity to improve. At the same time, although the limits of normal activity vary greatly across individuals, the temptation is to impose exercise regimens on clients that seem perfectly reasonable based on your own physical condition and experience. Unfortunately, these prescriptions may be too severe.

One challenge confronting you is to recognize what constitutes an overload for other people and to be enthusiastic about achievement that may seem insignificant. Rather than pretending to care or be impressed, you must learn to appreciate the fact that it takes considerable effort for some individuals to exercise for even 15 min a day. Additionally, because exercise typically involves groups, you will have to work unusually hard to convince beginners that they are making good progress. So often, the tendency for these individuals is to look around at seasoned members in awe, failing to appreciate all it took for them to become trained individuals. Such reactions can be instrumental in the development or verification

*The temptation is to impose exercise regimens based
on your physical condition.*

of weak physical self-concepts. At this juncture, let's examine the important concerns when prescribing intensity.

Guideline 1.   When prescribing work intensity, remember that the exercise must constitute an overload: It should exceed the demands of what typically constitutes normal activity for any given individual.

Regulating Physical Strain

The first principle of an aerobic prescription is knowing how to regulate the level of physical strain for a given individual and then imparting control over this stimulus to the client. Fortunately, heart rate response during exercise corresponds nicely with demands on the cardiorespiratory systems. Thus, proper regulation of work intensity involves two basic steps: (a) determining each client's heart rate reserve, and (b) determining the demand to place on this reserve.

Calculating target heart rate ranges.   To calculate heart rate reserve (HRR) for clients, you need to know their individual resting heart rates and maximum heart rate responses during exercise stress. The heart rate reserve is the difference between these two values. To determine resting heart rate, teach your clients how to palpate their radial (wrist) pulse. You can then have them record this response for three consecutive mornings just prior to getting out of bed. The middle heart rate of the three is the best estimate of clients' true resting response. As a general principle, you should discourage clients from palpating the carotid (neck) artery. Excessive pressure on this site can create bradycardia (slowing of the heart), a procedure that would distort the resting value. Furthermore, through massage of the carotid artery, it is possible to trigger a reflex that can induce arrhythmias and/or dizziness. The most accurate method of arriving at an individual's maximum heart rate is through a graded exercise test to exhaustion. In the absence of such test results, however, you can estimate maximum heart rate by subtracting a person's age from the value 220. In fact, this latter method is preferred when working with sedentary individuals and elderly populations.

Determining the stress level you want to place on the heart rate reserve is typically accomplished by setting a training range for heart rate. From your professional training, you probably learned that this range should span from 60% to 80% of the heart rate reserve, a range that yields an average intensity of 70%. Thus the actual training range would be established by adding 60% and 80% of the heart rate reserve to the resting heart rate. Let's take an actual example to clarify the procedure.

Mary, a 60-year-old tax accountant, has a resting heart rate of 60 and a maximal response during a graded exercise test to exhaustion of 160. Her heart rate reserve is 100 (i.e., 160 − 60). Sixty percent of 100 is 60 (i.e., .6 × 100) and 80% of 100 is 80 (i.e., .8 × 100). When each of these two values is added to her resting heart rate, Mary's training range becomes 120–140. Because it is desirable to have clients take exercise heart rates in 10-second intervals, the 10-second training range should be between 20 and 23 (i.e., 6 × 20 = 120 and 6 × 23 = 138). Mary now has a convenient method of monitoring her own work intensity to make sure that she experiences an aerobic training effect.

Is 60% to 80% the correct range?   In recent years, the American College of Sports Medicine has recognized that the 60% to 80% range may actually overestimate or underestimate an appropriate stimulus due to differences in physical condition (American College of Sports Medicine, 1986). You would not expect a client whose cardiovascular function has been compromised by heart disease to require the same training intensity as an executive who actively competes in corporate challenge road races. Therefore, you must adjust the training range as a function of clients' initial functional capacity ($\dot{V}O_2$max, or aerobic power). The American College of Sports Medicine suggests that you first measure or estimate clients' functional capacity in metabolic equivalents (METs). In case you are a bit rusty, a MET is equivalent to an oxygen consumption of 3.5 ml/kg•min. Thus, if your initial aerobic power is 35 ml/kg•min (this is the maximum amount of oxygen that you can consume per kilogram of body weight each minute of exercise), it represents 10 METs (i.e., 35 ÷ 3.5). To determine the average intensity for an individualized training stimulus, you simply add the functional capacity in METs to a baseline of 60. With a functional capacity of 10, your average training stimulus becomes 70 (i.e., 10 + 60), whereas a functional capacity of 5 METs would lower this value to 65 (i.e., 5 + 60). You can create a training range by adding and subtracting 10 from this average value. In the first example above, 70 + or − 10 would yield a training range of from 60 to 80. You can probably see why 60% to 80% is the often cited target range; it is based on a relatively unfit individual who has a functional capacity of 10 METs. By the way, the American College of Sports Medicine suggests that people never train beyond 85% of their functional capacity. Above this ceiling, the risk of cardiovascular complications increases greatly.

Guideline 2.   Target heart rate ranges should be set individually based on a client's level of cardiovascular fitness. This can be done most effectively if you have an estimate of the individual's aerobic power.

Choosing the Appropriate Activity

Some of the reactions you will get from clients may sound something like this: "Hey, I know I missed the program for a couple of weeks, but I wasn't exactly idle. After all, I played 72 holes of golf during that period." Or, "John seems to get a good workout from racquetball, why can't I?" In general, aerobics include all activities that involve vigorous, rhythmic movement of large muscle groups. However, your job requires much more than making a master list of these. You will have to make decisions and explain to clients what constitutes an appropriate aerobic stimulus, and why this varies from one individual to another. You will find it helpful to discuss activity from the perspective of skill level and functional capacity. If your average training stimulus should be 70% of heart rate reserve, then, according to our calculations, your functional capacity is 10 METs. Put in different terms, you should exercise at 70% of 10 METs, which involves activity requiring 7.0 METs.

Scientists have determined the mean and range MET requirements of a variety of activities. The most common activities asked about are listed in Table 3.1. Thus, for a sedentary, deconditioned individual who has a functional capacity of only 5 METs, an appropriate training stimulus would be 65% of this value or 3.25 METs. For this individual, low-level conditioning exercises would actually provide an aerobic stimulus! Once this individual is reevaluated at a 3-month interval, a change of activity may be indicated. Actually, if feasible in your specific setting, a very good use of this table is to offer a choice of four or five options from which clients select an activity. Research in psychology has shown that personal involvement in the decision making process enhances compliance.

Guideline 3.   Appropriate options should be individually prescribed based on an estimate of one's aerobic capacity. Helping clients select activities that provide challenge, fun, and aerobic benefit is possible!

Table 3.1   Demand of Selected Leisure Activities in METs

Activity	Mean	Range
Running		
12-min mi	8.7	—
11-min mi	9.4	—
10-min mi	10.2	—
9-min mi	11.2	—
8-min mi	12.5	—
7-min mi	14.1	—
6-min mi	16.3	—
Rope jumping		
60-80 skips/min	9.0	—
120-140 skips/min	—	—
Swimming	—	11-12
Cycling		
Pleasure	—	3-8+
10 mi/hr	7.0	—
Aerobic dance	—	6-9
Conditioning exercises	—	3-8+
Stair climbing	—	4-8
Paddleball, racquetball	9	8-12
Handball	—	8-12+
Hiking (cross-country)	—	3-7
Backpacking	—	5-11
Golf		
Cart	—	2-3
Walking (carrying bag or pulling cart)	5.1	4-7
Mountain climbing	—	5-10+
Waterskiing	—	5-7
Snowskiing		
Downhill	—	5-8
Cross-country	—	6-12+
Tennis	6.5	4-9+

Determining Training Duration and Frequency

In addition to the principle of exercise intensity, overload applies to both duration and frequency of training. Duration refers to the length of a daily workout or training session, whereas frequency pertains to the number of times clients exercise per week. The reason that overload is so critical to both duration and frequency is that the rate of improvement in functional capacity drops off quickly when duration is below 20 min or if frequency of training is less than three times per week. This assumes that a proper level of intensity is prescribed.

It is true from a purely physiological perspective that a client could lengthen individual sessions to 40 min of an aerobic stimulus and accomplish in two sessions what another person exercising for 20 min would accomplish in four. In effect you make a trade. By intensifying the overload of duration, you are able to back off on frequency. The problem with this rationale is twofold. First, for someone with a low functional capacity, it would take an unusual tolerance of discomfort to hold a proper percentage of heart rate reserve for more than 30 min. In fact, 20 min is a more realistic duration for most beginning clients. From the standpoint of compliance, therefore, extending duration is a highly undesirable strategy. And second, for low to moderately fit individuals, there are upper limits in both duration and frequency of training that drastically increase the risk of orthopedic injury. This risk begins to increase beyond 30 min of exercise and a frequency greater than four times per week and accelerates rapidly beyond 40 min of exercise or a frequency of greater than five times per week (Ribisl, 1984).

Guideline 4. Optimal range in duration for low to moderately fit individuals is between 20 and 30 min of an aerobic stimulus. Optimal frequency for this stimulus is three or four times weekly.

Although research has yet to confirm the fitness advantage of scheduling a day of rest between exercise sessions, this strategy is currently recommended for use with beginners. This provides a period of recovery between exercise bouts, facilitates physiologic adaptation, and is a means of keeping musculoskeletal discomfort and injury to a minimum.

Monitoring Progression of Activity

Progression is a critical component of exercise prescription, particularly as it applies to the concept of overload. For example, concern for progression was what led to the practice of varying the aerobic stimulus as a function of clients' fitness levels. It is also this principle that influences decisions regarding the degree of overload in both the duration and the frequency of training. In addition, progression may play an integral role in the actual selection of activities themselves. As a matter of fact, you may find in the early stages of aerobic programs that it is necessary to violate established principles of exercise prescription. Special considerations such as medical limitations or extreme levels of inactivity may require that initial training intensities fall below theoretically desired targets or that duration of activity is discontinuous. The purpose of such strategies is to avoid the problem of dropout that results from musculoskeletal injuries and/or psychological distress.

Follow stages of development.   At least three general principles apply to proper progression. First, it is well recognized that exercise programs involve the shaping of behavior. You don't climb Mt. Everest without careful graduated preparation. Similarly, getting people involved in physical activity demands that they adhere to concrete stages of development. These include the following: (a) a *starter phase* during which emphasis is placed on getting the musculoskeletal systems accustomed to the new demands of physical work (during this period of time, improvement objectives should be discouraged); (b) an overload or *growth phase* with a focus on distinct improvements in aerobic or muscular function; and (c) a *maintenance phase* that involves sufficient stimulation to prevent the loss of acquired conditioning.

Allow enough starter time.   A second principle of progression is that the length of time in the starter and growth phases can vary considerably. For example, it has been estimated that, for each decade after the age of 30, there is a 40% increase in time required for adaption to occur (Pollock, Wilmore, & Fox, 1984). If you accept the view that 15 sessions is a reasonable term for the starter phase with young adults (< 30 years old), then for a 50-year-old sedentary executive, the starter phase should be 27 sessions in length.

Similarly, there is good reason to believe that it takes much longer for this 50-year-old to experience the gains made by a 25-year-old in the growth phase. This is very difficult for people to accept and it is discouraging. Many will want to jump in where they left off 20 years before, or they may expect to whip themselves into shape in a month or two. It won't happen. You must present your clients with the facts and urge them to accept them. At the same time, however, don't force clients into an extended starter phase if they have a history of fairly recent activity. It should now be clear why interviews with clients are so critical.

Progression is a difficult concept to implement, yet its role in the dropout syndrome is substantial. The story of Joe, a 52-year-old executive, is an excellent case in point. He started jogging due to mid-life crisis and creeping signs of obesity. Fortunately, or so Joe thought, he had played football in college and was no stranger to the physical discomforts of hard work. So Joe began an exercise program that consisted of jogging 3 mi every other day. Much to his surprise and despair, the pain never really dissipated, and after 3 weeks there was little evidence of progress. If anything, his joints and muscles were pleading to quit and so he did. Now, 5 years after this initial attempt, Joe is 20 lb heavier and headed for severe hypertension.

Establish increments that encourage growth.   The third principle concerns the dilemma of establishing increments in the growth phase. Should clients walk or run, and what is the proper length of time for the aerobic stimulus phase? We see discouragement among exercise leaders brought about by a few clients who seem to favor walking or discontinuous activity patterns. These clients stop and rest after 10 min or so of exercise. Personnel are concerned not only for the individual, but because they fear that this behavior will set a bad precedent. Will discontinuous exercise patterns become the next epidemic? Is such discouragement warranted? After all, aerobic exercise is supposed to be continuous activity for at least 20 min and jogging is what it's all about, right?

Not exactly. Rate of adaptation is influenced not only by age but also by individual differences such as activity history, orthopedic restrictions, and psychological problems. The main point is not to become obsessed with maximizing the rate at which growth occurs, but to encourage growth that is both understood and accepted by the client and you. And what about setting a bad precedent? Can discontinuous work or some other behavior negatively influence other clients? Actually, if clients understand from orientation that programs are individualized and they are even given examples of what they might see others doing, there is no need for alarm. You may find that your less fit clients will receive significant social support from those who are more fit. The bottom line—keep clients informed.

A Comment on Specificity

How often have you heard comments like, ''Gee I just can't believe that I got so sore from doing a little hoeing in my garden. I've been doing this adult fitness routine now for almost 3 months. It makes me wonder whether the program is doing me any good at all." What underlies this expression of frustration is the principle of specificity. That is, the body adapts to training in a manner that is specific to the demand placed upon it. Some recent research in which swimming was employed as a primary mode of activity for aerobic training indicated that there was little or no improvement in the response of the leg muscles to a treadmill test! It is no surprise, then, to find that running does little for the endurance or strength of someone's arms (Magel, Foglia, McArdle, Gutin, Pechar, & Katch, 1975).

A knowledge of specificity in aerobic conditioning becomes very critical to clients who may want to improve their functional capacity, but also have an interest in developing aerobic power as it relates to some work or leisure activity. For example, if a work task or leisure sport demands repetitive movement of the arms, it would be a mistake to rely totally on running as a form of training. You may want to forget about running and rely on swimming or arm ergometry provided by the Schwinn Airdyne.

The Psychology of Aerobic Prescription

If two individuals who differed in level of fitness performed an exercise test to exhaustion at 80% of their heart rate reserve, the person in superior condition would outlast the other. If the subjects were equivalent in level of fitness, yet one had excessive body fat, wouldn't local discomfort in the legs or respiratory distress restrict the obese individual from keeping up with his leaner competitor? The fact is, there are numerous physiological and anatomical characteristics that contribute to the perceived difficulty of physical work. There is no reason why you should try to juggle all of these variables in the prescription process when research has indicated that clients can accurately monitor and integrate the demand of physical work for themselves.

Using Borg's Perceived Exertion Scale

In the early 1960s, a Swedish physiologist named Gunnar Borg found that people were actually quite good at perceiving the physical costs of various workloads. Through several years of research, he constructed the following self-report scale to assess these perceptions.

Borg's Perceived Exertion Scale

6	No exertion at all
7	Extremely light
8	
9	Very light
10	
11	Light
12	
13	Somewhat hard
14	
15	Hard (heavy)
16	
17	Very hard
18	
19	Extremely hard
20	Maximal exertion

Note. From *An Introduction to Borg's RPE-Scale* (p. 26) by G. Borg, 1985, New York: Mouvement Publications. Copyright 1985 by Mouvement. Reprinted by permission.

Notice that Borg's Perceived Exertion Scale ranges from 6 to 20 (Borg, 1985). If you multiply a person's perceived level of exertion by 10, the product is an approximate heart rate. In addition, establishing training ranges based on ratings of perceived exertion (RPE) reflects a natural and individualized integration of information. This information is relevant to the perceived demands of exercise such as heart rate, ventilation, the by-products of metabolism, environmental temperature, and even boredom. How does one use the scale? It has been recommended that, during aerobic work, intensity remain somewhere between 12 and 16 units on the Borg scale.

Limitations of the Borg Scale

We have found three limitations in using the scale that are worth passing on to other practitioners so that this valuable instrument can be used appropriately to enhance the exercise experience and the safety of participation.

Lack of experience.   It is unlikely that novice exercisers have the experience to control work intensity purely by subjective perceptions. Thus, in the early phases of an exercise program, we suggest using heart rate reserve and introducing clients to the role and eventual use of RPE. In fact, even during the later stages of training, there is merit in maintaining spot checks on both methods (heart rate reserve and RPE). The reason is that large discrepancies and/or changes in the relationship between HRR and RPE can constitute a meaningful signal. It has been shown that, in the absence of sufficient external stimulation, people focus more on physical symptoms (Pennebaker, 1982). This would lead to an elevation in perceived work intensity relative to heart rate response. If this happens, it may be time to alter social interaction patterns, change the running environment, and/or vary the mode of training.

The Type A perspective.   Second, even after making repeated attempts to wean people from HRR and onto RPE, you will occasionally find isolated clients who simply don't respond well. From our perspective some of the most problematic are extreme Type A individuals who have a strong commitment to exercise (Rejeski, Morley, & Miller, 1983). The term *Type A* implies that an individual is excessively achievement oriented, highly competitive, impatient, and prone to hostility. In situations where Type As are highly involved, they have a tendency to suppress or ignore physical symptoms. In checking their RPEs against HRRs, you should not be surprised if they are at or above the upper threshold of their training range. The danger is that these people are often at increased risk for cardiovascular disease. The following scenario describes a similar problem.

Not long ago, one of our Type A colleagues trained for and ran in the Marine Corps Marathon. He finished in a very respectable time—just under 3 hr. The problem was the way in which he ran the race. As it happened, he was a victim of heat stroke and actually crawled across the finish line! Heat stroke can be life threatening and for some unknown reason appears to increase your risk for subsequent thermal regulatory problems. When asked how he could have allowed himself to get into this type of trouble, he responded, "You know, the funny thing about it was that I never really felt that bad." Even more remarkable was the fact that his time qualified him for the Boston Marathon and he fully intends to compete!

At this point, you may be wondering whether there is an effective means of resolving the potentially destructive behavior of the Type A. One approach that we have found useful in a cardiac rehabilitation setting is to present the exercise prescription in the form of a challenge. A typical explanation might proceed as follows:

You know, it is often difficult to exercise in a prescribed heart rate range; for example, you seem to overshoot your upper limit with some frequency. However, if there is anyone who can master this task, my feeling is that it's you. I'll check back every now and then to see how things are progressing. Remember, a sign of failure is consistently finding yourself beyond the upper limits of the range that we have set for you. Take periodical heart rate checks during your workouts and pay close attention to this exercise response. See if you can achieve the control I am talking about; it's a significant achievement if you can. Good luck!

Notice that in this strategy we have used the compulsive style of the Type A to achieve a constructive end. When committed to proper goals, Type As can be model clients (Rejeski, Morley, & Miller, 1984).

Does not reveal feelings about exertion.   The third and final limitation with the RPE scale is that it does not provide any insight into how people feel about exercising at a particular intensity. For example, we have encountered subjects in our laboratory studies who enjoy *very hard* (RPE of 17) physical work. A competitive cyclist once told us, "I really feel good when I train between an RPE of 15 and 17. If I intend to get better, that is where I have got to be." In contrast, there are those who find working at an intensity of 15 or 17 on the Borg scale distressful. So, in some respects, the RPE scale can put you in the same bind as HRR; you have people working within a range that is unpleasant for them.

Using the Feeling Scale

Recently we have been experimenting with a different type of scale called a Feeling Scale. It is an 11-point scale that ranges from +5 (very good) to −5 (very bad). To use the scale, you simply tell clients to record a number that corresponds to how they feel while exercising. It is useful to indicate that there is no expected pattern and that they may find themselves going up and down the scale as they exercise. There may be change in a specific direction, or no change at all.

This type of measure is even more effective than the RPE scale in detecting problems like boredom or dissatisfaction with exercise. In addition, when things are not going well for someone, it provides a good mechanism for initiating discussion. People often use it as a subtle way of asking for help.

Our recommendation is that you use the Feeling Scale in combination with Borg's RPE scale. Instruct clients to make two or three recordings per exercise session, evenly spacing these across the 20 or 30 min of a workout. RPE and the Feeling Scale provide different kinds of information. Also, you can start using the Feeling Scale

Feeling Scale

+5	Very good
+4	
+3	Good
+2	
+1	Slightly good
0	Neutral
−1	Slightly bad
−2	
−3	Bad
−4	
−5	Very bad

from Day 1. By the way, you have to be committed and consistent in the use of these scales. If clients perceive a lack of concern on your part, it will be reflected in very poor compliance with using the scales, and the information obtained will be suspect.

Conditioning for Strength and Muscle Tone

To this point in the chapter we have focused entirely on aerobic conditioning. Although cardiovascular fitness is of critical importance to individual health, too often no consideration is given to strength or muscle tone. Some of the clients who come to your centers will be extremely naive. They have no concept of what your exercise programs can do for them, but each one knows exactly what kind of changes he or she would like to make. In our experience, a large number of clients have expressed an interest in muscular tone, but in the past we have not provided rigorous programming of this nature.

Not long ago, we had a patient in cardiac rehabilitation who was moderately compliant with his aerobic conditioning program. In retrospect, we recall that he made numerous references to the Nautilus equipment, and he frequently approached exercise personnel about starting a weight training program. Generally, his references to strength training were not taken seriously by exercise leaders. Attempts were made to discourage his involvement in such activity; he obviously needed exercise specific to the cardiovascular system. At about the time he was ready to quit the program and exercise on his own, an alert exercise leader made a deal to structure an appropriate strength program if he continued aerobic exercise. The change in this person's behavior was dramatic. Not only did he thoroughly enjoy Nautilus training, but his compliance to aerobic exercise was the best ever! This is an example of the importance of responding to individual client needs.

Unfortunately, guidelines for developing muscular tone and strength are less objective than those for aerobic conditioning. However, there are some general principles that you should share with interested clients. In many respects, concepts applied to aerobic conditioning can be transferred to the development of muscular tone and strength. The important elements include workout intensity, duration and frequency, and progression and specificity. It is often necessary, however, to point out the distinction between muscle tone and strength. Clients need to realize that exercises designed to firm the abdomen or chest (muscular tone) may not necessarily increase the size of these muscle groups, an effect tied to muscular strength.

Each client knows the kind of changes he would like to make.

The next few sections briefly summarize an approach to setting up and explaining the programs directed at increasing muscle tone and/or strength.

Intensity and Type of Exercise

Improvements in muscular strength and tone are accomplished through resistance training, and both involve the principle of overload, yet there are important differences in program structure. If the objective is to stimulate muscular strength, then the general rule for any exercise is high resistance and a low number of repetitions; muscular endurance requires low resistance and high repetitions. *Resistance* refers to the amount of weight lifted. *Repetitions* indicate how many times a given exercise is to be performed. The absolute number of repetitions for a given resistance is known as *repetition maximum* (RM). Usually there are 6 to 12 different exercises in a resistance program, and 2 or more bouts (called *sets*) of this circuit are performed during a single training session.

In the 1960s, there was a series of research studies on strength that led to the position that 3 sets of a resistance circuit at 6 RM performed on nonconsecutive days three times per week produced the greatest increase in muscular strength (Berger, 1962). More recently, however, research has indicated that a stepwise protocol performed with the same frequency is more effective (Stone, O'Bryant, & Garhammer, 1981). This would involve a program such as the following: (a) 3 weeks of from 3 to 5 sets at 10-20 RM, (b) 4 weeks of 3 sets at 5 RM, and (c) 4 weeks of 3 sets at 3 RM. Upon completion of this cycle, either it is repeated or the individual moves to a maintenance phase. A typical maintenance program might involve 3 sets at 10 RM performed two times per week.

It is important to note that it is best to exercise larger muscle groups before smaller ones and that heavy resistance training for strength will necessitate a period of recovery between exercises (e.g., 2-4 min). Also, many bodybuilders do not perform the exercises as a circuit. Thus they might perform all 5 sets of a bench press before moving to the next exercise. You should realize that not many clients will want to subject themselves to this level of training, and modifications are often necessary. At the same time, however, it is wise to present clients with the facts. This can be extremely valuable in reaching realistic goals.

As individuals increase the repetitions they perform of an exercise and decrease time between sets, the focus is shifted in the direction of improved muscular tone/endurance rather than strength.

For example, you will frequently find programs for enhanced muscular tone to involve 15 to 30 or more repetitions of an exercise circuit. Clients usually perform 1 or 2 sets, and they move sequentially through all exercises prior to repeating a given movement.

Irrespective of whether you focus on muscle tone or strength, however, intensity is a key variable. Because it is impossible to control intensity of resistance work through heart rate or any other objective physiological measure, we strongly recommend the use of the RPE and the Feeling Scale. The system we recommend is as follows. First, you will need to establish appropriate exercise resistances based on client objectives. Remember, total weight lifted, number of repetitions, and sets performed are the key variables that you manipulate. Second, during workouts, rather than having clients focus on number of repetitions, have them work at an exercise until they reach an RPE between 18 (very hard) and 20 (maximal exertion). Every 2 weeks or so, have clients record ratings on the Feeling Scale prior to beginning exercise, midway through their workout, and about 15 min after the session is complete. You may uncover some interesting trends. For instance, significant decreases in Feeling Scale ratings may result in early identification of a decline in motivation. This would warrant immediate follow-up with an appropriate intervention. And third, every few weeks have someone record the number of repetitions completed for each exercise and adjust resistances accordingly. This distracts participants from focusing on the number of times they perform an exercise. This approach is an effective system for optimizing client satisfaction.

Frequency and Duration

Two days of exercise training per week are sufficient to stimulate some change in muscular tone or strength; however, three is more desirable. For instance, many individuals seriously involved in strength training split muscle groups into two major areas—shoulders, arms, and chest versus back and legs. They alternate the two groups on successive days and work out 5 days per week. Because the 5th day of the first week would end with shoulders, arms, and chest, they would begin the next week with back and legs. It is not advisable to train the same muscle group on two consecutive days, because it does not provide an adequate period of recovery.

Duration of training can vary considerably, and this is due in large part to the recovery periods that play an integral role in strength training programs. In general, however, it is possible to train effectively for strength within a 1-hr session. Programs designed for improved muscular tone require less time; 20 to 40 min is usually adequate.

Progression and Specificity

You need to take the same precautions with resistance training as you do with aerobic conditioning. Most important is establishing starter, growth, and maintenance phases. Clients must understand that improvement objectives are on hold for at least 3 weeks, a time frame that should be adjusted upward after the age of 30 in accordance with the previously defined formula. Once again, another challenge you will face is to work with clients who have had experience with resistance training in their teens or early twenties. Often, they think they already understand the principles of resistance training and begin at levels that quickly lead to dropout due to soreness, injury, or disappointment. A good strategy for handling such individuals is to acknowledge their background during the interview process and then to educate them on detraining and the need to establish realistic objectives. In addition, it is worth pointing out to clients how failure to delay gratification may defeat long-term changes in fitness. In fact, you can make delay of gratification an explicit challenge in such a manner that they think they came up with the idea themselves. Consider, for example, the following interaction with a 38-year-old male who had weight trained during his college days.

"So you have had some experience with weight training in the past. Can you briefly describe it to me?" Irrespective of what the client says, the exercise specialist remarks, "Boy! That's really great! One of the advantages you have is that you seem to understand the concept of progression. You know, so many people we deal with are impatient. They fail to recognize that resistance training is a graduated process. You know, for example, that there is no way you can begin where you left off 15 years ago, and it's going to take a good 3 weeks before you are ready to handle a really rigorous program. Well, I don't need to go on, just let me show you what we have in mind and how it fits in with what you have done before."

Note that the exercise specialist in this exchange has reinforced the client for previous exercise experiences and recognized a level of knowledge that the client may not even have. However, the instructor will eventually share all the important principles of weight training with the client in a context where the client can pretend to know what is going on. Given that the information on resistance training almost appears to come from the client, starter programs and graduated growth is logical, realistic, and, most important, reinforcing.

In addition to the concept of progression, specificity is another consideration in resistance training. Clearly, to expect change in a given muscle group, exercises must involve the relevant movement pattern. We suggest that you use anatomical models so that clients understand the muscles involved in specific movements and how to create different exercises to achieve desired results.

Body Composition and Prescribing Exercise to Prevent Disease

We have specified the criteria that must be met if you are to expect improvement in cardiovascular and/or muscular function and indicated that overload is a central prerequisite in both instances. Of equal importance, however, is recognizing that clients can exercise with relatively low-intensity training for the purpose of lowering percent fat or reducing a health risk. This is in sharp contrast to our earlier remarks about the prescription process.

Body Composition/Weight Control

The key to managing weight effectively is the balance between calories consumed and those expended. Quite simply, if clients were to expend more kilocalories (a unit of measure that represents 1,000 calories) than they consumed, then they would experience a loss of weight. Without exercise, however, it is very possible that this loss would be in lean body mass (i.e., muscle). Thus exercise is beneficial in three respects. First, it increases the number of kilocalories consumed. Second, exercise increases the chance that weight loss will be due to a reduction in percent fat, rather than lean body mass. And third, it increases the rate at which kilocalories are consumed for several hours after a workout has been completed. Obviously, the mode of activity makes a difference. Those activities that are continuous and vigorous and involve large muscle mass result in greater energy expenditure. Table 3.2 lists the energy requirements of some popular physical activities for a 130-lb and

**Table 3.2   Energy Requirements (kcal/min)
for Several Physical Activities**

Activity (kcal/min/kg)[a]	130 lb	163 lb
Calisthenics (.073)	4.3	5.4
Cycling		
5.5 mph (.064)	3.8	4.7
Golf (.085)	5.0	6.3
Racquetball (.143)	8.4	10.6
Running		
Cross-country (.163)	9.1	12.1
9 min/mi (.193)	11.4	14.3
7 min/mi (.228)	13.9	16.8
Swimming		
Slow crawl (.128)	7.6	9.5
Fast crawl (.156)	9.2	11.5
Tennis (.109)	6.4	8.1
Walking		
Normal (.080)	4.7	5.9
Weight training (.116)	6.8	8.6

[a]To calculate the kcal expenditure for subjects whose weight is not close to 130 or 163 lb, simply convert their body weight to kilograms and multiply this figure by the values given in the parentheses.

163-lb individual together with a formula in the legend for calculating the energy expenditure of these activities for individuals with other body weights.

To illustrate the potential practical significance of this information, consider the following example. Maria has both a need and a desire to lose 10 lb from her current weight of 130 lb. Given her experience in adult fitness, she knows that she has to expend approximately 3,500 extra kcal to burn 1 lb of fat. Thus, to lose 10 lb she will have to expend an additional 35,000 kcal. Her plan is as follows:

1. Each day, for 5 days a week, Maria decides to burn around 300 kcal through aerobic exercise. As an activity, Maria has decided to run for 30 min at a 9 min/mi pace. This will lead to a total daily expenditure of around 342 kcal (11.4 kcal/min × 30 min).

2. Every day she exercises, Maria makes a commitment to cut her dietary intake by 200 kcal. Thus, each day will result in a negative energy balance of 500 kcal (i.e., 300 kcal from exercise and 200 kcal from diet).
3. Weekends are considered vacation time; therefore, she indulges in desserts (200 kcal/day) and doesn't exercise!
4. By dividing 35,000 kcal by 500 (the number of calories expended through daily exercise and diet), Maria calculates that it will take 70 days to lose 10 lb. This means that in 14 weeks (70 ÷ 5) Maria will reach her desired goal!

Exercising for Disease Prevention

Although we are not trying to downplay the potential health benefits of an aerobic stimulus, research evidence suggests that mortality can be reduced simply by increasing the number of weekly kilocalories expended through physical activity. In other words, as is true of weight control, the *amount* of exercise has a significant impact on health, irrespective of work intensity.

Support for this position has come from extensive study of nearly 17,000 Harvard University alumni that was led by Dr. Ralph Paffenbarger, Jr. In his research, Paffenbarger and his colleagues (Paffenbarger, Wing, & Hyde, 1978) observed 1,413 deaths among Harvard alumni across a 12- to 16-year period. Although the causes were extremely varied, the important observation was that death rates due primarily to cardiovascular or respiratory disease increased among those who were inactive. As a matter of fact, the decline in death rates was more dramatic as the number of weekly kilocalories expended through walking, stair climbing, and playing a sport activity increased from 500 to 3,500 kcal. Although this decline was fairly steady from 500 to 2,000 kcal, the benefits were less marked after the 2,000 kcal mark.

From a health perspective these data suggest that one goal of fitness and wellness programs ought to be the promotion of all forms of physical activity. Unfortunately, there are times when fitness professionals develop an elitist attitude, promoting the view that to help, exercise has to hurt! This simply isn't the case.

Prescribing Exercise for Flexibility

The fact that flexibility remains as the final parameter of exercise prescription does not imply that it has low priority. To the contrary, lack of flexibility—that is, restricted range of motion in various body joints—or the failure to incorporate stretching into exercise routines can spell serious trouble for your clients. For example, restricted range of motion can detract from work efficiency or, as in the case of shortened hamstring muscles, may contribute to lower back pain. Flexibility also plays an important role in fitness, irrespective of goals individual clients may have. Pre-exercise stretching enhances the efficiency of working muscle, reduces soreness, and decreases the chance of injury. Moreover, without stretching, clients run the risk that long-term exercise habits will result in musculoskeletal dysfunction. When you think of it, this makes good sense. If specific muscle groups are shortened through chronic involvement in running or lifting weights, it's only natural to expect postural changes and restricted range of motion.

The challenge that you face is to make flexibility a priority for your clients. The tendency is for clients to perceive that their flexibility is just fine. However, flexibility is a prime target for unrealistic optimism. Most clients won't feel that they are vulnerable to disorders brought on by restricted range of motion. If flexibility does eventually become an issue of concern, they believe there will be plenty of time to act. The hitch in this thinking is that it may have taken clients months or even years to create a noticeable symptom for having neglected flexibility training. Unfortunately, the discomfort isn't going to go away overnight, and the easy way out may be for clients to rationalize, "Well, I guess it's time I recognize my limitations and quit these workouts. After all, I'm not getting any younger."

Increased flexibility isn't something that most of us are overly enthusiastic about. You have probably heard people envy the shape of another's hips, waist, or chest, but you just don't run across comments like, "Boy, I would give my eye tooth for flexibility like hers." So it is best to assume from the onset that clients aren't interested in flexibility. Take the time to develop a good sales pitch for why flexibility is needed, assess it in the routine evaluations, and have a few reminders around to emphasize its importance. Remember, flexibility naturally declines with age!

Static and Ballistic Stretching

Improved flexibility may involve change in the structure of the ligaments, tendons, and/or musculature and is accomplished either through static or ballistic stretching. Static methods are passive and thus do not involve movement. The muscle is put in a position where it is stretched, then held in this stationary position for 6 to

15 seconds or more. Sitting on the floor and bending your upper body forward as far as possible is an example of this approach. In contrast, ballistic stretching is active. An example would be repetitive toe touches.

Physiologists have presented a strong case for the superiority of static over ballistic methods because the action of ballistic stretching actually causes the muscle to tense. This is a reflex response that is designed to protect the muscle from injury. We should point out, however, that ballistic stretching can still increase flexibility, and many practitioners find it to be useful. Therefore, in Tables 3.3 and 3.4 we have provided some general guidelines regarding both approaches. We would be remiss, however, if we did not add that flexibility is improved best through distributed rather than mass training. In other words, the ideal situation would be to stretch several times a day for very short periods, rather than conducting all stretching activity in a single block of time. Although this is an unlikely schedule for most individuals, it may be very reasonable for those who are using flexibility as a method of combating a health problem such as lower back pain.

A Stage Approach to Exercise Prescription

Based on chapter 1 and the principles of exercise prescription, there are several stages to physical fitness training that cannot be ignored. These include the following:

1. Clarification of clients' needs and establishment of appropriate exercise.
2. Education on mode of exercise and underlying principles of the training regimen.
3. Specification of progress assessment intervals and feedback mechanisms.
4. Planning and implementation of client-specific motivational strategies.

Because much of the material presented to this point in the text fits nicely into the first two stages, let's briefly review these. Stages 3 and 4 will be understood only after you have read chapters 4, 5, and 6.

Table 3.3   Target Zones for Static Stretching

Intensity	Time	Frequency
A muscle must be stretched beyond its normal length.	Hold the stretch at least 6 to 15 s.	Stretch all muscle groups daily if possible.
You can use a partner, your own body weight, or another type of weight to help stretch the muscle.	For best results repeat each exercise three times each time you exercise.	

Note. From *The Ultimate Fitness Book* (p. 100) by C. Corbin and R. Lindsey, 1984, New York: Leisure Press. Copyright 1984 by Leisure Press. Reprinted by permission.

Table 3.4   Target Zones for Ballistic Stretching

Intensity	Time	Frequency
A muscle must be stretched beyond its normal length.	Bounce against the muscle 6 to 12 times.	Stretch all muscle groups daily if possible but at least three times weekly.
Slow, gentle bouncing or bobs using the motion of your body will help stretch the muscle.	For best results, do three sets of 6 to 12 repetitions each time you exercise.	

Note. From *The Ultimate Fitness Book* (p. 100) by C. Corbin and R. Lindsey, 1984, New York: Leisure Press. Copyright 1984 by Leisure Press. Reprinted by permission.

Clarify Client Needs to Establish Appropriate Exercise

The formal interview process allows you to determine exactly what the client expects from your exercise program. The caution here is twofold. First, clients may have misconceptions about what is required to produce a given effect or they may desire an outcome that they cannot possibly achieve. In either case, failure to resolve such discrepancies will guarantee increased problems with noncompliance and dropout. Whereas the task of changing misconceptions about exercise usually can be resolved by sharing information with clients on the physiology of fitness, modifying clients' expectations and needs can be tricky. Given that we have not addressed this latter issue in any detail, let's consider several options that are available during the interview process.

Discuss needs and expectations. First, there will be many times that you will find clients quite willing to accept modified outcomes from their involvement in exercise. Their needs and expectations are not as rigid as you might expect. But unless you take the time to discuss these changes at the onset of their programs, there is the chance of breeding disappointment and hostility. There will be clients who speak up and those who will not. When you attempt to explain that they should not have expected a particular type of change, they will want to know why they were not informed earlier. Feelings of entrapment are common, and they may accuse you of trying to milk their pocketbooks. The bottom line, for both you and the client—it is best that expected results are clearly worked out early in the prescription process.

Set attainable goals. Second, it may be that desired outcomes are realistic but not in the time frame presented by a client. In this case, goal setting is particularly powerful. Although the details of why goal setting works and what is involved in the process are a topic of chapter 5, at this time we would like to reflect on just one feature—goal setting is used to divide a seemingly monumental task into more manageable units. It is a common experience for people to begin exercise only to feel 1 or 2 weeks later that they were in worse shape than they thought. You may have even heard statements like, "I am never going to get where I want to be anyway, so why waste my time and yours?"

Monitor and renegotiate. Finally, clients may truly want changes in their physique that are impossible. Many times, however, there is a simple method of convincing people that they need to adopt a more realistic perspective. That is, present the ideal, a case in which someone has the right genes. Explain in detail the work required in this model to make the changes in question. Most of the time clients will not be willing to put in what it would take and will quickly modify their aspirations. If someone is really stubborn, then experience is the best teacher. The trick, however, is to catch clients before they become completely devastated by failure and try to renegotiate realistic objectives with them. You are going to lose a client every now and then. Nobody is perfect, but if you take clients' needs seriously and work at reaching realistic objectives, we think you will find a great deal of improvement in client compliance and satisfaction.

Educate Your Client!

Once you and your clients have defined desired outcomes and agreed upon a particular type of activity, the second step is to be sure clients understand (a) why they are involved in a specific program, (b) the principles underlying their prescription, and (c) that other clients' prescriptions may differ from theirs. Although we have discussed Parts (a) and (b) at some length, a brief comment is warranted on Part (c). Clients must be discouraged from comparing themselves to other individuals. Differences in such areas as fitness level or extent of disease, as well as phases of conditioning, invalidate social comparisons. Furthermore, clients have varied objectives that often require different approaches to prescription.

Additionally, in the education process, particular attention needs to be given to defining starter, growth, and maintenance phases. There should be no improvement objectives in the starter phase; clients should have a clear understanding of the rationale for this procedure. We also recommend that intensities for the growth phase of resistance training be assessed at the end of the starter phase. This will provide a familiarization period for specific exercises and result in the prescription of a much more effective training stimulus.

Summary

Too often exercise prescription is treated purely as a physiologically based process. And even as a physiological craft, most attention has been restricted to aerobic forms of training. It is time that we move beyond the limitations of a physiologic model and recognize the breadth of physical conditioning.

This chapter has been an attempt at instituting such change. We don't have all the answers, but there isn't a cookbook resolution to prescribing effective physical training. There is too much diversity in human behavior. However, if you take the principles seriously and integrate these with the information in the remainder of the text, you will place yourself in the best position possible to promote fitness.

Suggested Readings

American College of Sports Medicine. (1986). *Guidelines for exercise testing and prescription*. Philadelphia: Lea & Febiger.

Anderson, B. (1980). *Stretching*. Bolinas, CA: Shelter Publication.

Haskell, L. (1984). Overview: Health benefits of exercise. In J.D. Matarazzo, S.M. Weiss, J.A. Herd, N.E. Miller, & S.M. Weiss (Eds.), *Behavioral health: A handbook of health enhancement and disease prevention* (pp. 409-423). New York: John Wiley & Sons.

Pollock, M.L., Willmore, J.H., & Fox, S.M. (1984). *Exercise in health and disease*. Philadelphia: W.B. Saunders.

Ribisl, P.M. (1984). Developing an exercise prescription for health. In J.D. Matarazzo, S.M. Weiss, J.A. Herd, N.E. Miller, & S.M. Weiss (Eds.), *Behavioral health: A handbook of health enhancement and disease prevention* (pp. 448-466). New York: John Wiley & Sons.

Skinner, J.S. (Ed.). (1987). *Exercise testing and exercise prescription for special cases*. Philadelphia: Lea & Febiger.

Chapter

4

The Basics of Building and Repairing Commitment

Every chapter of this book concerns the concept of commitment and is intended to teach you something about clients' decisions to comply with fitness programs. If you think of the client as an engine in a car, your role may be likened to that of a spark plug for the ignition of client enthusiasm. It is no easy function. There may be little fuel in the cylinders, and no standard plug will make every engine function properly! Indeed, clients come to you with varied expectations and needs. However, as chapter 1 described, there is a coherent logic as to why clients comply with your requests. This common thread woven through all human behavior allows you to construct a systematic approach to building and repairing commitment.

In this chapter you will learn strategies designed to make exercise meaningful in the lives of your clients. Although the content is based on the framework presented in chapter 1, the approach has five broad objectives: to learn (a) how to tailor exercise programs so they are perceived to fulfill valued personal needs, (b) how to foster a belief that exercise is well worth the potential costs, (c) how to create a positive attitude during individual exercise sessions, (d) how to counter negative reactions during exercise, and (e) how to deal with the difficult client.

Initial judgments regarding appropriate principles to apply with any given client are largely determined by the evaluation session (chapter 2). It will become evident, however, that building and repairing commitment are ongoing, dynamic processes.

Guidelines for Securing Exercise Commitment

The most basic line of defense against noncompliance is to concentrate on promoting the positive side of specific fitness behaviors, particularly their reinforcing properties. This is especially valuable in recruiting new clientele; however, it also plays an important role in the interview process and continues to be a concern throughout the remaining months and years of clients' involvement. For those of us who are sold on health and fitness, a regular exercise program entails putting aside approximately 4 hr a week to enhance our physical and psychological well-being. However, nonexercisers may perceive that we are asking them to take time out of their busy day to engage in some form of primitive self-punishment. It is also entirely possible that potential clients do not value the outcomes of exercise or are unaware of the consequences of not being physically active.

This extreme negative view of exercise may be the exception, but it illustrates the type of mind-set you can run across. In addition, although many nonexercisers may share a positive attitude toward the general concept of physical fitness and health, they may not necessarily have a positive attitude toward the specific behaviors you are promoting. For example, a walk/jog program for aerobic fitness conducted at 7:30 a.m. may not be tempting at all! Don't be fooled when clients say, "I really think fitness is a great idea. I am so glad someone finally has something structured to offer!" They might quickly change their minds when they realize what being fit really involves! After all, exercise will require physical effort and time on their part. What then, does this first line of defense involve?

Many clients perceive we are asking them to engage in a primitive form of self-punishment.

Establish Positive Beliefs and Note Personal Needs

The first guideline is to establish several positive outcomes and features of the specific exercise behaviors. Furthermore, it is important that the outcomes you establish are specific, realistic, and objective by design (chapter 5).

Though the benefits of exercise have recently received a lot of good press, it does not guarantee that people have accepted these benefits as attainable or relevant in their lives. For some individuals, the costs of exercise in dollars, sweat, time, and so forth may be more salient than the benefits. In addition, the benefits promoted may have no meaning to particular individuals. For example, a lean nonexerciser is unlikely to be interested in the role of exercise as a means of losing weight. In fact, this belief often has negative connotations. A person who is normotensive will not be motivated to exercise to combat the threat of hypertension. In educating individuals about the benefits of exercise, you should emphasize those benefits that will have meaning to individual clients, explaining exactly what it will take to achieve these in terms of both time and effort.

It is also important to explain the significance of certain changes that take place with exercise. Why is it advantageous to have a low resting heart rate or a high HDL? Although this knowledge may be second nature to you, the nonexerciser may be unaware of these facts. Also, keep in mind that information you share with individuals should be designed to

- catch their attention,
- be simple, and
- be easy to remember and act upon.

For example, visual presentation of a clotted artery offers much more in the areas of attention and retention than mere description of the condition. In simplifying the beneficial role of HDL, you might depict this substance as a truck, picking up extra cholesterol and carting it to the liver for processing before that cholesterol can clog up the arteries. Similarly, plotting clients' data on a risk factor continuum with decreasing risk of cardiovascular disease on one end and increasing risk on the other is both simple and easy to remember. Don't rush through in a mechanical manner but personalize the discussion so it will hold clients' attention.

If one of the strategies you employ to promote fitness is positive health, you will want to consider the following (Rosenstock, 1974).

- The target population should be encouraged and educated to have concern for their general health.
- The audience should be made aware of their vulnerability to the development of specific health problems. The initial evaluation of clients (chapter 2) may provide you with ammunition to develop this point. If you are involved in large-scale recruitment of clients, it is advisable to administer health risk profiles or other screening devices to emphasize clients' perception of risk.
- The health problems must be viewed as carrying negative consequences. If the problem is severe, debilitating, and immediate, client response, at least in the short term, is more positive to exercise.
- The exercise behaviors you promote must be perceived as being effective in reducing susceptibility to the diseases or illnesses in question.

Meet Peripheral Goals

As a second guideline, appreciate the fact that exercise will not constitute a number one priority in most people's lives. You will want to include features or outcomes that make exercise more attractive.

For example, take time to highlight perks such as locker room facilities, saunas, and whirlpools. Many of our colleagues could not stomach the thought of such promotional campaigns. To them, such paraphernalia degrades the concepts of health and fitness. Don't fall prey to this belief. By offering such services, you are simply increasing the reinforcement value of exercise, a behavior that, for many people, doesn't have much inherent attraction.

Also, you may want to consider establishing tangible reinforcements for clients' exercise behavior. For example, given that clients attend a minimum number of sessions, several corporate enterprises now sponsor all or a portion of employee fitness memberships. In some cases, involvement in exercise results in a reduction in health care costs and/or leads to the accumulation of well days—vacation days earned by employee involvement in preventive health.

Another approach is to offer forms of exercise that are more appealing. There are numerous cases of women who despise running, yet are incredibly dedicated to aerobic dance or water aerobics. In fact, with certain groups you may want to offer a free trial session. When at all possible get potential clients behaviorally involved.

You will discover that a number of people join fitness facilities for reasons other than exercise. Some may be looking for a place to meet people. Others may be seeking a cure for their tension headaches, disenchantment with life, or smoking behavior. Exercise itself cannot meet all these needs; however, supplying relevant services, or at least information on how clients may satisfy these needs, will benefit your facility by giving it an image of concern for the total health of its clientele. Contracts can be made with outside organizations or individuals so that on-site programs are available in smoking cessation, stress management, or weight reduction. Most fitness facilities are already equipped to offer regular blood pressure screening, and in many centers, staff members are qualified to offer seminars on various health topics ranging from nutrition to the proper selection of footwear for different sports.

In a related example, the manager of a corporate fitness facility in New York City approached a large corporate client and offered to do several training seminars for their employees before a corporate challenge road race. The seminars covered training principles, warm-up and cool-down procedures, proper clothes and shoes, and racing strategies. The information was well received, resulted in an increased membership for the facility, and improved attendance for some of its members who had slacked off a bit. By linking exercise to the pursuit of peripheral interests, you can strengthen commitment to exercise.

As a final comment in this section, it is worth recalling the common needs that were identified in chapter 1. Most people are in the pursuit of mastery, attention, recognition, social approval, health security, or social interaction. Creating outcomes and/or features in your program that permit individuals to satisfy these needs can only increase the value that clients attribute to it.

Counter Negative Beliefs and Present Consequences of Not Exercising

A third guideline is to counter negative beliefs associated with specific exercise behavior and to emphasize the negative consequences of not exercising (Ajzen & Fishbein, 1980). Many of the negative beliefs you encounter are really fallacies. Two examples: Exercise has a masculinizing effect on women, and it predisposes one to arthritis later in life. Neither is true. In fact, exercise is now prescribed for certain patients who have arthritis. Of course, there are certain negative aspects of exercise. It does take time out of your day, and there are times when you may be able to name nine other things you would rather be doing. Most often, however, these beliefs can be restructured with a little thought. As an example, rather than dwelling on the fact that exercise is consuming valuable time during your day, you may consider the fact that it actually enhances daily output. When you add to this improved health and in most cases fewer sick days, time dedicated to fitness is well spent.

Similarly, educate clients on the negative consequences of not exercising (Ajzen & Fishbein, 1980). A person may be lean now, but does that individual know that with every passing year the ratio of lean body tissue to fat is changing in favor of the fat? If diet remains stable, there is no way to stop this process except with exercise. Do women know that lack of physical activity is a risk factor in osteoporosis? This type of information can prove to be the cornerstone in building commitment. As mentioned above, however, the consequences of not exercising have to be viewed negatively by clients. They must be led to recognize their vulnerability to the consequences in question.

Although some of this information can be passed along to potential clients in recruiting sessions or during the interview process, it can also be effectively transmitted through brochures, posters, and even check stuffers on payday! For instance, prior to the grand opening of an in-house fitness facility, AT&T primed its employees (and potential clients) with all sorts of health information, stressing the role of exercise in improving health and dispelling exercise fallacies like "no pain, no gain." AT&T found that by educating its employees, it increased interest and membership in its fitness facility and has continued to serve its members successfully.

Making the Most of Social Influence

An important ingredient in motivating people to become physically active is social influence (Andrew et al., 1981). This section outlines ways to enhance that support, a fourth guideline to building commitment to exercise.

Help clients plan social influence.   Because exercise requires a time commitment, it may interfere with family responsibilities, peer interaction, or business schedules. Unless significant others know about and support the arrangements made for physical fitness conditioning, conflicts are bound to arise. Lack of social support is a frequently cited precursor to noncompliance. Thus communication between clients and significant others is essential if social influence is to work for rather than against a lifestyle that includes a regular fitness program. Clients need to be encouraged to identify those who will and will not support their exercise habit and how this will occur. In addition, it is useful to determine the extent to which clients' behavior is influenced by a particular social force. For example, in attempting to get mill workers to join a corporate fitness program, one exercise specialist decided to use the influential verbal support of the company president. As it turned out, however, the workers were disgruntled with this particular executive's behavior, and the message had the opposite effect! So, be sure that the client in question is motivated positively by a given significant other.

Subsequently, you should work toward developing active support from those who are willing to help. For example, if a friend or spouse expresses an interest in your progress and takes the time to pat you on the back, it is going to be much more potent in motivating you to continue than silent or implicit support. We remember a student who sensed that her roommate was supportive of her weight loss, but she never actually received any overt signs. We developed a simple strategy for more effective support. The girl was asked how her roommate could demonstrate her support. She decided that the best form of support would be for her roommate not to eat sweets in front of her and to agree to help in buying the right foods. The request was made, the roommate was excited to be a part of the weight control program, and the success 6 months later was remarkable. The girl lost 30 lb! The point is that social influence should be planned. Don't rely on chance.

Helping clients identify those people who are a hindrance may enable you to plan strategies to prevent problems before they occur. In one case we had a client who scheduled his exercise at a certain time each day and would slip out of the office with a feeling of guilt, never telling anyone where he was going. His perception was that office personnel would resent his taking time out from work to exercise. More than once his secretary caught him leaving the office and assertively announced an appointment that had come up just that morning. Finally, this client realized the necessity of informing his secretary about his workouts. Not only was she supportive of the idea, but together they managed to schedule his exercise sessions on a weekly basis, treating that time as a regular appointment. The support from significant others needs to be not only moral support, but physical support in the adjustment of schedules and plans.

Organize events for clients, family, and friends. One way to encourage social support for your exercisers is to organize events to which they can bring their families or friends. For example, we know of an employee wellness program that advocates employees' bringing their families in for the regular cholesterol screenings. Making cholesterol reduction a family affair may be contributing to the decreases that have been observed in employee cholesterol levels. Our cardiac rehabilitation program has regularly scheduled social events so that family and friends of patients can meet each other and perhaps share some of the adjustments they have made as a result of their parent or spouse's heart disease. Again, those patients whose families actively participate in these events are the same ones who come regularly to the program and are the first to sing its praises.

Encourage a sense of belonging. In addition to obtaining support from significant nonexercisers, you should be aware of motivational factors that stem from group dynamics at the center. Corporate fitness programs often rely on these factors to assure their program's success; however, several require planning. For instance, identification with a group inspires a commitment to that group, but it also requires that a person feel comfortable with the group. Introducing newcomers on the exercise floor or in the locker room will make them feel more at home and a part of things. Once a feeling of belonging has been established, clients are more likely to encourage and support one another. After exercising faithfully for 6 months at about the same time three times per week, one of our clients came up to us glowing with pride. One of the clients who also exercised at that time had congratulated her on her hard work and complimented her on her weight loss. That praise meant more to her than anything we could have said.

Foster **positive** *competition.* Introducing a little competition into a group can also be a catalyst to better adherence, although for some it may be sufficient reason to quit! The key is to use competition as a secondary goal to having fun. You aren't trying to create another Olympic event. For example, establishing teams to compete for total monthly mileage can foster support among team members. At a major hospital in the southeastern United States, a weight loss contest was organized around decreased consumption of calories and increased exercise. It was a major success in large part because two teams competed for the total number of pounds lost over a 3-month period.

In summary, the potential motivational power of social influence remains largely untapped, and nonsupport, which is often a misperception, continues to play a major role in noncompliance. In developing strategies to address this area, you have several options:

- You can work together with the client to identify what should be done with whom to properly shape social influence.
- You can attempt to acquire support for your programs from business and industry and have them communicate their position directly to employees.
- You can involve clients' significant others in events that encourage positive social influence.
- You can use social forces within the exercise setting to enhance positive outcomes.

Any or all of these options will help you help your clients build their commitments to exercise.

Techniques for Building and Repairing Commitment

Establishing and maintaining commitment is not a problem exclusive to fitness promotion; most organizations are faced with this challenge. Historically, solutions to the enigma of creating commitment to an activity or group have been varied and not always pleasant. For example, fraternities and military establishments have traditionally employed long and difficult orientation periods with tasks that humiliate and exhaust their potential members. Perhaps you could try similar approaches to fitness promotion. Drag your clients into the weight room for the first 3 weeks and really force them through tough multiple sets or push them aerobically with interval training until they wheeze and drop. Sound ludicrous?

Of course it is! You don't want to eliminate the weak, promote obsessiveness with physical activity, or acquire a reputation as a center for fanatics. You should neither expect that most clients will view exercise as their number one priority nor attempt to convince them that it should be. In addition to being unhealthy, the goal of making everyone a fanatic is as unrealistic as the beginning exerciser who has the lofty goal of running a marathon after training for just 6 months.

In the final sections of this chapter, you will be introduced to a variety of techniques that have been proven useful in both building and repairing commitment to fitness. Although several of them can be incorporated into standard practice, many are best viewed as options that will vary in effectiveness for different individuals.

Getting the Hesitant Client Started: Shaping

Once you have captured the attention of hesitant clients, you will want to be very cautious about how you introduce them to exercise. One useful approach is *shaping*, which is similar to goal setting (Martin & Dubbert, 1984). It assumes that at the onset of a fitness program some clients will view the activity you introduce, through either observation or discussion, as too demanding or complex. Therefore, it is necessary to establish a series of clear-cut steps that gradually move these clients toward a program of regular exercise.

Although this may sound identical to the starter phase of an exercise prescription, early steps of shaping may actually involve behaviors that precede any exercise. For example, at a corporate fitness program in New York City, clients' first step is simply to make an appointment for an interview and submaximal fitness test. The second step involves scheduling an orientation session during which clients are familiarized with exercise equipment. At the completion of this orientation, with the help of their exercise leaders, clients are encouraged to plan three exercise sessions for the upcoming week. These will be very low-level, starter-phase exercise bouts. At each of these sessions, clients will work with exercise leaders to set up specific exercise goals that they believe they can meet. The goals may consist of a certain number of minutes on the treadmill or the addition of another resistance training station. This sequence of events eventually culminates in clients committing themselves to a 3-day-a-week exercise prescription that will lead to desired change in specified fitness parameters. Such a procedure builds confidence, insures that clients do not incur early overuse injuries or excessive soreness, and personalizes the prescription. All indications would suggest that this use of shaping is successful in enhancing 3-month attendance rates.

The first rule in shaping is to start with behaviors that are simple enough for clients to perform easily. In the example just described, the initial required behavior was making an appointment to talk with someone and to participate in a submaximal bicycle test. Whatever the required behavior, it should be accompanied by a considerable amount of reinforcement. Praise, feedback on performance, or something as simple as a membership card would serve nicely. Remember, our primary goal is to make exercise a habit. For this reason we want to be sure that programs worked out for beginning exercisers are within their comfort zone, not too difficult but still challenging. As mentioned in chapter 3, RPE and Feeling Scales are helpful in determining appropriate exercise levels at any time, but especially during these first few weeks.

Creating Positive Exercise Experiences

In the beginning of this chapter we addressed the promotion of positive beliefs, refuting fallacies associated with exercise, and educating clients to the benefits of physical activity. Of equal importance is that during exercise itself clients learn to accentuate the positive and downplay the negative. The following are several methods designed to achieve this end.

Point out the positives.   For the novice, it is only natural that the costs of exercise are apt to be more salient than the benefits. After all, many of the positive effects of exercise are long-term (e.g., increased muscle tone, better figure), whereas several potential negative features of exercise are immediate and can have a high frequency of occurrence (e.g., muscle soreness, sweating, and the sacrifice of time). Thus, along with insuring that clients' exercise programs are within their comfort zones, clients must be taught to interpret some of the symptoms associated with exercise as positive signs of a good workout. They must be encouraged to approach exercise consistently with a favorable attitude.

Reinforce clients by complimenting them on their appearance as they are laboring during physical work. For example, to change attitudes toward a potentially negative physical effect such as sweat, present a brief explanation of the function of sweating in the regulation of body temperature. We once had a client who enjoyed exercise, yet constantly expressed guilt for taking time away from her responsibilities both at work and at home. With minimal effort on our part, she was convinced to view exercise as a time-out that she had earned. If anyone objected, she was urged to think in terms of their unfairness or lack of understanding and not her failure to accept responsibility . After this brief intervention, she found exercise to be more relaxing.

Share your enthusiasm.   Another strategy for maintaining a good attitude is to help clients focus on the positive aspects of a single exercise session as they warm up. For instance, remind them of the number of calories they will be burning, or mention how nice it is to shed business clothes for a brief spell, and emphasize how relaxed they will feel when they complete their session. By planting these seeds, you will find that clients adopt a more enthusiastic frame of mind.

Your own enthusiasm and positive thinking can be very powerful. To prove this to yourself, try this little experiment. During stress testing, as clients get close to maximum effort, ask one sample group of clients,"Are you ready to come off?" And to another say, "You are doing a great job! Can you go another minute?" We bet you will find, as we have, that when you ask people if they are ready to quit, 80% of the time or better they will. On the other hand, if they are reinforced and asked if they can go longer, most will respond, "Yes." Positive mind-sets not only increase client enthusiasm, but also increase client output, which means that goals will be achieved more quickly, making exercise a more rewarding event.

It is impossible for you to set the proper mind-set every time a client exercises. If you are serious about creating a positive environment, however, it will not be long before clients themselves act as educational therapists. They will encourage one another and may actually understand and repair a fellow participant's negative thinking more effectively than you can. The end result is that you create strong bonds of social influence.

Remember interview information.   It is important to take note of the labels clients use to describe themselves during the interview and other informal interactions. These can be telltale signs of people who require special attention. Examples are clients who refer to themselves as "unathletic" or who have never been "physical fitness oriented." Getting started on the right foot is critical. Encourage your clients to be generous in evaluating their performance and not to be too hard on themselves. Suggest that they pat themselves on the back often—otherwise they may become their own worst enemy.

Teaching Self-Monitoring and Self-Reinforcement

All of us are at times unaware of what we say to ourselves and how we feel. Even though these thoughts and feelings are not part of conscious awareness, they do influence how we think, feel, and act. This built-in response is designed to make life more spontaneous, conserving our mental and physical energies.

Unfortunately, this automatic pilot can be destructive. In the case of your clients, they may be unwittingly short-circuiting their own efforts to become physically active. In other words, through negative private self-talk and emotion they gradually eat away at their self-motivation. These people eventually quit. Self-monitoring and self-reinforcement are two techniques that can be used to deal with this problem (Taylor, 1986).

Self-monitoring.   Self-monitoring can be used during the course of a day or limited to an exercise session. For example, if used in the latter context, you would ask clients to pay close attention to every detail of a workout from beginning to end. Have them record every thought, feeling, and action. The result will be a script of what really goes on in the mind of each client. Self-monitoring is normally reserved for use with clients who are experiencing difficulties, and you will gain valuable insight into the origin of their problems. In a number of cases, we have had clients immediately recognize a pattern of negative thinking and/or the absence of any self-reinforcement. It can be a very powerful incentive to change behavior.

Self-reinforcement.   You and the client can use the self-monitoring record to plan alternative lines of thinking or possibly modify the mode of exercise. It is also useful to incorporate self-reinforcement for playing out the new script. For a cardiac patient named Pat, a bright red dot was placed on the upper right corner of her running watch. She was told that this dot represented the "new me," the person in the revised script who didn't get down on herself. Each time Pat performed an agreed upon change in her exercise behavior, she was instructed to glance at the red dot as a way of complimenting herself. It was not long before Pat noted that each subsequent time she looked at the red dot, it seemed to get brighter—a simple symbol had suddenly acquired strong personal meaning.

Countering the Discomforts of Exercise

Exercise can have associated discomforts, and this is particularly true for individuals who are not physically conditioned (the major portion of American society). Even for those who do exercise, there is a substantial group that does so in spite of the physical discomfort. If you asked these individuals why they exercise, they would probably respond, "Well, if I ever did stop running, I'd have to quit eating or else just get fat!"

Another consideration in improving compliance is to reduce or eliminate unpleasant cues associated with the discomforts of exercise. Three valuable methods available to accomplish this objective are (a) dissociation, (b) relaxation, and (c) reinterpretation (Kenney, Rejeski, & Messier, 1987).

Dissociation.   Dissociation is based on the principle that one can attend to only a limited number of stimuli at any given moment. Thus dissociative tasks are designed to distract individuals' attention away from sensations produced by exercise. You have probably used this technique without knowing its technical label. Perhaps the most widely used dissociative tool is music. A variety of cassette tapes are now marketed exclusively with walking and jogging in mind. We recall one client whose children gave him a portable cassette recorder for his birthday. At first, he joked about the idea of using this crutch, but before long he found that exercise was more enjoyable with it. He also achieved greater output.

Things like composing a letter in your head, exercising on a wooded trail, or daydreaming can serve the same function. Have you ever noticed how much your clients enjoy your conversation while they are exercising? You are their distraction!

In designing and implementing dissociative tasks, you should consider the following points. First, the task has to be relevant and enjoyable to the client. The use of earphones can make the task more enjoyable and serve a dual purpose. Aside from delivering the music, they keep the person locked into the dissociative mode by shutting out distractions.

Second, the more involved the client is in the task the better. Have you ever become engaged in an intense discussion and found that you lost track of time? Your level of involvement distracted you from any other considerations. This is true for exercise as well.

Third, it is best to keep dissociative tasks constructive in nature to support a commitment to positive thinking. You may find that negatively oriented people choose to dissociate using negative content. And fourth, the use of distraction as a form of coping requires a little common sense. For example, it would be inadvisable to suggest dissociation for use by those who run on public roads. This would dampen or perhaps totally block out clients' sensitivity to important external cues. Also, it is not recommended for clients in cardiac rehabilitation and others who, for medical reasons, must pay close attention to physical symptoms.

Although a technique like dissociation may appear obvious, you will come across people who are oblivious to the efficacy of music, daydreams, or other forms of distraction that can make their exercise more enjoyable. Clue them in and hopefully you will be supplying them with an effective buffer against noncompliance.

Relaxation.   Muscular tension in the working muscles is a natural by-product of exercise; however, it is also true that many novice exercisers tend to have unwanted tension in nonworking muscles. This excess muscle activity can actually work against desired movement patterns or can be expressed in the bracing of adjacent body segments, both of which reduce efficiency and intensify feelings of exertion. Although some of this unwanted muscular tension is due to lack of skill with movement patterns, it is likely that a portion of it is tension that clients bring to the exercise setting from work or home.

To counter these effects, consider two separate methods. First, educate clients on proper exercise technique, taking opportunities

You'll come across people who are oblivious to the efficacy of enjoyable distractions.

during activity to make comments to specific individuals. For example, if you have a treadmill and a large mirror, use them to allow clients to see the differences you are talking about. A second strategy is to incorporate a modified relaxation training session into daily warm-ups. We suggest *modified* because you will not have the time to get clients into full-blown relaxation programs.

One way to modify relaxation training is first to target muscle groups rather than specific muscles. For example, treat the legs as one unit, the arms as a second, the torso as a third, and the neck and face as a fourth. The relaxation training is planned for the first 5 min of the warm-up period. Clients should lie down on their backs with their arms placed comfortably by their sides. One at a time, each muscle group is contracted isometrically at a moderate intensity for 10 s. Instruct clients to release the tension, saying as they do so, "Let all the tension go." Relax passively for 20 s or so and then proceed on to the second group. Encourage clients to notice the difference between a contracted and a relaxed state and urge them to attempt to achieve the relaxed feeling in nonworking muscles (e.g., muscles of neck or hands) during exercise.

In addition to priming clients in the concept of relaxed muscles, you can use this period of time to establish positive pre-exercise mind-sets. For example, at the end of the active muscle phase for the four groups, you can ask clients to take a few moments to think about the importance of this time for their own personal health and well-being. Be enthusiastic and challenge the clients to try to stir up some good feelings. Use some variety from one session to another. Prior to relaxation, you may want to give clients a few moments to think of something pleasing, which they can then focus on when asked to do so later.

If this modified relaxation training is planned as a regular part of the warm-up, it should become habitual, and the effects will increase over time. We should add that, in our cardiac rehabilitation program, relaxation training has also been integrated into the cooldown phase of exercise. This is a passive form of relaxation—no attempt is made to contract muscles. One real plus in using relaxation at this point is that it allows clients a brief opportunity to appreciate the calming influence of exercise. Once again you can take this opportunity to reinforce those good feelings!

Reinterpretation.   A final strategy for combating the discomfort of exercise is to use some form of reinterpretation. Put simply, take the unpleasant symptoms of exercise and convert them to cues that signify something pleasant. This concept was introduced previously in the discussion about changing reactions to something as basic as sweating. A clearer example comes to us from a friend who is a bodybuilder. Humphrey recently had surgery on his clavicle and is recovering in physical therapy. He had a mild setback, which he explained like this:

When I started to feel a little stronger I started to push myself in therapy. You know, ordinarily muscular discomfort is a sought-after feeling for the bodybuilder, because that is when you really make the progress. Feeling the effects of muscular overload normally has a positive influence on me. Well, I guess I did a little damage! I suppose for now, I had better learn to reinterpret discomfort as something bad.

If you are going to use this technique, you will soon learn that it does not work with everyone, and, as in the example of Humphrey, reinterpretation can be harmful. In our experience, it seems to be most effective if a person feels either neutral or somewhat positive about the discomfort at the start. Thus reinterpretation may be limited to situations in which you are trying to enhance the performance of someone who is already doing fairly well. Experiment a little with the technique, and if it doesn't work you always have other options available to you.

One last point. A question that invariably crops up is, "Should clients be encouraged to push through discomfort barriers? Aren't you increasing the possibility of injury?" What we are promoting is the use of these techniques to manage the discomfort associated with sound exercise prescriptions. We do not support their indiscriminate use with untrained individuals to extend maximal performance.

Encouraging Regular Attendance

One of the most effective techniques for making exercise a habit is to encourage clients to set aside a specific time each day and to maintain this schedule from week to week. If 4:00 p.m. on Monday, Wednesday, and Friday is designated as an exercise break for a particular client, then you increase the chances that significant others will remember and accept this. For the client, there is no decision to be made—it is exercise time! In fact, in the early phases of clients' exercise programs, you might advise them to leave reminders around that a certain day and block of time has been reserved for exercise. Such reminders might include leaving eye-catching notes/symbols on calendars and keeping exercise gear in a highly visible location. Discuss alternative plans for days when the schedule may have to be adjusted unexpectedly. It is good to plan in a little flexibility.

Exercisers should be taught how to recognize, avoid, and react to high risk situations. For example, for a business executive, travel can pose a continued threat to regular exercise. The best solution is to locate hotels with exercise facilities. However, business trips are often brief and so highly structured that getting to exercise facilities may be problematic. In this case, have preprogrammed on-the-road maintenance programs consisting of doing calisthenics, jumping rope, or running in place for 20 min in the hotel room prior to a morning or evening shower.

When clients return from a trip and it is clear that they made a special effort to schedule some exercise, take time to compliment them and encourage them to enter this event into exercise logs. Simple interventions such as this make a big difference in overall enthusiasm and compliance rates. Let's explore some of the more common reasons clients have for missing exercise and what you can do to help them improve or maintain their attendance.

Discuss inevitable conflicts and slips.   In stressing the importance of regular attendance with novice exercisers, you must also discuss the inevitability of adherence slips. Your clients must understand that a slip in attendance does not imply failure. Exercise does not operate on an all-or-none principle, though frequent periods of abstinence can place clients at risk for failure. However, even the best laid plans are often disrupted. In preparing for chronic absenteeism, you will need to develop a system for contacting individuals. In our cardiac rehabilitation program, which meets three times a week, patients who miss two consecutive program days are contacted by phone. At one large corporate fitness program, a 2-week interval is allowed to pass before phoning clients. Inform clients about your procedures during the initial interview and ask where they can be contacted if you should need to do so.

Certain clients may resent being contacted at work. If they do give a business phone extension, however, you may be forced to leave messages with secretaries rather than talking directly with clients. Although this is less desirable, at least the client receives some form of reminder, and often the secretary can give you an idea as to where the client has been.

When clients have been absent for an extended period, set up an appointment for reevaluation of their program and assure them that they will not have to start all over again. The sooner you can get them to return the better! At the very least, welcome returning exercisers and make a point to adjust their workouts appropriately. Overenthusiasm or attempts to catch up after a layoff can result in injury or excessive muscular soreness, consequences that only spell further trouble.

Using the decision balance sheet.   There are times when it is apparent that absenteeism is due to waning commitment and that further problems are inevitable. In these situations, you may find it useful to use a *decision balance sheet*, a technique normally used to strengthen the initial decision to change behavior (Wankel & Thompson, 1977). This procedure requires that clients reevaluate, either verbally or in writing, the benefits and costs of their participation in your fitness program. This may reveal that some re-education is required or suggest the need for specific intervention. Perhaps a change of time or prescription is indicated. Maybe there is an urgency to repair social support networks. At times, simply asking clients to rethink why they were trying to establish a program of fitness in the first place is sufficient motivation to trigger a healthy restart.

You might think that the cost of participation would show up on the decision balance sheet as a benefit of dropping out, but this is not always the case. Thus, in conducting the decision balance process, you should instruct clients to include the costs and benefits of not performing the behavior as well. Typical costs might be an increased risk for cardiovascular disease, the inability to control weight, or loss of muscle tone, whereas benefits might include the loss of guilt or annoyance from interruption in the workday.

The following is an example of how to make practical use of the decision balance sheet. Becky had been an avid fan of aerobic training (jogging) for almost 6 weeks. From the very beginning of her involvement in the health club she exhibited a lot of interest and dedication, exercising four times each week. However, during Becky's 7th week of participation her schedule was interrupted for 5 days due to a business trip, and upon her return she came to aerobics only once the following week. Immediately, Becky was contacted by phone to find out what was keeping her from the program. Was she ill, discouraged, or just too busy? In an effort to clarify the problem, the exercise leader framed her telephone interaction within the context of a decision balance sheet (see Tables 4.1 and 4.2).

Table 4.1   Decision Balance Sheet: Participation

Benefits	Costs
Relaxation	Shin splints
Toned muscles	Loss of noon lunch
More energy at end of day	

Table 4.2   Decision Balance Sheet: Nonparticipation

Benefits	Costs
Lack of discomfort	Gain in weight
Return to noon lunches	Stress at end of day
Time to run errands	Potential loss of friends
A little extra money to spend	

In the course of the discussion, Becky noted that she was suffering from shin splints as a result of aerobics and that the business trip provided immediate relief. She also remarked that having some spare time during the day allowed her to take longer lunch breaks and to complete errands that would otherwise have to wait for the weekend. On the other hand, Becky was still very concerned about her weight and lack of muscular tone. She also indicated that since she had quit aerobics, she actually felt more stressed and fatigued at the end of her workday. In contemplating these costs and benefits, Becky decided that she really did want to be involved in some type of program. With the assistance of her exercise leader, Becky returned to lunchtime aerobics, but only two times each week. Oftentimes she resorted to brisk walking rather than jogging. Becky also exercised one other time weekly, but on a flexible schedule where she varied the activity, usually choosing to ride the bicycle or swim. Additionally, Becky was given specific exercises to strengthen her calf muscles, and more time was spent on flexibility. Becky returned with her initial enthusiasm and continues to be a dedicated exerciser.

Initiate behavioral contracting.   A final approach in dealing with the difficult client makes use of social influence and/or increases the costs of noncompliance. This approach is known as behavioral contracting (Epstein, Wing, Thompson, and Griffin, 1980). A behavioral contract is a written agreement binding two people. Common units consist of you and the client, two clients, or a client and spouse. The behavior to be changed is clearly and objectively defined within the contract so one can easily determine when it occurs. For example, the required behavior may be defined as aerobic exercise of a specific intensity performed for 30 min, three times a week for 3 months. Moreover, the consequences of performing and not performing the behavior must be clearly outlined. In a sample contract, an 85% compliance rate across the 3 months might be rewarded by a husband's agreeing to do the evening dishes for 3 months, whereas failure to fulfill the contract might mean that the husband gets a 10-min back rub for the same interval. You can also use money and tangible goods such as running shoes or the free use of some additional service. However, behavioral contracts seem to be more fun and influential when two people engage in behavior modification. We knew of a secretary who gave up a day of smoking in the office for every day her boss exercised. This contract benefited both parties; the boss ended up with a daily commitment to exercise and the secretary quit smoking completely!

Clearly, one of the advantages of this technique is that clients play a major role in the planning of their contracts. This emphasizes the development of personal control (chapters 1 and 2). Furthermore, in making a contract with another person, the client experiences self-presentation effects; that is, the individual is motivated by the desire to look good in the eyes of someone they admire. Finally, a contract elicits a formal commitment to perform a particular behavior, making it that much more difficult to break. This can be especially influential for those in business who deal with contracts regularly.

Several cautions are issued in using behavioral contracting. First, participants must have the skills or equipment necessary to perform the desired behaviors. Second, there must be a specific time period for which the contract is valid, and an objective measure of performance is necessary. And third, in designing the contract, you must take precautions to insure that participants will not engage in unhealthy practices to meet stated requirements. For example, if in the previous sample contract the requirement had been written as 1½ hr of aerobic exercise weekly, it is conceivable that a client might elect to do this all in one day! Used correctly, contracting can be a very effective motivational technique, using an often ignored resource—social influence.

Summary

Motivation is a process that needs to be treated as a system rather than a series of strategies applied indiscriminately. Commitment to exercise will fluctuate as other appointments and responsibilities take priority. In trying to help you learn how to build and repair commitment, we emphasized the role of beliefs and personal needs, supplying a number of techniques that can directly influence these.

You must remember that clients' apparent commitment in the initial interview may be tempered by the actual exercise experience.

Also, goals may be met or forces that are motivating at one point may lose their impact at some later time. In order to keep commitment strong, you will need to reevaluate it regularly. If you treat compliance as an ongoing battle, and if you come back to the basic principles of human behavior (chapter 1), you will greatly increase your chances of emerging victorious.

Finally, be mindful that you will be working with a variety of individuals, from novices to veterans. What works for one may not work for another. Chapter 5 details the principles of goal setting and feedback. In conjunction with what you have learned in this chapter, we think you will better understand what we mean by individual programming and how with some effort you can respond to a wide range of clientele.

Suggested Readings

Ajzen, I., & Fishbein, M. (1980). *Understanding attitudes and predicting social behavior.* Englewood Cliffs, NJ: Prentice-Hall.

Wankel, L.M. (1980). Involvement in vigorous physical activity: Considerations for enhancing self-motivation. In R.R. Danielson & K.F. Danielson (Eds.), *Fitness motivation: Proceedings of the Geneva Park Workshop* (pp. 18-32). Toronto, ON: Orcol Publications.

Wankel, L.M. (1981, August). *Social psychological dimensions of physical activity involvement.* Paper presented at the Third Canadian Congress on Leisure Research, University of Alberta, Edmonton.

Setting Goals and Providing Feedback

Goal setting and feedback are indispensable motivational strategies for use with clients in fitness settings. You may think that this is old news and decide to skip this chapter. Please don't! Over the past 5 years we have come to understand the complexity of these two strategies. We have learned through our mistakes and offer the benefit of this knowledge to you. It takes careful planning to make the most of goal setting and feedback, but you will find that both are irreplaceable components of successful programming when used properly.

This chapter begins with a discussion of why goal setting works. You will learn the things that are necessary for goal setting to be effective, and this will greatly enhance your ability to counter complications that occur. The chapter then discusses how to get the most out of your goal-setting programs. Finally, special attention will be focused on feedback. The chapter distinguishes between specific and objective feedback and lists some of the major stumbling blocks in communicating feedback. Goal setting and feedback are closely related, and the ineffectiveness of one the other can easily destroy the value of both. We will provide seven guidelines for setting goals and giving feedback.

Why Goal Setting Works

In a previous section on the client interview, we discussed the necessity for fitness programs to take a client-centered approach; that is, interventions should be based on individual preferences and needs. In the next section, we will ask you to put yourself in your client's place for a moment.

Meeting Client Needs

Suppose your purpose in joining a fitness program was to lose 15 lb. You would probably feel much more enthusiastic about exercise training or other behavior change if weight loss were an explicit goal and if program personnel also made your weight loss their number one concern. This simple procedure gives you an initial impression that someone is listening and responding to your needs as an individual. Thus goal setting functions much like a contract, clarifying expected outcomes and reassuring the client of the fitness center's commitment to individually tailored programs.

Goal setting can also help to alter unrealistic or inappropriate expectations. For example, most clients do not understand the principles of exercise prescription and may expect changes to occur more quickly than is physiologically possible. Even the term *fitness* is quite vague. Also, outcomes need to be clearly stated because there is a good deal of specificity to training. Don't be afraid to recheck clients' comprehension. For example, after explaining the anticipated effects from an aerobic program, you might say something like, "Now you realize that this probably isn't going to improve your golf game." If they are surprised by this statement, they obviously have not understood your explanation.

Making Objectives Manageable

For years now we have watched individuals of all ages begin and quit fitness programs. At some point in your career, you will come to understand that a significant factor in attrition is disappointment or discouragement with progress. Let's face it, all of us want immediate results. If your goal is to gain muscle mass, then the mirror better reflect a satisfying change. However, fitness-related goals do not happen overnight. They require considerable effort and time. For most clients, your only hope will be to establish short-term intermediate goals, rather than emphasizing long-term objectives. Without the short-term goal, there is a good chance many clients will perceive the task as overwhelming, become discouraged, and quit.

The trick is to draw clients' focus away from final endpoints—the size-5 dress or that sleek, fit appearance. Help them to be oriented toward intermediate steps that are realistic—a principle result of sound goal setting. This is not to say that long-term goals have no value. The point is, goal setting needs to be viewed much like a ladder with an emphasis placed on reasonable distances between rungs. Later in this chapter we will outline a practical method of linking these intermediate goals to long-term objectives.

Present a Clear Vision of the Road to Success

A side effect of orienting clients toward manageable goals is that they begin to understand the sequence involved in realizing their long-term objectives. You may find it very helpful to use the analogy of a road map. Initially, clients will have a specific destination in mind, and there will be several available routes to reach this objective. If they encounter an impasse along the way, then it may be necessary to make alterations in travel plans.

Let's examine a concrete example. Not long ago, J.R. set out to lose 10 lb through diet and exercise. This was to be accomplished within a 2-month period. He knew at the beginning that his plan to cut back on desserts would be no easy task, but the 10-lb goal remained foremost in his mind. In the unlikely event that this course of action did not work out, the possibility was discussed of dropping the diet constraint and shedding the weight totally through increased caloric expenditure—exercise. One week after initiation of the program, J. R.'s diet broke down, and a reassessment was necessary. It was decided that biweekly desserts would be allowed in combination with the proper exercise program, which should lead to the desired weight loss in about 4 months. J.R. is on a new road now, content and every bit as motivated to regain his former sleek appearance. The critical point in this case is that goal setting provided alternative and acceptable behavior for reaching desired goals. In the absence of a specific progressive plan, long-term goals can actually strip the individual of self-confidence.

Keeping the Client on Track and Determined

An astonishing fact of the fitness boom in the United States is that most people don't know what the word *fit* means. They are involved in a process they do not truly understand. And so people run a little, walk, do some calisthenics, or ride a bicycle, and they fail to consider the possibility that perhaps they are putting their eggs into the wrong basket. The result is that many people lose their commitment to fitness because they do not get the expected results.If you don't use goals to maintain a specific direction for clients, you will find that they wander all over—working hard one day and not the next, perhaps even varying their exercise routines to the point of having no consistent stimulus phase whatsoever. One of the assets of goal setting is that it harnesses energy for a specific purpose.

Just as a central theme or purpose is critical to fitness programming, so too is persistence and daily effort. Based on the principles of exercise prescription, this should come as no surprise. Goal setting encourages persistence and effort because it creates mini-experiences of mastery, provides short-term rewards, and gives clients a feeling that they are moving in a desired direction. Consider the following experience that was related to us by a close friend.

Not long ago I had an opportunity to do some rock climbing. The cliff that was chosen by a seasoned climber (a real stress seeker!) was, at first glance, a bit frightening. As I stood at the base, I felt totally inadequate and had little desire to exert even minimal effort for the task. Had I begun in that state of mind, I never would have persisted in climbing because failure would have been imminent within the first 10 ft. Without further hesitation, I mentally divided the cliff into five sections and decided that I could quit after any one of them if I felt like it. Thus my total focus for the start of the climb was a section of rock that extended about 10 ft up from the ground.

I was duly psyched for reaching this first goal and put a lot of physical effort and concentration into the task. Well, I got there and it felt like I had conquered Mt. Everest! More importantly, the cliff didn't seem so threatening anymore, and I was determined to go further. As I progressed from section to section, the feelings of mastery became stronger. But, I must admit that I only got to the three-quarter mark. I became fatigued and couldn't go on. The need to readjust my final goal wasn't devastating in the least, though, because I had met several intermediate goals and had conquered the real obstacle—fear!

Clarify Client Expectations

Experts indicate that goal setting motivates individuals because it fosters feelings of self-worth. We believe goals do this in a very subtle but powerful way. When clients enter fitness programs, a significant number will have little idea of what constitutes a sound workout. Yet, like most of us, they want to please others—in this case, exercise personnel. They harbor feelings of guilt that they are not doing as much as they should, and they may be convinced that others joke about their lack of athletic ability. In fact, they may try to engage in activity that is totally inappropriate for their level of conditioning. One thing leads to another until finally these individuals are forced to admit failure to themselves, and then they quit.

Goal setting can counter this type of thinking and behavior by validating the worth of individualized activity. It clarifies to clients at the very beginning exactly what is expected of them. Clients need to understand that you accept and encourage varying levels of participation. Be careful, however, not to undermine clients' goals. It is easy to provide stronger reinforcement to those who choose to work harder. The old adage, "actions speak louder than words," clearly applies in this instance. You cannot give more attention to those who opt for greater challenge and then turn around and say in the same breath that your center emphasizes the importance of individualized programming.

It should be clear that goals work for very specific reasons. By way of review, the following is a list of what goal setting can help to achieve. For additional discussion of these and related points see Locke, Shaw, Saari, and Latham (1981).

- Communicate to clients your commitment to their fitness needs.
- Assist in altering and defining unrealistic expectations.
- Convert large, difficult tasks into smaller, more simplified targets.
- Unveil strategies for obtaining personalized objectives.
- Maintain behavior that is specific to stated outcomes.
- Serve as an incentive to short-term effort and long-term commitment.

The challenge that lies ahead is to understand how you can obtain these outcomes from the goal-setting process; they are not automatic.

Getting the Most Out of Goal Setting

Like any technique, goal setting is only as effective as the person who uses it. There is nothing magical about its ability to motivate behavior. So what are the tricks of the trade? Has any clear system emerged from research and practice? In the following pages we will discuss seven guidelines that you will find useful in setting goals and providing feedback.

There is nothing inherently magical about goal setting.

Goal Setting Is an Interactive Process

Most practitioners agree on the importance of including the client in the goal-setting process. You may be wondering who would ever try to set goals without taking the client's position into consideration. Unfortunately, many of us do. Not only do we lead people away from their primary purpose, but it is often true that we establish standards of progress that clients really don't accept. Why do we do this, and how can it be prevented?

As mentioned in chapter 2, it is a good idea to assess clients' needs prior to the interview. Also, assure clients that you are interested in knowing of any health- or fitness-related objectives they may have, irrespective of whether they believe the center is capable of responding to all of them. Once the interview is in progress and they have heard your comments, they may alter their objectives somewhat. This may not be an intentional form of influence on your part; the simple fact is that clients look for cues to make good impressions. With some experience you will be able to tell how strongly clients feel about certain goals. At times it is clear that clients acquire their stated needs from their doctor or peers. In these cases, there is a clear absence of any strong motive to achieve, and goal

setting is inappropriately timed. You first have to secure commitment relative to client-based needs. Goal setting will have little effect
if the final outcome has little personal value.

To help clients become committed to goals, you may want to show
them how these are related to other outcomes they value, a reason
why interviews are so important. For example, we know of an asth-
matic who quit walking due to respiratory discomfort. Initially, she
had a reasonable motive to lose some fat from her thighs, but even
the most carefully planned fitness goals would have been sabotaged
by such physical distress. What we helped her to realize, however,
was that further deterioration in fitness would actually compound
her asthma, and that although an increase in fitness might have
some short-term discomfort it should have a long-term respiratory
benefit. We set fitness goals based on a specific threshold of respiratory discomfort and had this client keep a daily record of respiratory symptoms and the level of activity at which they occurred.
Eventually she found that she could do more and felt less pain. This
brings us to Guideline 1.

Guideline 1.   Clients' stated needs can easily be distorted if they
   think you want to hear something different. Also, specific established goals may lack intrinsic value or become supplanted by
   competing needs. When the latter occurs, you might try linking exercise goals to areas of a person's life that are highly
   valued.

Outcome Versus Process-Oriented Goals

Most clients will talk in terms of outcome goals; that is, they will
say, "I want to lose 15 lb" or "I would like to have slimmer thighs."
They state an absolute endpoint. As mentioned earlier, one problem with such an approach is that it might take an entire year to
shed the desired weight or make a sought after shift in physique.
People have a difficult time delaying gratification, and these long-
range objectives will probably not work. Thus it is important to have
intermediate endpoints. For example, someone might have a 20-lb
weight loss goal for 9 months and set 7- and 15-lb losses at the 3-
and 6-month marks, respectively.

Despite these reasonable increments of growth, there is even a
greater problem with outcome goals. Specifically, you can never
guarantee with a particular individual that precise increments of
change will occur if some behavior is followed for a given unit of
time. In addition, even with quarterly goals, you are still dealing
with objectives that are more long-term by design. In other words,
you just don't get reliable increments of change in health-related

outcomes on a daily or weekly basis. So, what do you use to motivate clients in the interim? The answer is process-oriented goals.

Process-oriented goals deal with specific exercise behavior. For
example, you need to run 30 laps or do two sets of 15 leg lifts with
120 lb. Note that these goals provide a daily guide to fitness activity
and create a mechanism for obtaining desired outcomes. Your purpose in employing process-oriented goals is not to replace health-
or fitness-related outcomes. After all, observable changes in physique or health often serve as powerful motives for exercise behavior. On the contrary, process-oriented goals provide the needed
short-term behavior that enables clients to fulfill their personal
needs. When clients experience the link between process-oriented
and outcome goals, the former acquire very strong reinforcing
properties.

But what about those instances in which process-oriented goals
are adhered to, yet clients fail to reach stated outcome objectives?
There is no getting around the frustration and disappointment that
this scenario creates; however, you will find that adverse reactions
are minimized if you encourage clients to be patient. For example,
we have found it useful to convey the following:

> Although we have set some specific quarterly targets for you,
> it is important to be flexible in your fitness program. For in-
> stance, we may find that you improve faster or somewhat
> slower than anticipated, and adjustments in prescriptions or
> quarterly goals may be required. Remember, you are physio-
> logically unique, and without some experience it is difficult to
> know how you will respond to exercise. Please be patient and
> keep in mind that you are making a long-term commitment to
> healthful living. No matter what kind of problems you run into,
> chances are that together we can work them out. It may require
> some modifications of behavior on your part, but we definitely
> have the expertise it takes to treat a wide range of individuals.

Guideline 2 describes the principle behind this statement.

Guideline 2.   It is important to set both outcome and process-
    oriented goals; however, care should be taken in establishing
    outcome goals that are not too rigid.

As always, continued interaction with your clients throughout their
process of achievement is vital.

Goals Should Be Specific, Clearly Defined, and Realistic

At the very beginning of this chapter, you were introduced to several different explanations of why goal setting works. The central theme of this discussion was that objectives must be both concrete and obtainable. In other words, fitness goals must be specific, clearly defined, and realistic (Locke et al., 1981).

Specificity and clear definition.   By their very nature, goals are specific and clearly defined. They involve obtainable achievements that can be monitored objectively. Yet, employing these principles in real-life goal-setting programs requires some planning. For the sake of simplicity, let us suppose that a heart patient says that he wants to get stronger—a commonly stated goal. Where do we begin? Well, the first task is to determine what the client means by the word *stronger*. To one individual it may mean being able to walk up a flight of stairs without labored breathing, whereas to another it may represent the ability to lift heavier boxes. Do not assume that you share a common language with your clients. Ask for plenty of examples to clarify terms like *stronger, less fatigued, better conditioned,* or *fit*.

Second, you must convert general terms like *stronger* into specific, measurable endpoints. These may involve goals such as 3-week increases in a specific number of laps or a specific amount of weight lifted. You are probably wondering how you could even set performance goals in the initial interview. Actually, in most cases you can't. But, if you remember the chapter on prescription, we discouraged goal setting until after the starter phase is completed. Explain the goal-setting process in the initial interview to a point that your only task after the starter phase of the exercise prescription is to agree upon concrete increments of growth. Don't try to set specific goals without having information on a client. You will make too many errors, and the end result will be the destruction of a very useful motivational strategy.

And third, make sure the originally stated need of the client is met by the goal-setting process and that this is reflected in short-term and long-term goals. This provides a sense of direction, clear vision of expected effects, and a means of realizing desired change.

Realistic goals.   There is no standard for setting goals, and even though it is well recognized that goals should be difficult, this is a relative term. That is why we recommend using the starter phase of an exercise prescription for determining realistic objectives. It gives you an opportunity to understand both the physiological and the psychological limitations of the individual. In our experience, the critical issue is whether clients are willing to accept specific increments of change. On the one hand, it is very important that individual goals represent a significant challenge; however, if challenges are too difficult, there is an increased chance of injury and/or burnout. On the other hand, if change is perceived to occur too slowly or goals are obtained without much effort, then dissatisfaction will occur. Above all, you want to impress on the client that goals are not etched in stone. They should feel that the goal-setting process is highly valued by the center and that change in goal structure is often times essential. Realistic goals can be set by following the third guideline.

Guideline 3.   Goals need to be stated in objective terms. The original needs of the client must be clarified, there must be agreement that reformulated objectives are consistent with original statements of need, and increments of growth should be based on performance in the starter phase of an exercise prescription.

Lack of Support Undermines the Goal-Setting Process

Goal setting does not occur without planning. To impress upon clients how much goals are valued by exercise personnel, provide adequate support. For example, suppose you suggest that, as a re-lated goal, specific clients restrict their caloric intake, let's say to 2,000 cal/day. Without providing some education and offering appropriate interventions, you have not done your job; there is no mechanism to achieve this desired goal. If particular goals cannot be supported, and if you do not have the resources to facilitate specific objectives, then do not pretend that you do.

To be serious about goal setting, you need to do some thorough self-examination. Do you have the resources to make goals obtainable? For example, is there adequate equipment or programming? Can clients obtain proper training, or is ability apt to be a restricting factor? How do you plan to follow up on goals? What can be done to overcome client resistance? To reiterate, if you want to get the most out of goal setting, if you want clients to value the process, then it has to be clear to them that you believe that goals play a critical part of fitness programming. What better way to communicate this message than through goal-setting support structures? Guideline 4 stresses the importance of these support structures.

Guideline 4.   Program and facility support are necessary if goal setting is to work properly. Consideration needs to be given to equipment, physical space, and training.

Goals Can Be a Risk

Although goals offer a powerful means of motivating fitness behavior, there are some possible liabilities. First, there are those who argue that goals create a ceiling on performance. In other words, even though they have the capability, clients do not work any harder than their goals specify. On the one hand, perhaps you want to create a ceiling effect. After all, you are trying to instill a lifestyle change in activity level. Why should clients be encouraged to enter some sort of competitive race towards their goals? On the other hand, if ceiling effects do occur and they significantly hamper progress, then you probably have been too rigid in presenting goals. Remember, goal setting needs to be characterized as a dynamic process, one requiring constant input from the client.

Second, some clients may become obsessed with their goals and begin to take shortcuts or drastic measures just prior to reevaluation. For example, in haste to reach a weight goal, we saw a client fast for 2 days and run in a rubber suit for over 30 min just prior to testing! Obviously, this is not the type of behavior you are attempting to shape. So how do you discourage this type of response? It all begins in an educational phase of goal setting. We emphasize to clients that gradual progress is much more desirable than large, short-term gain. If clients are having difficulty reaching intermediate goals, it should be sufficient warning that some renegotiating is necessary. If you don't renegotiate, then you encourage shortcuts because clients have no alternative, unless they choose to accept failure.

And finally, perhaps goals take the fun out of fitness. Are you making exercise all work and no play? To answer this question, you have to evaluate the intensity of a goal-setting program. If you use sound principles of exercise prescription, fitness is not a "no pain, no gain" experience. Also, workouts do not have to be plagued by self-monitoring and recording for goal setting to work. For instance, 10- or 15-min intervals between heart rate checks of an aerobic workout are more than adequate. If, of course, particular clients are interested in high-level training for whatever reason, then they have to be willing to accept the consequences, which at times may mean that exercise does seem more like work than play.

Guideline 5.   Goals can actually limit performance and encourage clients to take shortcuts (e.g., starvation diets) when used

Are you making exercise all work and no play?

improperly. Furthermore, an overemphasis on performance through excessive focus on demanding goals creates the risk of establishing a work- rather than a leisure-oriented environment. This will be unacceptable to many clients.

The Goal-Setting Process: A Case Study

To illustrate how to get the most out of the goal-setting process, we will describe the first few weeks of interaction with a client we will call Bill.

Assessing Needs and Defining Major Objectives

During his first visit, Bill was asked to complete the "Needs Assessment Questionnaire" (chapter 2). His reasons for joining the program were threefold: (a) to lose some weight in his midsection and tighten his stomach muscles, (b) to quit cigarette smoking and develop greater respiratory function, and (c) to become disciplined about exercise.

During the semistructured interview, the exercise specialist talked with Bill about his intentions for exercising and indicated that they needed to make them more specific and to tie them to a very structured exercise program. Bill agreed. The following points were made: (a) The best way to lose weight is to cut down on daily caloric intake and eventually burn about 2,000 cal/week through aerobic exercise. (b) To tone the abdominal muscles, Bill was told that he would have to spend a few minutes each day working out on the Nautilus abdominal and lower back stations. (c) The aerobic program would help him with his wind, but the center did not offer formal programs in smoking cessation. Several ideas were presented with regards to how and with whom he could get help in this area. And (d), the idea of self-discipline was discussed. Why was he having difficulty making exercise a part of his lifestyle? As it turned out, Bill disliked the isolation of exercising on his own, and it seemed as if he always had more pressing things to do. This information was valuable in that it hinted at possible sources of noncompliance.

The Prescription

Bill's prescription was implemented around a model of goal setting that involved the following steps:

Step 1.   It was emphasized to Bill that his objectives could be achieved, but that it would take between 9 and 12 months to make the desired changes.

Step 2.   Two types of goals were discussed: outcome- and process-oriented. Outcome goals were long-term and would be evaluated at 3 months, 6 months, 9 months, and the 1-year mark. These required caliper measurement of fat tissue on the abdomen, a subjective measure (1-10) of respiratory distress at the 7-MET level of the submaximal exercise test (about 90% of his maximum aerobic capacity at entry), and assessment of compliance with the exercise program. This was accomplished by documenting percent attendance and the percent of time that Bill adhered to his prescribed exercise intensity. Whereas the compliance goals were set at 90%, Bill was told that within 1 year his abdominal skin-fold should be reduced from 15 mm to 5 mm. This would require about a 2.5 mm decrease at each testing period. To follow respiratory distress, ratings were always taken at the 7-MET value, and Bill was told to expect an improvement of about 1 unit at each testing period; of course, he was told this could be influenced in either direction by changes in smoking habits. Finally, average daily calories burned through exercise were calculated from the number of laps completed each session. The initial goal was 1,000 with a 300-calorie increase each testing period. A summary outcome goal record was discussed with Bill (Table 5.1).

Process-oriented goals were short-term in nature (daily), the purpose of which was to keep Bill on a course that would yield the desired outcome goals. Fitness goals were punched into a computer and included the following: (a) date of attendance, (b) 15-min and 30-min RPE and HRR, (c) number of laps covered, and (d) RPE at last repetition of abdominal and lower back machine. At the end of each month, prescriptions were updated and this information was also placed on the computer. Bill was asked to maintain his present dietary habits for the first week of the program, although this was not computerized. At the end of this time interval, several specific, yet realistic goals were agreed upon: (a) He would restrict the number of business luncheon cocktails to one per meal and (b) he would include desserts only on Sundays and Wednesdays. He was asked to enlist the help of his peers and family to achieve these objectives.

Step 3. Bill was encouraged to look at the first 3 weeks of exercise as an adjustment phase. It was suggested that he view it as a breaking-in period for his muscles and an opportunity

Table 5.1 Summary of Outcome Goals

Goals[a]	Entry	3 months	6 months	9 months	12 months
% Attendance	NA	90% ( )	90% ( )	90% ( )	90% ( )
% Intensity (aerobic)	NA	90% ( )	90% ( )	90% ( )	90% ( )
% Intensity (abdominal)	NA	90% ( )	90% ( )	90% ( )	90% ( )
Skinfold	15 mm	12.5 ( )	10.0 ( )	7.5 ( )	5.0 ( )
Respiratory distress (7 METs)	9	8.0 ( )	7.0 ( )	6.0 ( )	5.0 ( )
Exercise cal (daily average)	NA	1,000 ( )	1,300 ( )	1,600 ( )	2,000 ( )

[a]Achieved values are placed in parentheses.

to have some hands-on experience with various components of the exercise program (e.g., instruction with the Nautilus equipment and learning how to monitor exercise intensity using heart rate and RPEs). He was told that he would not be given his formal workout schedule until this period of time had elapsed. Therefore, there was no need to keep data on process-oriented goals except attendance and dietary restrictions.

Step 4.   After taking a look at Bill's exercise history and listening to why his attempts to exercise had failed, we determined that commitment was, at best, moderate. We devoted a considerable amount of this text in the last chapter on how to enhance commitment, and with Bill three strategies were appropriate. First, from the medical screening process, it was evident that Bill was borderline hypertensive. Thus, there was an additional incentive to lose weight. After talking with the medical director, we had good reason to suspect that exercise and control of salt intake and the like would remedy Bill's problem. This became an explicit outcome-related medical goal: to lower resting blood pressure response within 6 months. Process-oriented goals at this point included replacement of normal table salt with a suitable alternative (e.g., light salt). Second, it was necessary to get Bill on a regular exercise schedule and to encourage social interaction. He was introduced to other clients who had formed a car pool, and exercise was set at 6:30 each morning.

Step 5.   Finally, Bill was encouraged to view outcome goals as ballpark figures. They were designed to be challenging, but for a variety of reasons might require modification as time passed. Above all, it was emphasized that gradual change was the ideal and that no attempts should be made to alter diet or exercise schedules without first talking with an exercise leader.

Goal Setting and Feedback

It is meaningless to talk about goal setting exclusive of feedback or to think of feedback without setting goals; they are closely related. In fact, from a motivational standpoint, research supports the view that goal setting and feedback go hand in hand; both are necessary to enhance performance, yet neither in and of itself is sufficient. There are three reasons why feedback is treated as a separate issue. First, the type of feedback that clients receive needs to be specific to their individual goals and must be objective by design. Second, clients need to be made aware of feedback schedules, and special attention has to be given to the significance of these sessions. And third, knowing how to communicate feedback is perhaps as critical as the information itself.

Making Feedback Specific and Objective

Kim, an enthusiastic client, began exercising with a concrete objective in mind: to lose weight. She seemed to work hard for nearly 3 months until one day she suddenly quit. Baffled by her behavior, one of the exercise personnel placed a follow-up call in an attempt to understand what had gone wrong. In talking with Kim, this person discovered that she was dissatisfied with her failure to lose weight. Kim was happy with some of the changes she had made, but the feedback she craved was in actual pounds lost, and the observation by exercise leaders that she looked better wasn't enough.

The above situation is not atypical. As mentioned before, clients come with specific needs and expect results. It is possible in Kim's case that her goals were unrealistic; however, let's examine how the feedback process could have been enhanced. The problem may have originated in the baseline feedback session. Kim should have been told that with exercise sometimes you see no change in weight, yet an improvement in physique occurs because the fat lost is replaced with lean tissue. Thus a better indication of progress is change in percent body fat. In fact, it would be advisable to take multiple measurements and note the change in each site (expressed in millimeters) rather than pooling the results into a single value. And second, it would have been desirable to have intermediate goals that were based on caloric intake and expenditure. For example, Kim could have been encouraged to lower her caloric intake gradually by keeping weekly food records and to burn more calories progressively through increasing her aerobic exercise program. Of course, actual target values for these goals would have been based on her food consumption and fitness level at the onset of the program. Notice how this enhances the quality of feedback that you are able to give to clients. It is very specific and objective.

Guideline 6. Feedback should involve objective methods of assessment that are specific to clients' goals and sensitive to even minor changes in improvement.

Feedback Schedules and Their Importance

Obviously, you won't have the time to make daily contact with every client, and it is impossible to work up detailed feedback sessions on a weekly or monthly basis. Remember, however, that process-oriented goals are designed with self-regulation in mind; that is, clients should monitor their own progress, making daily entries into some type of formalized log. A summary of process-oriented goals along with long-term outcome goals is only provided at each subsequent 3-month interval. It is essential, however, that clients understand clearly how and when feedback occurs. Using a "Summary of Outcome Goals" sheet (Table 5.1) provides an excellent means of ensuring this. A copy should be given to the client at each testing interval.

In addition to firmly establishing feedback schedules, you cannot overemphasize to clients the importance of quarterly feedback sessions. You might consider some type of computer-assisted countdown that alerts clients to the length of time remaining before their next evaluation. Monthly personal reminders and charts posted in exercise rooms can be used to heighten the value and purpose of feedback. You want clients to anticipate and get psyched up about evaluation; it will greatly increase the motivational qualities of the information fed back to clients.

Guideline 7.   You need to impress upon clients the critical role of self-responsibility for process-oriented goals. They need to understand the feedback process. Special care must be taken to heighten the importance of quarterly feedback sessions.

The Art of Communicating Feedback

As mentioned previously, how you communicate client feedback is as crucial to the process as the quality of the information itself. With this in mind, we offer the following suggestions.

Provide immediate feedback.   It is doubtful that there is anything more frustrating to a client than to wait days or even weeks before hearing test results. It not only leads to client dissatisfaction, but also reduces the perceived importance that you as exercise personnel place on the information. If for technical reasons a delay is unavoidable, inform the client ahead of time. Remember, if at all possible, provide test results immediately.

One approach that we have found useful in corporate fitness settings is to attach test results to clients' exercise logs. A note is included to the effect that questions are anticipated and should be directed to individually assigned exercise leaders. When evaluations such as graded exercise tests must be interpreted before results can be discussed, it is advisable to make appointments immediately following testing sessions. This protocol reassures clients that they will receive specific feedback, and it reinforces the importance of the information to be received.

Discuss process-oriented goals first.   Take time early in quarterly feedback sessions to review clients' process-oriented goals. Have they adhered to suggested behavior change? To make a thorough review, it will be necessary to monitor the specific exercise behaviors in question. This might include summary data on attendance, intensity, and duration of daily workouts. Such information can be used to explain why particular outcomes have or have not occurred.

Emphasize achievements first and then discuss weaknesses. Clients tend to be more receptive to facing weaknesses in one area if achievement in another has been duly noted. Also, weaknesses are most effectively discussed when phrased in a manner that places control in the hands of the client. For example, we can distinctly recall one client who was strongly praised for making a total weekly increase in his running of from 10 to 20 mi. At the same time, however, it was noted that his smoking habit would eventually restrict subsequent achievement. If he was interested in making additional gains, the cigarettes would have to go, he was told. The next day he quit cold turkey and remains a convert.

Reemphasize the flexibility of outcome goals.   In discussing outcome goals, recap clients' objectives, then point out and reinforce how specific data support the view that they are moving in the proper direction. Emphasize to clients that direction of change is more important than meeting a specified increase or decrease in some targeted area. You want to reinforce consistent, gradual change. The message clients should hear over and over again is that the long-term changes in behavior are the ones that produce meaningful results.

In several respects, health behavior change can be likened to a savings account. That is, no matter how small monthly deposits may seem, consistent efforts to save yield surprising results across a 10- to 20-year period. Also, just as we break our dietary or exercise goals every now and then, for most of us there are those periods when a savings deposit is missed or an unexpected event results in dipping into existing funds. These breaches of informal contracts can be devastating when feelings of failure and negative thinking predominate; "Oh, what the heck, I might as well forget this. I knew I could never do it on a consistent basis to begin with. As usual I was fooling myself."

Don't elaborate on irrelevant goals.   In discussing appropriate goals, you should not establish client objectives that are beyond the capabilities of your facility. For example, it would be foolish to establish smoking- or dietary-related goals if there were no formal program to facilitate behavior change in these areas. Therefore, during feedback sessions, don't get caught up in discussing how clients are progressing with behaviors that are not part of stated program objectives—leave this for some other time. It is easy for feedback sessions to be consumed by irrelevant topics. Aside from being unproductive, they are dangerous because clients may be disappointed about some shortcoming that had absolutely nothing to do with their quarterly evaluation. In a flash, the motivational power of feedback and goal setting can be destroyed.

Documentation of progress and overall plan.   Make certain that clients leave with a copy of the evaluation data. Any adjustments in prescription or goals should be documented. The data should be concise and include both past achievements as well as future objectives.

Summary

This chapter has attempted to make you aware of the fact that goal setting and feedback are indispensable to effective fitness programming. At the same time, great care is required to get the most out of these techniques; both necessitate sound organization and planning. If you take time to understand why goals and feedback do motivate behavior, then you will become adept at resolving problems that periodically arise. As a fitness educator, you need to understand why people behave as they do and how various techniques work to augment or modify these behaviors. Much of the time when methods fail, it is not the method, but the manner in which it was applied, that is at fault.

Suggested Readings

Locke, E.A., Shaw, K.N., Saari, L.M., & Latham, G.P. (1981). Goal setting and task performance: 1969-1980. *Psychological Bulletin*, **90**(1), 125-152.

O'Block, F.R., & Evans, F.H. (1984). Goal-setting as a motivational technique. In J.M. Silva III & R.S. Weinberg (Eds.), *Psychological foundations of sport*. Champaign, IL: Human Kinetics.

Chapter
6

Establishing
the Proper
Environment

The environment in which people exercise offers one of the best means of motivation at your disposal. Consider how joggers seem to come out of hibernation in the springtime. Or perhaps you have experienced the difficulty of running on rainy days. In both of these cases, the weather influences behavior. Although you cannot control Mother Nature, you can manipulate many characteristics of the exercise setting to promote desired client behavior. The term *environment* encompasses much more than temperature or an attractive room. In addition to physical features, it includes impressions given by exercise personnel and organizational structure. The environment does facilitate exercise. For example, the spouse of one of our cardiac patients explained that, without the education and support provided to her by the program, she probably would not exercise even though she enjoyed it! This essentially relates to one of the propositions introduced in chapter 1: Exercise behavior is controlled in large part by the reinforcement value it has for the person.

In this chapter, we will explore some basic principles of establishing a proper environment for exercise, principles that are currently operative in a number of successful fitness centers. Of four distinct areas that will be considered, first is the behavior of exercise personnel. Should you formulate some basic policies about appearance and client interaction? Second, what about reinforcements? Are extrinsic rewards taboo? Third, how are environmental cues manipulated to facilitate exercise behavior? And fourth, does facility decor and organization really make a difference? In many respects, the environment offers a unique dimension to motivation. The reinforcement value of exercise behavior is as much a function of the setting as it is of the client; in fact, the two are inseparable.

Setting Standards for Exercise Leadership

Through objective evaluations of fitness programs, we consistently find the behavior of program personnel to be a key to client satisfaction. It upsets people when what you do is inconsistent with what you say. A relaxed environment should not be confused with a tolerance for unprofessional habits. You are expected to be an expert, and clients pick up on evidence of personalized care. Although most of us acknowledge the importance of these areas of concern, we often don't recognize violations. Placed in the role of a program director, you may assume that the proper interface between personnel and clients occurs naturally; if it does not then you terminate employment and rehire! We disagree with this approach. Proper exercise leadership is planned, and it is important to have built-in mechanisms to insure its success. If not, it could be the basis of failure for the facility. At the very least, you will encourage a restricted membership.

Practice What You Preach

The exercise leader is a natural role model for exercise behavior; therefore, what you do on the job will have a strong influence on your clients. It is your responsibility to portray an enthusiastic, dedicated exerciser. This doesn't mean that you must have a bubbly, cheerleader-like demeanor, but if you aren't excited and committed to exercise, it is going to show. Obviously, the most direct way to portray a favorable image is to spend some time exercising with your clients in daily sessions. Additionally, as in our cardiac rehabilitation program, it is not uncommon for exercise leaders to enter city- or business-sponsored road races to pace clients. Others may show up to watch and cheer. The fact that these personnel take time from their own schedule to support the exercise habits of patients has a profound effect on creating strong bonds between exercise leaders and clients. Those who aren't sure they want to give up their precious time off to serve clients free of charge should understand that we really aren't talking about an extensive commitment. This type of interaction occurs only once or twice a year. It is very little to give for what you receive in return.

Another example of practicing what you preach has been instituted at a corporate fitness program in New York City. They require that all exercise leaders have a structured daily workout themselves in their facility. This practice led to numerous comments by clients that indicated that they were glad to see they were not alone in their efforts.

In addition to modeling actual exercise behaviors, you will find it helpful to display some of the touted benefits of exercise, particularly a positive self-image and zest for living. Good posture and grooming are essential to projecting the desired self-image, whereas a smile and genuine interest in people and events around you suggests the latter. It is necessary for exercise leaders to practice good health habits as well. For example, smoking should be prohibited. Drinking soda or eating candy while on the exercise floor should

You can show your interest and enthusiasm by cheering clients at community events.

also be considered unacceptable. Such behaviors are not only unprofessional, but also convey a disregard for health. Although no one is perfect or feels like smiling all the time, when at work every effort needs to be made to model the behavior you want your clients to imitate. A classic illustration of this principle can be found at Disneyland. Although not connected with fitness, personnel there are constantly reminded that their roles at work should be handled like parts in a play. It takes conscious planning and effort to develop and maintain the proper image.

Professionalism—A Must

There is no substitute for professionalism. Without it, educational effectiveness is severely handicapped and the future of any organization is jeopardized. The first major component of projecting a professional image is personal appearance. Even in a fitness setting there is a need to look the part; therefore, some sort of uniform dress is mandatory. It is also important that you appear fit and well groomed. After all, the physical status of exercise personnel is one of the strongest marketing schemes at your disposal. We know of fitness facilities at which personnel are required to correct poor hygiene immediately, and there is even an insistence on proper dress when traveling to or from work. Although this may seem a bit extreme, it is best to take a conservative approach.

In addition to appearance, professionalism involves the avoidance of bias, a knowledge of facility equipment and procedures, and a respect for co-workers. With regard to bias, it is important not to stereotype different exercise behaviors as masculine and feminine or to be judgmental and communicate to clients the belief that certain routines or activities are less demanding and therefore less worthy of recognition. For example, aerobic dance has traditionally been viewed as a feminine activity, whereas weight lifting has an aura of masculinity. This can result in the fragmentation of participants and unwanted labels, such as the "serious group." Perhaps the best antidote for such bias is to require that exercise personnel participate, if not instruct, in all areas on a routine basis.

Professional exercise leaders should be trained on every piece of equipment and in all activities, from weight machines to the aerobic dance floor. Furthermore, in instructing clients on the use of equipment, exercise leaders should be clear and concise, detailing the procedures for adjusting equipment and repeating important instructions frequently. If, as an exercise leader, you do not have the answer to someone's question, always ask a colleague who does. You do not want clients to compare notes only to find that they were given conflicting information. Also, the safety of the client must always come first.

Finally, exercise leaders need to show respect for each other's work. It is unlikely that everyone employed at a fitness facility will have the same training. If strict training is not offered at the facility, differences in programming are bound to arise. For example, there are several accepted ways of doing sit-ups. Some are more appropriate for different populations than others. Nevertheless, if one leader works with a client on a specific method and later someone comes along and tells that client she is doing her sit-ups improperly, the client will likely be confused and annoyed, and this is a poor reflection on the facility. Rather than confronting the client and changing methods, the second exercise leader should question the first and, if required, allow the original exercise leader to suggest modifications. Challenging one another's abilities in public detracts from everyone's credibility.

Bending the Rules—Be Flexible

Many rules exist in exercise prescription regarding the appropriate stimulus for people with various physical limitations. For example, weight lifting is not recommended for people with high blood pressure because of the potentially excessive demand placed on the heart. Rowing is generally not recommended for those with back trouble. Despite these restrictions, you need to listen to your clients and construct adaptive programs when appropriate. For instance, it is conceivable that you will come across individuals who complain of back trouble, but regularly use a rowing machine without pain or injury. Would you inform these individuals that they cannot use the rower at your facility because such practice violates the rules of prescription? We hope not.

We have found that inflexible restrictions on use of equipment for particular medical problems can destroy motivation. Individuals may perceive these rules as punitive. In the situation described above, we would suggest an adaptive prescription. For example, allow clients to cool down on the rower, after performing their main workout on the treadmill or bicycle. In this way clients can still use the equipment, but at a low intensity. This should prevent injury and give the client a sense of control.

After you have established clients' prescriptions, follow-up is vital to insure that medical problems do not arise later on in their programs. Modification may be required if an injury does occur. The following story illustrates this point.

Nancy's medical history yielded a clean bill of health. She enjoyed walking and chose to spend a good deal of her workout time on the treadmill. Her exercise leader established a suitable protocol and Nancy was off! After a week or so, however, Nancy began experiencing cramps in her calves. She was given some specific stretches for her problem, but they did not help. Nancy remarked that she only experienced cramps while on the treadmill; she was walking 20 blocks to work each morning at a similar pace and never had a cramp. After considering her problem, the exercise leader suggested that Nancy bring the walking shoes she wore to work to use on the treadmill. Nancy did just that. Interestingly, her cramps disappeared, and Nancy remains a dedicated exerciser.

The walking shoes Nancy brought to the facility were not your typical athletic shoes. In fact they were ugly, black, and had heels. However, because they freed her from discomfort, she enjoyed exercise more and remained a loyal client. She even convinced two of her friends to join. A little flexibility and timely intervention really paid off. And so it will for you if (a) you nurture a good relationship with your client and (b) you are not afraid to bend the rules on occasion to set up an exercise program that really fits your clients' needs and desires.

The Individual Touch

In our computerized world, there are many situations in which our social security numbers are sources of identification. Because we are so often depersonalized by this number game, it should come as no surprise that taking time to learn names and getting to know clients can be an extremely effective way to motivate them. Something as simple as greeting the clients as they come into the facility can set the stage for a positive workout. Clients will be thinking, "Someone knows me by name and cares I'm here!" When a personal greeting is impossible, messages written informally in exercise logs serve to reinforce the feeling of personalized care.

By the same token, if clients have to skip a session or two, they like to know that they were missed. We have heard many clients complain after returning from an extended vacation, "No one even knew I was gone!" To combat this, a number of fitness facilities notify clients that they will be contacted if absent for 2 weeks or more. Unfortunately, during the starter phase, such a length of absenteeism is the telltale sign of a dropout. During the first 6 weeks, therefore, you will want to contact clients every time they don't show up as scheduled. During this crucial stage, the more contact between exercise leaders and clients the better.

Personal notes can be just as effective as phone calls, sometimes more so. Dropping a client a note is easy, and, if kept, the note can serve as a constant reminder to that client to return to exercise. In fact, personal messages are useful even prior to the development of compliance problems. In a 10-week weight loss program run as part of the Total Life Concept program, a comprehensive health program offered at AT&T, classes are held once a week. During the delivery of one such module an instructor increased class attendance by contacting each member every week between classes by way of a visit, a call, or a note.

While the efficacy of regular client contact during the first 6 weeks cannot be overstated, pampering can lead to problems. For example, at a large corporate fitness program, an exercise leader we know offered to call a client three times a week as a reminder to exercise. The client told a friend and soon the leader was making two sets of phone calls. These individuals lost any sense of self-responsibility and before long quit. To avoid this problem, keep interactions with clients on a professional level. Do not go too far out of your way for any one client; often that will lead to having to do the same for another. Also, express an interest in your clients, but avoid involvement in personal matters, particularly work-related ones. Remember, you may have many other clients. You will certainly have clients that become personal favorites, but they must not claim all your attention. At all times, encourage clients to take charge of their own exercise program and to challenge themselves. If interactions are kept professional, with an emphasis placed on client independence, then it is unlikely that you will run into the problems created by excessive attention.

The Cardio-Fitness Corp. in New York City came up with a clever way to optimize individual attention and increase membership renewals. At this particular facility, members numbered over 1,000. Managers developed what is known as the PEP program. This involves the assignment of a Personal Exercise Physiologist to each client. Exercise physiologists are required to get to know their assigned clients and to provide personalized follow-up. The PEP takes care of the orientation and designs the exercise program. During their first 6 weeks, clients are tracked daily. Their PEP notes when they arrive and strives to make personal contact each time they come in to work out. In the starter phase, if clients miss even once, they are contacted by their PEP. Once clients are beyond this initial stage, their PEP reviews exercise logs periodically and speaks with them as often as possible. In addition, clients are encouraged to seek out their PEP with questions or problems and are instructed to let their PEP know if they experience any discomfort, plan to be out of town, and so forth. This process insures that lack of personal care is not a reason for noncompliance.

Considering the ratio of members at Cardio-Fitness to exercise physiologists, we can see that keeping up with clients is no small feat. A single physiologist may be responsible for as many as 200 clients! In order to keep track of those who are temporarily inactive (normally due to vacation or travel), phone call follow-ups are made on any client who is absent for 2 weeks or more. Each exercise physiologist is given at least a half-hour a day to complete this task. They are responsible for contacting each person in their inactive files weekly and are required to maintain a log of who was called and when. Managers meet weekly with physiologists to insure that they are keeping up with their clients. Exercise physiologists are evaluated on their ability to track their clients and are offered incentives for membership renewals. The result of this elaborate procedure—happier clients and an increase in number of renewals!

Tips for Effective Exercise Leadership

This is a brief summary of the previous discussion. Use it, as we do, for quick reviews.

- Take time to model the behaviors you want your clients to adopt.
- Professionalism is essential. There is no substitute for well-groomed appearance and positive regard for fellow workers and administrative personnel.
- Establish a system for personal exercise consultants.
- If it is recommended that clients not engage in a particular activity due to physical restrictions, but the activity has value to these people, find a way to adapt the activity.

In our next section, we'll discuss the extensive history of both research and clinical interest in the use of reinforcement and punishment to shape behavior. The contributions of this theoretical approach to the modification of health behaviors are well recognized by a variety of scholars (e.g., Martin & Dubbert, 1984). Although there are those of you who probably have a grasp of basic concepts in this area of psychology, anyone can benefit from an examination of how reinforcement and punishment can be most effectively used in fitness settings.

Approaches to Shaping Behavior

Before we begin our discussion, it is important to acknowledge that reinforcement and punishment can either be given (+) or taken away (−). Thus there are four different consequences that can be used to shape behavior. These are

- + *Reinforcement*—giving a reward for behavior
- − *Punishment*—retracting a reward for behavior
- + *Punishment*—administering punishment for behavior
- − *Reinforcement*—terminating punishment

For example, a reward for corporate executive involvement in fitness has been the use of well days. Whereas time off with pay (+ reinforcement) is given for attending a specified number of exercise sessions, some corporations retract well days when the same employees skip scheduled workouts (− punishment). Similarly, an organization might charge higher rates for health benefits if employees smoke (+ punishment) and reduce personal charges to normal levels when they quit (− reinforcement). In the opinion of most professionals, the administration of punishment is undesirable; therefore, you are limited to using either + reinforcement or − punishment; that is, either giving or retracting rewards.

Positive Reinforcement: The Role of Contests and Incentives

Within the exercise environment, the most popular form of shaping behavior is providing reinforcement, an approach that typically involves some form of contest or challenge. Although research in social psychology (Deci, 1975) warns that extrinsic rewards have the potential of undermining the intrinsic value of an activity, this threat is most severe when rewards are perceived by clients as being used for manipulative purposes (chapter 1). When extrinsic rewards are viewed as feedback—"you deserve recognition"—they are much less problematic. In fact, extrinsic rewards have been used with great success in both getting people started and maintaining their exercise behavior beyond the first 6 weeks of involvement.

One attraction of contest and incentive programs is the element of fun that they can give to exercise, an effect that strengthens the intrinsic value of activity. For example, in the LifeFit™ program at Bermuda Village, a retirement community in Advance, North

Carolina, instituting a "walk across America" concept in the walking program led to an increase in the number of participants and the number of miles charted each week. Residents choose a city somewhere in the country as a destination, and for every mile they actually walk, 25 miles are plotted on the map. In a few weeks, one resident on route from Winston-Salem, North Carolina to San Francisco, California had already reached the border of Kansas! The race continues.

In the Champions for Life Program, a system developed by Champion International, participants are challenged by a monthly honor roll. To get their name on this prestigious list, participants must attend at least 15 exercise sessions in a single month. Although this may seem like a trivial accomplishment, it is pursued with great vigor by a large number of participants. They also have 100, 200, 400, 600, and 1,000 clubs. These numbers signify the number of exercise sessions attended; participants receive a gift at each mark that becomes increasingly more valuable to reflect an increased commitment to exercise. Finally, Champion International employees who are interested can be trained to become fitness leaders. These employees have full-time jobs in other departments, but also work in the fitness center on a volunteer basis. In exchange for their hours, the employees receive special instruction in areas of personal interest. For example, an employee fitness leader may receive additional instruction in weight training in exchange for hours in the fitness facility. For avid exercisers who are not interested in becoming fitness leaders, there is the opportunity for appointment on an advisory committee that gives feedback to the staff of the health club. This position is one many exercisers at a variety of facilities would find enviable.

Several other uses of + rewards warrant mention. Cardio-Fitness in New York City offers the fiercely sought-after title of "Client of the Month." This incentive requires that a participant exercise every day of the month that the facility is open. Though a small prize is awarded for this achievement, clients claim to participate just to see if they can do it. A large corporation that we know of pays one-half the cost of employees' membership renewal to a corporate fitness program on the condition that they attended a minimum number of sessions the previous year. And at Wake Forest University, clients in their cardiac rehabilitation program have their names printed in the monthly newsletter if they had 100% attendance the previous month. It is our observation that it is in the best interest of any fitness facility to work internally and with local companies to establish similar types of incentive programs.

Some Rules for Using
+ Reinforcement Effectively

You should observe a couple of simple rules for + reinforcement to work effectively. First, never assume that what you think are rewards have reinforcement value for clientele. What appeals to one person may be distasteful to another. For example, you will run into a number of clients who will have little interest in acquiring a program designer T-shirt; yet, these same individuals may find it very reinforcing to be given a physiological explanation of what type of changes occurred with their performance gains. This is why a variety of options must be available. As mentioned in chapter 2, one purpose of the initial interview is to develop a reinforcement menu for each client. It is extremely valuable to know ahead of time what button to push when and if incentives are used.

Second, + reinforcements can be administered on a variety of schedules. Initially, exercise behaviors need to be reinforced every time they occur—a continuous schedule. This is when personal contact and praise play such a vital role in client satisfaction. You may recall, for example, that in the PEP program at Cardio-Fitness there is constant attention for the first 6 weeks of involvement. Once a behavior is established, however, it is advisable to move to a fixed or variable schedule. Examples of a fixed schedule are the clubs at Champion International that involve attendance of 100, 200, 400, 600, and 1,000 exercise sessions. Participants know exactly when they will receive their next reinforcement. However, with variable schedules, there is no predictable interval between reinforcements.

Variable schedules have been found to be very powerful in controlling behavior. A case in point: after the first 6 weeks of the PEP program, patients are contacted personally by exercise physiologists, but on a random schedule. How is a random schedule arranged? One method that we have found to be effective is to identify a list of 10 to 30 clients whom you will make contact with in a given week. This can be done by simply running your finger down the list and stopping at whatever interval you like. Subsequently, their names are deleted from the list and the next week you select another random group. This is repeated until the entire list is completed. The same procedure can be performed again.

Behavioral psychologists suggest that variable schedules are superior to those that are fixed. Based on our experience, however, both have turned out to be useful. As support for fixed schedules, you will find little that is more powerful than 3-month evaluation sessions. Clients want and expect some system of predictable feedback.

Negative Punishment

Of course, not everyone will be motivated by a gift or other forms of + reinforcement. In fact, in the executive program of a large corporation with clients earning $60,000+, the program director has been hard-pressed to find appropriate cost-effective incentives. Another option is the use of − punishment. For instance, we are aware of a very successful program in which employees are allowed to pursue exercise on company time. The hitch is that those choosing to use the fitness center are told that unless they use the facility at least 30 times in 12 weeks and participate in a posttest, they will never again be allowed to use the facility. The result has been a decrease in noncompliance.

In the Cardiac Rehabilitation Program at Wake Forest University, there are three levels of participation: beginners, advanced, and cardiac fitness. Graduating from one level to another carries considerable weight. Currently, there is discussion of instituting a system of − punishment. The problem we are having is that once some of our patients reach the advanced or fitness stage, they develop a graduate mentality. That is, although they continue to appear at the exercise sessions, the quality of training frequently drops and other negative health habits return. Our − punishment would involve demoting patients to advanced or beginners' status.

Perhaps you are thinking that − punishment is bound to erode intrinsic motivation. After all, there is a strong element of control and little in the way of feedback. In our experience, the trick to using − punishment properly is to *explain the operation in detail prior to implementation, emphasizing why the procedure exists* and to *apprise clients of their status.* You must set up − punishment structures such that clients view the consequences as self-inflicted and for their benefit, rather than something you did to them. For example, in a rehabilitation program, clients could be told that these procedures exist to optimize safety. That is, as patients graduate from beginners' to advanced status, the assumption is that they are less of a medical risk. If, for reasons of noncompliance, their risk once again increases, then it is advisable to have them under closer supervision (i.e., to return them to a beginners' status). There is a great deal of similarity between − punishment and what Adlerian psychology terms *natural consequences of behavior.* The reason we point this out is that the use of natural consequences in curbing dysfunctional behavior has an excellent record of success in clinical practice.

Tips on Shaping Behavior

Here is another brief summary we hope you will use as a future guide for client success!

- + Reinforcement and, in some cases, − punishment is preferred over + punishment or − reinforcement.
- Clients will not resent − punishment as long as they realize that they brought it on themselves. When used properly, − punishment can instill a strong sense of self-responsibility for positive health behaviors.
- There is a lot of individual variability in what clients view as rewarding.
- Care should be taken to insure that extrinsic rewards are not perceived as controlling, and every attempt should be made to develop intrinsic reinforcement value.
- Whereas the use of continuous reinforcement is valuable in the early stages of shaping exercise behavior, you will want eventually to move to fixed and variable schedules.

Next we will examine the measures you can take to make setting an important element in your motivational program.

Setting the Stage for Exercise

In the theatrical world, a wide range of props is used to create a particular mood or feeling. The same technique can be applied to the fitness setting. Objects, eye-catching displays and posters, and carefully planned facility layouts create an environment that fosters positive attitudes, increases desired behavior, and inhibits antagonistic ones. Manipulation of these variables is called *stimulus control*.

The Exercise Scene

To create the type of environment that will elicit exercise behavior, start with the basics. Decorate walls with pictures of people exercising. At Cardio-Fitness Corp.'s Pan Am facility, even the window panels have action scenes of sailing, cross-country skiing, and running. Similarly, in the exercise equipment room at Bermuda Village in North Carolina, motivational posters are hung on the walls. Such decor motivates exercise behavior or, at the very least, reinforces it.

Eye-catching posters can foster positive feelings.

Wall mirrors can also be functional in setting the stage for exercise. Mirrors not only enable clients to make sure they are doing exercises correctly, but also keep the focus on exercise behavior. The only problem you can run into is that mirrors increase self-awareness, a situation that some clients may find undesirable. For example, mirrors may increase the embarrassment experienced by a client who happens to be excessively overweight. In general, it is best to have mirrors available, but not unavoidable.

Locker rooms should not be neglected in setting a proper stage for exercise. Before people actually begin an exercise session, they are vulnerable to distractions that can keep them from their exercise. On a particularly stressful day, a client may be more attracted to the sauna than to the exercise floor. Or perhaps there is a comfortable chair or even a sofa in the locker room—what a temptation for a tired client! Locker rooms should encourage clients to change clothes and get out to exercise. Simple benches are enough in the way of furniture and such luxuries as sauna and steam room should be located near showers rather than in the dressing area. Exercise pictures or symbols on the walls are appropriate here as well. Finally, as the music is more easily heard in the locker rooms than on the exercise floor, upbeat tunes can raise one's spirits and act as an invitation to get out and get going.

Other Useful Stimuli

Additional stimuli that traditionally serve as cues for exercise behaviors are bulletin boards and newsletters. In reserving a place to post information about road races, the benefits of exercise, the latest research findings, and so forth, you have created a useful motivational tool. Although many people have a sincere interest in fitness and health, few have time to read up on it. By condensing interesting facts to posting size, you will reach a lot of clients as the board catches their eye at some point in their workout. By attracting their attention to other aspects of health and fitness, you may also provide them with alternative motives to continue exercising.

The same is true of newsletters. This literature is typically short and easy to read. The focus is usually on one topic in detail, whereas others are treated in more general terms. In making these letters short and simple enough to read, even on the subway, you insure that more clients will actually read them. In addition to supplying information, the newsletter is a great way to recognize clients who are doing particularly well or are just deserving of some acknowledgment. As almost everyone enjoys seeing their name in print, this personal touch to your newsletter will most likely have more impact than you may expect.

Beyond the Facility

Stimulus-control procedures like the ones just described are not difficult to practice and have proven effective in many fitness centers. However, the success of these procedures is predominantly realized once clients are already in the facility. They do not necessarily get them there in the first place. For the latter to occur, stimulus-control techniques must be practiced outside the facility, at work, and in the homes of clients.

It is easy to manipulate the setting to inspire exercise for companies with in-house fitness programs or corporate memberships to fitness centers. A poster of the fitness center's logo strategically placed in the lobby can be extremely helpful in prompting people to exercise. Setting up a pamphlet library on health topics in the employee break room or occasionally stuffing paycheck envelopes with exercise information are other ways to stimulate exercise behavior. One company found that offering a low-calorie item on their cafeteria lunch menu helped to motivate people to take advantage of their corporate fitness program as well. The company concluded that their employees thought counting calories and exercise went hand in hand.

To reach individual clients at home, you will want to teach them some basic stimulus-control techniques. For example, individuals can be taught to set aside a specific time to exercise, making a daily ritual of physical conditioning. Laying out exercise clothes, coordinating meal plans, and writing a message on the mirror have all served as useful motivators. Perhaps the best stimuli, however, are other people. Be sure to get secretaries and family members involved, or better still have clients make a date with a colleague or club member. There is no better form of stimulus control than *social reminders.*

The staff of a fitness center can also stimulate exercise behavior in the community by taking an active role—offering exercise seminars and participating in health fairs at malls, libraries, or schools. Pamphlets left for distribution in drug stores is another good way to increase awareness in those who may be oblivious to the benefits of exercise. The role of public awareness merits close attention. For example, a restaurant in Greensboro, North Carolina, has resorted to labeling certain items on the menu as heart-healthy and/or low-calorie. This simple form of identification has increased the popularity of these foods tremendously. In the same way, you can use symbols in mass communication to support your own cause. In a recent building we visited there were eye-catching illustrations near every elevator. There was a picture of a man walking the stairs in a healthy heart and one of a man in the elevator encased in a weak and frail-looking heart—very effective!

The Setting—
Stacking the Adherence Deck

Although exercise leaders have responsibilities to reinforce behavior, the setting itself can be further manipulated to motivate the desired behavior and to help insure the success of a fitness facility (cf. Oldridge, 1984). Have you ever entered a restaurant or hotel and been immediately impressed by the atmosphere? What was it that impressed you? The decor? The cleanliness? The people in the setting? What happens when you are not pleased with the ambience? Doesn't it put a damper on your enthusiasm for what is taking place? Would you consider leaving? As with anyplace a person is going to spend time and/or money, the first impression of a fitness facility is extremely important in the decision to begin an exercise program. Even though this idea may not be new to you, we have compiled a checklist against which you can evaluate your own facility for appearance, convenience, and enjoyment.

Appearance

One of the first things people notice is the cleanliness of the setting. This is particularly true in fitness facilities, because most people will be showering after their workout. Similarly, the working condition of equipment and the appearance of personnel contribute to that critical first impression.

Understandably, people worry about picking up infections when they share a small locker room space and shower facilities. Evidence of pests only confirms this fear. Going out of your way to insure a clean facility will pay off in terms of keeping established clients and attracting new ones. There are several other items you will want to consider in creating a good first impression. For instance, does your facility supply towels? Soap? Shampoo? Are exercise clothes available? Supplying toiletries, towels, and exercise wear to clients provides some degree of reassurance that these items aren't left around to create unsanitary lockers. Comfortably bright lights, light-colored walls, and bright carpets all suggest a clean environment, because with such decor there is no hiding mildew or dirt. By not allowing food or drink in the locker rooms or on the exercise floor, you should have less trouble maintaining the clean environment. In addition, smoking should not be allowed in the facility. The odor and waste associated with smoking is often unsightly and is certainly not in keeping with a fitness philosophy.

That brings up yet another point: odor. Does your facility have a good ventilation system and control over temperature and humidity? If not, it will smell like a gym, and you can expect a certain amount of dissatisfaction among clients. The reputation of the facility depends on keeping standards high in all areas of maintenance.

Finally, let's consider equipment upkeep. Heavily used equipment is bound to break down occasionally. Regular maintenance for all equipment should be standard procedure, as should some means of marking those pieces of equipment that are temporarily out of order. Of course, having too much equipment under repair suggests poor facility management. If several pieces of equipment happen to be down at once, remove those you can until they are repaired. In addition to maintaining the mechanics of the equipment, you should pay attention to its appearance. Regardless of how long a piece of equipment has been around, if it is to be available for client use, it should be routinely painted and oiled, not to mention cleaned. Towels should be available on the exercise floor for wiping down equipment. It was a regular complaint among the female clients at a fitness center in North Carolina that the sit-up boards were always coated with sweat. They refused to use them. Leaving a towel out by the boards solved this problem.

Convenience

When people elect to put time and money into some venture, you can bet that convenience factors play a key role in how long they will stay with it. Yet, convenience involves more than mere location. It includes hours of operation, auxiliary services, crowd control, and flexibility of programming. These are basic issues in structuring effective exercise environments, but they are frequently overlooked. Let us examine the critical considerations in each category.

Location.   Location is a central concern for fitness programs. This is evidenced by the popularity and positive impact of in-house facilities such as those provided by AT&T and Johnson & Johnson. From a recruitment standpoint, it makes good sense to concentrate your attention on restricted geographical boundaries. If getting to a fitness center means fighting 20 additional minutes of traffic and risking delays in getting home or to work, support structures will begin to deteriorate. When this is compounded with the personal frustrations of the client, you can easily predict the outcome—dropout. In fact, we always bring up the issue of location in the orientation interview, even if we don't think of this as a potential problem. Remember, it is clients' perceptions of location that are important. If you suspect that location is going to be a barrier, it is best to confront this in the beginning. Who knows, you may be able to offer some solution that will alleviate the perceived difficulties of location (e.g., catching a ride with someone who doesn't mind the traffic). At the very least, it is worth pointing out to clients the risk of noncompliance that exists when location is an inconvenience. After all, neither the client nor you succeeds when dropout occurs. There is also a positive feature of discussing these types of problems with clients. It gives them the feeling that you are not just after the fee, but that you want their experience to be rewarding.

Hours of operation.   A second aspect of convenience concerns hours of operation. To accommodate everyone, a facility would have to be open 24 hr a day. Because this is not cost-effective, hours of operation have to be based on requests made by the majority of clientele and the location of the facility. For example, in New York City where the business hours of stock brokers and other financial personnel are well established, most clients choose to work out before or after work. This means that fitness facilities have to open their doors at 6:00 a.m. and operate at least until 7:30 p.m. Fitness personnel may have to get up as early as 4:00 a.m. to get to work on time!

Many times, hours of operation are constrained by the availability of personnel or space. If you are in the process of getting a fitness program off the ground, or feel that you could attract a larger group of clients with more flexibility in hours of operation, do a feasibility study first. You may learn that there is not as big a demand for some specified time period as you originally thought.

Auxiliary services.   In an earlier section on the exercise environment, we talked about the role of items such as towels, shampoo, soap, and even clothing in establishing an impression of cleanliness. These same provisions can add an element of convenience as well. It is nice not to have to remember to gather the appropriate paraphernalia at six in the morning. Furthermore, it may be very inconvenient to haul exercise gear on subways or find adequate storage at the office for dirty socks, shorts, and the like.

If you do elect to supply clothing, then you have the added responsibility of making sure that you are well stocked, particularly during rush hours. Also, don't forget those who are overweight or otherwise hard to fit. The last thing you want to do is to set someone up for an embarrassing experience. Auxiliary supplies can contribute significantly to client satisfaction, thus they constitute a consideration for optimizing compliance.

Crowding and flexibility of programs.   The final aspect of convenience deals with crowding and flexibility of programs. Every facility has its prime time, which leads to the problem of equipment and space overload. If clients have to wait in line for a piece of equipment or are forced to slow down on the track, you can expect problems because they are not getting what they paid for. Take some time to organize workouts. If necessary, rope off lanes in the pool or track for different paces and alternate aerobic and weight training phases of workouts to accommodate larger groups.

Some centers have opted for structured monthly appointments. Although this resolves crowding, it does hinder those who do have flexibility in their daily schedules. Having the option of attending exercise either in the morning or at an unpredictable hour in the afternoon is a real luxury for some clients. In New York, one program director has clients establish a specific 3-hour-a-week exercise plan at the time of orientation, yet allows clients the option to change as the need arises. This assists in the general organization of exercise, yet permits that important ingredient of flexibility.

Not unlike location, hours of operation, or auxiliary services, crowding and flexibility contribute to the overall convenience of fitness programs. Whereas any one item alone may not be the straw that breaks the camel's back and increases the frequency of dropout, taken together these areas of convenience constitute a major concern for the problem of noncompliant behavior.

Enjoyment

The comment, "it is not fun until you stop," is a reaction to exercise that occurs with greater frequency than many of us may like to admit. However, the exercise experience for a significant number of clients is more like unpaid labor than play. As research in exercise adherence indicates, such perceptions relate to the problem of dropout (Oldridge, 1984). Therefore, a reasonable question to ask is, "What can you do to increase the pleasure/fun associated with exercise?" Following are some ideas that may work for you.

Games.   Regardless of age, most people find games to be enjoyable, and they can be used to introduce an element of playful competition into the exercise setting. In addition, many games can be easily integrated into the exercise prescription. For example, in the Wake Forest University Cardiac Rehabilitation Program, volleyball has been employed as one optional activity during the cool-down. For medical reasons it is used primarily with those who are well stabilized medically. This activity is so popular that many of the exercise leaders contend it is the major motivational force behind the regular attendance of the old guard. An interesting observation is that patients who are in the early phases of their care have verbalized that they eagerly await entrance into the fitness group so they too can play volleyball! We should add that no one ever wins these games—it is the chiding given to one another for making mistakes and the group experience that provides the enjoyment.

In addition to using volleyball as a cool-down or shooting baskets as a warm-up, fitness personnel have introduced other playful activities into preventive and rehabilitative exercise settings. For example, towels and neckties are manipulated to stretch and tone musculature in both the upper body and legs. One typical challenge is to increase flexibility in the hamstrings by lifting stretched towels higher, or to shorten the length of necktie between your hands and feet in a lower back stretch. Also, balls can be passed from patient to patient in an increasingly faster pace to gradually increase heart rate as part of warm-up. Dribbling balls with either the feet or the hands from one place to another is also a challenging and fun way to begin an exercise session.

Variety.   It has been said that "variety is the spice of life," and the realm of exercise is no exception. Indeed, 90% of the people polled at the 1980 Ironman Triathlon said they began training for all three sports because they were no longer challenged by a single event (Perry, 1987). Some exercise facilities have the capability of offering clients a wide range of training options. For example, for aerobic work, there may be stationary bicycles, a track, treadmills, rowing machines, a Stair Master, bicycle paths, and perhaps even a pool. Each activity or piece of equipment offers a novel experience and will be very attractive to some clients.

Other strategies that are less costly involve such perks as introducing novel approaches to stretching or muscular toning. Offering short minisessions on topics like building a strong abdominal wall, tips on toning the hips and thighs, or snacking for fitness provide meaningful information for clients and help to break the monotony of a routine. Relaxation sessions following exercise can be extremely pleasurable and offer an opportunity to create positive experience through suggestion. In a particular retirement community, the participants were involved in a stretching program that included facial exercises. Participants in the class were asked to sit close to the mirror and manipulate their faces into various positions to exercise the muscles in their jaws, eyelids, cheeks, and chins. Though these exercises were difficult and sometimes silly, the challenge and laughter that accompanied the sessions were particularly memorable for everyone involved.

Music.   Music has the potential of not only distracting clients away from exercise distress, but also providing enjoyment. For example, a particular style of music can make or break an aerobic dance class. In teaching aerobics to a group of retirees, we found that the pop music of the 1980s not only was too fast, but wasn't really music by their standards. As we devised aerobic dances to tunes like "Beer Barrel Polka," "Red River Cha Cha," and the "Charleston," the class became very popular. The activity had excellent reinforcement value, and the intrinsic outcome expectancy of having fun was strong!

By the same token, the background music played on the exercise floor in most fitness settings should be targeted to the clients and not the staff. For example, in cardiac rehabilitation, we have found big band music to be very popular in the beginner program. Patients can often be found snapping their fingers or singing along as they exercise. Before long this behavior becomes contagious and everyone is having fun! It also increases social interaction, which can have a significant impact on both reinforcement value and clients' beliefs concerning particular outcomes (see chapter 1).

Your own behavior.   Your own behavior has a strong impact on whether your clients have fun during their exercise session. Be outwardly enthusiastic, smile, laugh, and make a joke or two while leading exercise classes or supervising the exercise floor. This will go a long way towards making exercise fun. Remember, you are a role model. If you are enjoying yourself, you will soon have others doing the same.

In this regard, a former exercise leader deserves special mention. No matter what was going on in his own life, Mike always managed to bring a smile and a joke or two to the program. He also enjoyed wearing jams (long printed shorts in wild colors), the wildest ones he could find! Before long, the patients began trying to anticipate which shorts Mike would wear on a given day. Perhaps even more significant was that in a matter of a month or so, several patients followed Mike's lead and started wearing jams to exercise themselves. The competition was stiff, with patients trying to outdo one another in wild colors or prints. This certainly added a lot of color and laughs to our early morning exercise program! Although a uniform would stymie this kind of fun in many programs, this example should bring home the point that you can easily play an integral role in making and keeping exercise fun for your clients. Remember, none of us exists in isolation. The fun surrounding exercise, therefore, need not come from the activity itself. Take time to have some brainstorming sessions with personnel on new strategies. Not only will your clients benefit, but you will find that staff involvement on a problem such as this can increase job satisfaction and improve group cohesion—effects that have a very important influence on client behavior.

The Computer Age and the Exercise Setting

With the rapid advances being made in computer science, soon computers will be available for commercial use at a minimal cost.

Computers are already being used in several fitness facilities, resulting in a decrease in the amount of paperwork inherent to exercise programs and an increase in the effectiveness of exercise leadership.

By way of an example, we would like to close this chapter with a description of the role of the computer in Champion International's Champions for Life fitness program. It is possible that this program marks the trend of the future, so we believe it warrants special attention.

Champions for Life

In the Champions for Life program, participants are given a comprehensive evaluation that includes a medical history, body composition analysis, risk factor analysis for cardiovascular disease, and submaximal bicycle testing. Once completed, these data are entered into the computer and analyzed according to age group norms so that each participant has a fitness profile. From this initial analysis, a personalized exercise prescription is developed. Participants are then carefully oriented to all equipment, including the computer, which is used by all on a daily basis.

Participants at Champion are not required to maintain exercise logs—this is done by computer. Instead, they carry exercise prescription cards. These cards not only serve as identification on the exercise floor, but contain clients' heart rate ranges and a general idea of the work required to reach target intensities. In addition, participants may choose to carry a throwaway card, which allows them to record heart rates and the amount of work done on different pieces of equipment for later input into the computer. Exercise programs in this center are generally unstructured and not extremely goal oriented, though the option for a structured program with specific exercise goals does exist.

Each day, after completing an exercise session, participants plug into the computer and enter the data they collected during their workout. They are asked to input warm-up and cool-down procedures, heart rates during the stimulus phase of their workout, their weight, and any other pertinent information they would like to save. In turn, the computer gives participants immediate feedback on their exercise session, including mileage covered, change in weight, heart rate response, and the ever-popular number of calories burned. These data are saved and tabulated for reproduction in major interval reports.

The major interval reports also include reassessment of body composition, major risk factors, and fitness level. The time lapse between reports is a function of a specified number of visits rather than weeks in the program. Interestingly, the computer tracks attendance and is thus used as a mechanism for scheduling retests. It also generates a list of participants who have been absent for 4 or more weeks. Exercise leaders are still responsible for the scheduling of retests and contacting those who have been inactive, though much of paperwork inherent to these duties is reduced considerably. Indeed, the computer supports the exercise leader's job by supplying daily reinforcement to every participant through the feedback that accompanies the storage of training information after a workout. In a way, the computer even motivates recreational activities outside the facility, for these too can be plugged in and analyzed in terms of heart rate response and calories burned.

Summary

So there it is, the motivational power inherent to the exercise environment and a glimpse at the future of computer support. The environment offers a tremendous opportunity to attract and maintain membership in various fitness-related enterprises. Self-examination of programs and facilities by personnel is as central to understanding noncompliance as the mental and physical make-up of clients themselves. Whereas one impact of the computer should be an increase in the precision and scope of information typically available in most traditional fitness settings, the use of computers should not imply a lack of human contact. If used in this manner, the results will be most disappointing.

Suggested Readings

Martin, J.E., & Dubbert, P.M. (1984). Behavioral management strategies for improving health and fitness. *Journal of Cardio-pulmonary Rehabilitation, 4,* 200-208.

Orlick, T. (1976). *The cooperative sports games book.* New York: Pantheon.

Taylor, S.E. (1986). *Health psychology.* New York: Random House.

Chapter 7

Dedication Does Pay Off

As we discussed in chapter 1, one of the greatest professional challenges you will ever encounter is confronting the problem of noncompliant behavior. Unfortunately, it is a challenge requiring skills that are not taught by most formal training programs in exercise science or program administration. You can always ignore the reality of noncompliance or pretend that it isn't your responsibility, but a nagging question will always remain: Do you really want to face the consequences of remaining passive? How many clients who truly need your services will fall victim to inadequate programming? Noncompliant behavior is a major problem for all health professions. *You* are a key player in the fight against its destructive power.

A System for Motivating Clients

In this book, we have provided a system for enhancing motivation in exercise settings. A basic assumption is that motivation should be a cornerstone of all program structure. Contrary to popular belief, intervention for noncompliant behavior is not something you do when things go wrong; rather, it is best viewed as preventive. If you follow the structure established in this book, three significant results will occur. First, those clients who would have been satisfied without a formal motivational program will be more impressed, satisfied, and committed than ever. Second, there will be a group, probably unknown to you, that will remain committed largely due to the motivational steps you have taken. Without such structure, however, this group would have never persisted. And third, there will still be those noncompliers. The difference now, however, is that you have a jump on the problem. You know what makes these clients tick, and there are a variety of weapons that you have in your arsenal to deal with their problems. Sure, there will be casualties. They can never be totally eliminated. But noncompliance will be less troublesome, the exercise environment will be much more rewarding for both you and your clients, and standard programs lacking this approach will pale in comparison.

The approach we have offered consists of four broad propositions:

1. It is wise to adopt a common structure for intervention. For this purpose, we have offered the rigorously tested principles of social learning theory. These were presented in chapter 1.
2. Evaluation is essential. As pointed out in chapter 2, it is important to establish clients' baseline physiological profiles, clarify individual needs and beliefs, define program objectives, and explore potential barriers to exercise.
3. Give careful consideration to the exercise prescription. In chapter 3, we explained how to match client needs to various exercise regimens, discussed the importance of educating clients on the anticipated costs and benefits of different prescriptions, and removed several myths about the concept of "no pain, no gain."
4. Psychological interventions designed to deter noncompliance should take full advantage of both the individual and the environment. Chapters 4, 5, and 6 offered specific suggestions on how to accomplish this two-pronged attack.

The Benefits of a Systems Approach

The planning and effort required of a formal approach to motivation involves far more than haphazard intervention with an occasional motivational gimmick, but you would probably agree that most things in life worthy of possession have their costs. Indeed, it is the rewards that make any sacrifice worth the effort. Although we have implicitly discussed the benefits of a structured motivational approach throughout this book, let's take a moment and examine the most important advantages for both the client and yourself.

Advantages for the Client

It all begins with the interview process. From the onset, clients are led to develop realistic goals and to understand the nuts and bolts of fitness training. Do they really have a clear concept of what they are after, and are they willing to make necessary commitments? The interview also affords you, the exercise leader, an opportunity to learn about the reinforcement value structure of your clients and to establish a rapport that is characterized by mutual respect and trust. This critical phase of awareness leaves a lasting impression on many clients. It sets the stage for subsequent feedback and in and of itself may be the most constructive step taken in the fight against noncompliance.

Similarly, experiencing exercise as a series of graduated steps helps insure continued progress and increases clients' level of confidence. Communication is key to maintaining this confidence. That's where goal setting and specific feedback can be so useful. As described in chapter 5, clients will put forth more effort if they view objectives as obtainable. By setting goals and providing fixed intervals of feedback, you establish a clear avenue for effective interaction. Clients will notice the attention, feel the powerful influence of social approval, and sense that long-term objectives are under their control. Also, goal setting can remove a great deal of anxiety. The reason that anxiety often occurs is because clients want something badly, yet do not have confidence in the means available to achieve the desired end. Goal setting offers the means that these anxious clients have been looking for.

Finally, clients will experience an environment that is directed toward the constant reaffirmation of purpose and the development of constructive feelings and thoughts. It is pleasing to be associated with an enthusiastic group and to feel part of an association committed to the development of constructive lifestyles. It breeds optimism and a sense of what being alive is all about. What more can you offer anyone?

Advantages for the Exercise Leader

It is possible that you may still question what benefits a formal motivational system has in store for you. Why invest the added time and effort? For starters, consider a self-centered interest: If clients are more satisfied and believe they have a good thing going with involvement in your fitness facility, then they are going to spread the word. They will bring in their friends, a recruiting effect that may insure your job security and perhaps lead to a raise in pay! Second is the issue of job satisfaction. Fitness is a service-oriented occupation. People are looking to you for advice on improving their health, looks, and/or lifestyles. In large part, seeing people make those changes—helping others—is the key to job satisfaction. More clients will experience success in achieving fitness goals with formal motivational programming; thus, by giving to others you receive.

Increased job satisfaction will be accompanied by increased confidence in your own skills as an exercise leader or program director. Clearly, if you are helping people institute lifetime changes in their physical activity habits, then you must be doing something right. As with most skills, the more practiced you become with this motivational system, the better you will be at applying it. With time you may even make your own modifications to the system—there is nothing sacred about it. In using this system, you will begin to anticipate needs and apply appropriate strategies more quickly and effectively, identifying trouble spots before they become major problems. Your sense of control over noncompliance will increase daily. Rather than feeling frustrated and remaining passive about noncompliance, you will be armed to initiate steps for remediation of the problem.

This book provides you with weapons to do battle with noncompliance, something that, to date, has been an opponent too formidable for most. You may not win every battle even with this system, but you will certainly experience many victories that would have been impossible had you not used it.

Conclusion

Keeping clients satisfied and physically active is essential to the success of any fitness facility. The trick is knowing what the trade secrets are to achieve this end. This book demonstrates that so-called trade secrets involve far more than cookbook recipes. In reality, countering noncompliant behavior is a preventive process that is both dynamic and interactive.

We hope you have come to recognize the need for formal motivational planning. Our reasons are not selfish; rather, we believe that for many clients you alone hold the trump card in making the commitment to fitness a lifetime venture. All of us in the field of physical fitness have an enormous responsibility. If we can solidify the physical activity habits of the American people, we can improve their quality of life and the quality of their time spent with us.

Few clients will ever seek counseling for exercise-related therapy, despite the fact that some of their approaches to fitness are self-destructive. In the end, you create the first and last offensive move against noncompliant behavior. Doesn't it make sense then to assure that you have designed the best play available? We think so. We wish you success and personal satisfaction as you put these strategies to use in your game plan!

References

Ajzen, I., & Fishbein, M. (1980). *Understanding attitudes and predicting social behavior*. Englewood Cliffs, NJ: Prentice-Hall.

American College of Sports Medicine. (1986). *Guidelines for exercise testing and prescription*. Philadelphia: Lea & Febiger.

Andrew, G.M., Oldridge, N.B., Parker, J.O., Cunningham, D.A., Rechnitzer, P.A., Jones, N.L., Buck, C., Kavanagh, T., Shephard, R.J., Sutton, J.R., & McDonald, W. (1981). Reasons for dropout from exercise programs in post coronary patients. *Medicine and Science in Sports and Exercise*, **13**, 164-168.

Bandura, A. (1977). Self-efficacy: Toward a unifying theory of behavioral change. *Psychological Review*, **84**, 191-215.

Becker, R. (1977). *Introduction and development of "Life be in it" campaign. Minister's Paper, Government of Victoria, Melbourne*. Paper presented at the international TRIMM conference, Paris.

Berger, R.A. (1962). Effect of varied weight training programs on strength. *Research Quarterly*, **33**, 168-181.

Borg, G. (1985). *An introduction to Borg's RPE-scale*. New York: Mouvement.

Corbin, C., & Lindsey, R. (1984). *The ultimate fitness book*. New York: Leisure Press.

Deci, E.L. (1975). *Intrinsic motivation*. New York: Plenum Press.

Dishman, R.K. (1982). Compliance/adherence in health-related exercise. *Health Psychology*, **1**, 237-267.

Epstein, L.H., Wing, R.R., Thompson, J.K., & Griffin, W. (1980). Attendance and fitness in aerobic exercise: The effect of contract and lottery procedures. *Behavior Modification*, **4**, 464-479.

Kenney, E.A., Rejeski, W.J., & Messier, S.P. (1987). Managing exercise distress: The effect of broad spectrum intervention on affect, RPE, and running efficiency. *Canadian Journal of Sport Sciences*, **12**(2), 97-105.

Locke, E.A., Shaw, K.N., Saari, L.M., & Latham, G.P. (1981). Goal setting and task performance: 1969-1980. *Psychological Bulletin*, **90**, 125-152.

Magel, J.R., Foglia, F., McArdle, W.A., Gutin, B., Pechar, G.S., & Katch, F.I. (1975). Specificity of swim training on maximum oxygen uptake. *Journal of Applied Physiology*, **38**, 151-155.

Martin, J.E., & Dubbert, P.M. (1984). Behavioral management strategies for improving health and fitness. *Journal of Cardiopulmonary Rehabilitation*, **4**, 200-208.

Oldridge, N.B. (1984). Adherence to adult exercise fitness programs. In J.D. Matarazzo, S.M. Weiss, J.A. Herd, N.E. Miller, & S.M. Weiss (Eds.), *Behavioral health: A handbook of health enhancement and disease prevention* (pp. 467-487). New York: Wiley.

Paffenbarger, R.S., Wing, D.L., & Hyde, R.T. (1978). Physical activity as an index of heart risk in college alumni. *American Journal of Epidemiology*, **108**, 161-175.

Pennebaker, J.W. (1982). *The psychology of physical symptoms*. New York: Springer-Verlag.

Perry, P. (1987, March). Are we having fun yet? *American Health Magazine*, pp. 59-63.

Pollock, M.L., Wilmore, J.H., & Fox, S.M. (1984). *Exercise in health and disease*. Philadelphia: W.B. Saunders.

Rejeski, W.J. (1985). Perceived exertion: An active or passive process? *Journal of Sport Psychology*, **7**, 371-378.

Rejeski, W.J., Morley, D., & Miller, H. (1983). Cardiac rehabilitation: Coronary-prone behavior as a moderator of graded exercise test performance. *Journal of Cardiac Rehabilitation*, **3**(5), 339-346.

Rejeski, W.J., Morley, D., & Miller, H. (1984). The Jenkins Activity Survey: Exploring its relationship with compliance to exercise prescription and MET gain within a cardiac rehabilitation setting. *Journal of Cardiac Rehabilitation*, **4**(3), 90-94.

Ribisl, P.M. (1984). Developing an exercise prescription for health. In J.D. Matarazzo, S.M. Weiss, J.A. Herd, N.E. Miller, & S.M. Weiss (Eds.), *Behavioral health: A handbook of health enhancement and disease prevention* (pp. 448-466). New York: Wiley.

Rosenstock, I.M. (1974). The health belief model and preventive health behavior. *Health Education Monographs*, **2**, 354-386.

Rotter, J.B. (1954). *Social learning and clinical psychology*. Englewood Cliffs, NJ: Prentice-Hall.

Stone, M.H., O'Bryant, H., & Garhammer, J. (1981). A hypothetical model for strength training. *Journal of Sports Medicine and Physical Fitness*, **21**, 342-351.

Taylor, S.E. (1986). *Health psychology*. New York: Random House.

Wankel, L.M., & Thompson, C. (1977). Motivating people to be physically active: Self-persuasion vs. balanced decision making. *Journal of Applied Social Psychology*, **7**, 332-340.

Author Index

Subject Index

About the Authors

Jack Rejeski

Elizabeth Kenney

Jack Rejeski, PhD, is an associate professor at Wake Forest University, where he teaches courses in health and exercise psychology. Dr. Rejeski has published over 25 scholarly works on perceived exertion, stress, and exercise compliance in patients with cardiac problems. In 1985 he received Wake Forest University's award for research excellence. Dr. Rejeski has also been intensively involved in a cardiac rehabilitation clinical practice for the past 8 years. This dynamic combination of academic, research, and practical experiences has contributed to the development of the exercise adherence techniques described in *Fitness Motivation*.

Elizabeth Kenney, MA, joined the Appalachian State University staff in 1987 as director of the Adult Fitness Program. Her responsibilities include organizing and implementing class schedules; screening, teaching, and giving feedback to participants; and supervising student interns. Ms. Kenney also initiated a cardiac rehabilitation program in conjunction with a local hospital. She is the director of the Watauga Cardiac Wellness program and wrote its preventive and rehabilitation procedures manual.